Stress and Quality of Working Life

Current Perspectives in Occupational Health

Stress and Quality of Working Life

Current Perspectives in Occupational Health

edited by

Ana Maria Rossi
International Stress Management
Association in Brazil

Pamela L. Perrewé
Florida State University, Tallahasse, Florida

and

Steven L. Sauter
National Institute for
Occupational Safety and Health

INFORMATION AGE
PUBLISHING

Greenwich, Connecticut • www.infoagepub.com

Library of Congress Cataloging-in-Publication Data

International Stress Management Association. Conference (2005 : Porto
   Alegre, Brazil)
   [Stress e qualidade de vida no trabalho. English]
   Stress and quality of working life : current perspectives in
occupational
   health / edited by Ana Maria Rossi, Pamela L. Perrewé, and Steven L.
   Sauter.
      p. cm.
   Includes bibliographical references and index.
   ISBN 1-59311-486-9 (hardcover) — ISBN 1-59311-485-0 (pbk.)
   1. Job stress—Congresses.   I. Rossi, Ana Maria. II. Perrewe, Pamela
L. III. Sauter, Steven L., 1946-   . IV. Title.
   HF5548.85.I57 2005
   158.7'2--dc22

                                                           2006003118

Printed in the United States of America

CONTENTS

PREFACE

International Stress Management Association in Brazil

Ana Maria Rossi

This book was developed for the 2005 International Stress Management Association Conference in Brazil. The original book was recently published in Portuguese, but because of the popularity of the topics and the world-renowned stress scholars who contributed chapters, we are very pleased to have the opportunity to publish this work in English.

Stress has turned into an ordinary word, generally known to represent any type of distress or tiredness of the body or mind. We commonly hear people say: "don't upset me because I'm stressed out today" or "I have to get rid of this stress." Regardless of the use, people are right when they say they are distressed, tired, or upset. More than a state of mind, stress is an individual's reaction to an adaptation and could cause a number of symptoms—physical, psychological, and behavioral. However, unlike the common belief, we cannot get rid of stress and it is not an evil to be fought for that matter. Stress is necessary to mobilize people, give them a certain drive so that they can achieve their goals. The problem is that too much or too little stress undermines body defenses and affects health. Aiming at showing that it is possible to efficiently cope with stress, the International Stress Management Association in Brazil (ISMA-BR) was established, a nonprofit organization that studies stress and ways to prevent it. ISMA-BR is the Brazilian branch of ISMA International that was founded in the United States in 1973. In the beginning, it was called Association for the Advancement of Tension Control. The increasing participation of other countries and the interest of experts in studying the subject led the association to change its name to International Stress Management Association.

ISMA has had a branch in Brazil since 2000. Its mission is to disseminate the scientific knowledge on stress management and provide guidance on the technology applications for its diagnosis and treatment. Additionally, ISMA-BR works as a reference in training and updating of Brazilian and South American professionals, providing training, through workshops and conferences, scientific research and also by making people aware of the importance of diagnosis, preventive measures and proper treatment. And there is a lot to be done. A survey conducted by ISMA-BR showed that 70% of economically active Brazilians suffer from the consequences of too much tension in their daily lives.

A book on the subject is intended to be an additional tool containing information on stress and ways of dealing with pressures and demands, because we know that the level of stress will continue to increase. We believe that only through information—and here you will be able to find the experience and opinion of some of the greatest and best professionals of the world in this field—people will manage to live better and more balanced lives. This is what ISMA-BR wishes and hopes for. Have a good reading.

Ana Maria Rossi, PhD
President, ISMA-BR

FOREWORD

Job stress has become a worldwide concern. Surveys in the United States consistently show that from one-fourth to one-third of workers report high levels of stress on the job, and situation is quite similar in Europe.[1] Although a full and precise accounting of the costs and burden to society of such high levels of job stress are not at hand, the available evidence is sobering. In the United States, for example, the median absence period for disability due to job stress is several-fold greater than the median for all other injuries and illnesses combined (Webster & Bergman, 1999). Further, in a study of 46,000 workers, health care costs were nearly 50% greater for individuals reporting high levels of stress in comparison to risk-free workers. The increment rose to nearly 150% for workers reporting high levels of both job stress and depression (Goetzel, Anderson, Whitmer, Ozminkowski, Dunn, & Wasserman, 1998).

This volume provides a series of comprehensive summaries of what is now a fast-growing literature aimed at understanding the causes, effects, and prevention of stress in the workplace. It begins with three chapters on different sources of stress at work, ranging from organizational factors to attributes of workers themselves. In the opening chapter, Cary Cooper describes new organizational practices, such as flexible employment arrangements, that are common to advanced industrial countries worldwide. While the consequences of these practices are not fully understood, this chapter raises serious questions about potential risks they may pose both to the effectiveness of organizations and to the well-being of workers.

Although much of the literature on job stress focuses on the effects of working conditions, there exists a substantial body of knowledge on the role of individual factors. The second chapter, by Ana Maria Rossi, bridges these two domains, showing that perceptions of organizational stressors may differ for men and women. These types of findings raise concerns of possible biases in the literature on job stress resulting from a tradition of research in this field that involves mainly male-dominated study samples. In the final chapter in this section on risk factors for stress, Paul Rosch provides a fascinating summary and personal account of the seminal studies on "Type-A Behavior" and heart disease—perhaps the most heavily investigated individual risk factor in the job stress literature. This body of work ushered the way for what is now a burgeoning field of study on job stress and cardiovascular disease.

The next five chapters update our understanding of the toll that stress can take on individuals, their families, and organizations. In the first of these chapters (chapter 4), Christina Maslach reviews the familiar phenomenon of burnout, and summarizes research on individual and work related factors that lead to burnout. Of particular interest, the chapter concludes with discussion of a conceptual approach to preventing burnout that involves diagnosis and reform of workplace risk factors.

Chapters five and six deepen our understanding of job stress and family functioning. In chapter five, Johnathan Halbesleben and Kelly Zellars examine the rapidly growing literature on work-family conflict, and discuss job and family contexts that may influence the risk of conflict. Of special interest, Chapter five also raises the possibility of supportive or facilitative relationships between the work and family environments. Chapter six by Mina Westman continues on this theme, discussing the spillover of stress from one domain of life to another (e.g., between work and home) or crossover of stress from workers to peers and family. The burden of stress on society and the importance of prevention is greatly increased when we consider the possibility of this type of contagion.

Chapters seven and eight are of particular interest because they enlarge our appreciation of the implications of stress for worker performance and organizational effectiveness, a subject that has received far too little attention in the job stress literature to date. In chapter seven, Jason Stoner and Pamela Perrewé make a strong case that depressed mood resulting from stressful work may have serious adverse consequences for the organization, including impaired work performance, fewer organizational citizenship behaviors, and lower organizational commitment. In chapter eight, Steve Jex and colleagues expand upon this argument, suggesting that the impact of stress may be more apparent and destructive for discretionary worker behaviors (organizational citizenship behavior, prosocial behavior, personal initiative and innovation, counterproductive behavior) than for task performance.

The final cluster of chapters in the book has a more positive flavor, looking at the benefits of healthy work environments and ways to overcome and prevent stress at work. This series of chapters begins with an uplifting chapter (chapter 9) by Debra Nelson and Bret Simmons who advocate for greater attention to building human strengths and positive psychological states, with particular attention to "hope," as a pathway to health and performance in the workplace. Chapter 10 by James Campbell Quick and colleagues builds on this theme by emphasizing the importance of positive leadership qualities, such as emotional competence, empathy and commitment in promoting safety, health and well being in organizations. In chapter 11, Gerald Ferris and colleagues draw attention to organizational politics as a potential stressor at work and to the importance of political skill in nullifying stress in the workplace. As a relatively new topic of inquiry, recommendations are provided for further research to better understand the level and breadth of influence that political skill may have in preventing stress at work.

In chapter 12, Lennart Levi shifts the focus away from individual resources to prevent job stress toward national guidance and corporate responsibility to ensure safe and healthy workplaces. This latter approach is no more developed than among European Union Member States. Guidance and policy by several European and international bodies (European Commission, International Standards Organization, European Foundation for the Improvement of Living and Working Conditions; European Agency for Safety and Health at Work) on objectives and approaches in preventing stress at work are described. Sauter and Murphy provide complementary information on the scope of job stress and prevention approaches in the United States in the final chapter. As noted, the predominant focus has been on stress management in contrast to work redesign. The chapter describes needed research and information without which interventions to improve the work environment are unlikely (e.g., further evidence on the effects of organizational interventions and authoritative information on how to design, implement and evaluate interventions).

In sum, the present articles highlight both core knowledge and new developments within the rapidly growing field of research on work and stress. We are hopeful this information serves to raise awareness of the causes and costs of stress at work, and provides some incentive and insight for organizations to begin thinking about and acting in ways that lead to a less stressful environment for their workforce.

Ana Maria Rossi
Pamela L. Perrewé
Steven L. Sauter
Steve M. Jex

NOTES

1. See chapters 12 and 13 of this volume.

REFERENCES

Goetzel R. Z., Anderson D. R., Whitmer R. W., Ozminkowski R. J., Dunn R. L., & Wasserman J. (1998). The relationship between modifiable health risks and health care expenditure: An analysis of the multi-employer HERO health risk and cost database. *Journal of Occupational and Environmental Medicine*, *40*, 843–854.

Webster T., & Bergman B. (1999). Occupational stress: Counts and rates. *Compensation and Working Conditions Online*, *4(3)*, 1–4. Retrieved December 15, 2004, from http://www.bls.gov/opub/ted/1999/oct/wk3/art03.htm

INTRODUCTION

Reduce This Burden

Lennart Levi

Mental health problems and stress-related disorders are the biggest over-all cause of early death in Europe. Finding ways to reduce this burden is a priority (World Health Organization, 2001). Related declarations have been recently made by the World Health Organization (WHO) Executive Board, the European Council of Ministers, and, most recently, by the WHO European Ministerial Conference on Mental Health, in Helsinki, January 12–15, 2005. But what is meant by "stress-related disorders?" This volume represents an impressive and successful attempt to answer that question. The following is my own attempt to clarify the issues sur-rounding stress-related disorders (Levi, 2004; Levi & Levi, 2000).

Let us assume that an individual has the following problem: The com-pany she works for is operating at a loss and is planning staff cutbacks. Or the civil service department, school or care institution where she works has exceeded its estimates and is forced to economize by giving staff their notice. This will mean that she will either be unemployed or will be over-worked and more insecure to boot. She may then take her concerns home with her, have trouble sleeping, have difficulty unwinding, and get surly and irritated. Her family life is adversely affected, and her relationship begins to fray at the seams. If the course of events continues, this can affect her health and well being in a number of different ways.

Misinterpretation of the world around.   This individual may perhaps be developing a tendency to interpret everything happening around her for the worst. The usual laughter of a coworker is interpreted as a derisive sneer. She sees a neutral enquiry as to how she is feeling as an insinuation. A suggestion to replace some office furniture, she interprets as an attempt to undermine her position. In a nutshell, she is interpreting her surroundings as threatening and hostile. Such a chain of events can trigger strong and long-lasting stress responses with few or no possibilities for recovery.

Misinterpretation of proprioceptive signals.   A long time before the situation described above even occurred, this individual had perhaps felt occasional pressure across the top of the head. She sometimes fancied she was having difficulty catching her breath and needed to inhale deeply. Occasionally she has felt obviously tired. Sometimes she has noticed a mild pain in some part of the body. Much of all this is part of the normal functioning of every organism. This person need not necessarily be sick or even on the way to becoming ill. But if—under the influence of her tough life situation—she starts becoming all too alert to such perceptions or begins interpreting this normal "engine noise" from her perfectly normal "car engine" as "knocking," then she is beginning to have a problem. The pain across the head: can it be—a brain tumour? Finding breathing a little hard going: is she contracting lung cancer? The tiredness, perfectly normal perhaps, after a busy day at work: is this the first sign of burnout syndrome? The thought—indeed any *one* of these thoughts—can heighten her anxiety. That anxiety increases the tendency to dwell on things and worry. This tendency means that she increasingly detects the normal "engine noise," which increases her anxiety, thereby increasing her tendency to worry. The problem in this particular case is that completely normal proprioceptive signals (organ sensations) are experienced and construed as symptoms of various illnesses.

Emotional responses.   It is not surprising, of course, that an individual, in the difficult situation in which she finds herself, feels ill at ease, anxious, depressed, and helpless. But, is she experiencing symptoms of illness? It can become so if the responses are sufficiently intense, prolonged or frequently repeated. A little anxiety can be endured—that is one of the facts of life. But constantly living with feelings of worry, anguish, and depression is not normal in a reasonable context. All of these can very effectively disrupt the only life we will ever have. Furthermore, such chronic "gloominess" increases our tendency to experience vexation as disaster and feelings of discomfort in the body as symptoms of illness.

Physiological responses: When a teacher stands in front of his or her rowdy class or a salesman is faced with a tricky customer, the heart beats faster in many instances, the breathing quickens, the muscles tense. It not only feels so—it is so. The adrenal medulla produces more adrenaline, which releases the fuel from the sugar depots in the muscle system and liver (glycogenolysis). More noradrenaline is also secreted, which similarly releases the fuel from the fat deposits (lipolysis). And cortisol from the adrenal cortex affects the conversion of both sugar and fat. If these or related reactions become long-term and/or intensive and/or frequently recurrent, they can place a strain on the organism and result in damage not only to the function but also to the structure of various organs and organ systems. They can lead to individuals developing, for instance, cardiovascular and/or musculoskeletal disorder symptoms, metabolic syndrome, burnout syndrome, or a chronic pain condition. A majority of all people on long-term sick lists in many countries are characterized by a panorama of such conditions.

Cognitive responses: Another common effect is that an individual may have problems with her ability to think clearly and constructively. Her memory may begin to fade, she may find it harder to learn new things, or when she needs to make an important decision, she starts to vacillate and puts off making the decision interminably. All of this can exacerbate her situation even further.

Behaviors: Perhaps an individual starts to handle her discomfort by "self-medicating." After a really busy day, she staggers home and pours out a double whisky, and then another. That undeniably helps for the moment, but it is more of a hindrance in the longer term if she makes a habit of it. Or she manages her discomfort and restiveness by chain-smoking. Or she comforts herself with fatty, sweet, salty, and/or low-fiber foods. That source of comfort is nearly always available, after all, even when life no longer offers any other sources of happiness. A morel-spiced rustic pâté, a slice or two of delicious Black Forest gateau, or the taste of chocolate and whipped cream feel like a protective layer enveloping the quivering nerve ends. Unfortunately, they also deposit layer after layer around the midriff. And eventually they may have a negative impact on health.

If her existence is sufficiently dreary perhaps, she may try to break up the gloominess by seeking extraordinary challenges, taking risks, even really dangerous ones. And as for the good habits, exercising, meditating, and medicating according to the doctor's prescription, she cannot be "bothered" with those, she skips them, they are "forgotten" altogether. All these behavioral responses can damage individuals' health. The most desperate and unfortunately all too customary response has not been mentioned yet. That is, attempting to take one's life, committing suicide.

All these ways of reacting and behaving affect, and are affected by, the stress in the organism. All are likely to aggravate public and occupational health as well as the individual's health, if she is exposed to long-term stressors and does not cope with them successfully. As every doctor knows, the vast majority of diseases mentioned here do not have one single cause, one single explanation model. A single strain (unless extremely powerful or long-lasting) can no more induce sickness than the Bank of England's vaults can be opened with a single key. It normally requires a whole "bunch of keys." Furthermore, one and the same syndrome, one and the same pattern of symptoms, can be associated with entirely different diseases. Some of these are banal, others are life threatening.

A stitch in time is said to save nine. It would be better still to make sure that loopholes were never allowed to develop in the first place. The former is often referred to as secondary prevention, the latter primary prevention. Tertiary prevention involves trying to implement "damage containment" once the "loophole develops into a gaping gash" (cf. British Government, 1998).

Prevention can be specific or generic. The former pertains to intervention to combat a series of specific risk factors—for example, lowering blood fats, normalising blood pressure, reducing weight, weaning people off smoking and so forth, in order to prevent ischaemic heart disease. Generic prevention is based on the powerful interconnectivity displayed by many kinds of ill health—comorbidity. It is then worthwhile to try to tackle whole "clusters" of correlated problems, attempt to understand their common aetiology and pathogenesis, and intervene to combat joint risk factors and promote collective health factors by, for example, improving the social competence of entire population groups. Understanding the above and implementing it in primary, secondary, and tertiary prevention will be a major challenge for all stakeholders. This book is an important step to promote this.

REFERENCES

British Government. (1998). *Our healthier nation. A contract for health* (green paper). London: Author.

EU Presidency. (2001, Octorber 25-27). *Coping with stress and depression related problems in Europe.* Brussels, Belgium: Federal Ministry of Social Affairs, Public Health and the Environment.

European Council of Health Ministers. (2001, November 15). *Combating stress and depression related problems.* Brussels, Belgium: Council Conclusions.

Levi, L. (2004). Det sjuka Sverige [Sick Sweden]. *Läkartidningen, 101*(18), 1624–1627.

Levi L., & Levi, I. (2004). *Guidance on work-related stress: Spice of life or kiss of death?* Luxembourg: European Commission.

WHO Executive Board. (2002, January 17). *Strengthening mental health.* Resolution EB109.R8. Geneva, Switzerland: Author

World Health Organization. (2001). *Mental Health in Europe.* Copenhagen, Denmark: Author.

Ziglio, E., Levin, L., Levi, L., & Bath, E. (Eds.). (2002). *Investment for health—A discussion of the role of economic and social determinants.* Copenhagen, Denmark: World Health Organization European Office.

CHAPTER 1

THE CHANGING NATURE OF WORK

The New Psychological Contract and Associated Stressors

Cary L. Cooper

Many workplaces throughout the world are changing dramatically from over a decade ago, with more downsizing, outsourcing, joint ventures, mergers and acquisitions, and major restructurings to compete in the global economy. This has led to change fatigue, intrinsic job insecurity and a longer working hours culture in many countries as the workforce becomes more Americanized. The questions we have to ask ourselves and begin to find solutions to are: how can organizations continue to demand more and more of their employees, including loyalty, while providing less and less job security and support? Is the psychological contract between employer and employee worth the metaphorical paper it is written on? This paper explores the changing nature of work and what this will mean for all of us in the future.

Stress and Quality of Working Life: Current Perspectives in Occupational Health, 1–7
Copyright © 2006 by Information Age Publishing
All rights of reproduction in any form reserved.

THE CHANGING EUROPEAN WORKPLACE

The old adage that "change is here to stay" epitomizes the workplace over the last four decades (Cooper, 1998). The 1960s embraced changed and new technology, with the then British prime minister proclaiming that the "white heat of technology" was about to transform our lives, producing a "leisure age" of 20-hour working weeks. This was followed by the 1970s, a period of industrial strife, conflict, and retrenchment. The workplace became the battleground between employers and workers, between the middle and working classes, and between liberal and conservative thinking.

In most developed countries, the 1980s were described as the decade of the "enterprise culture," with people working longer and harder to achieve individual success and material rewards. We had globalization, privatization, process reengineering, mergers and acquisitions, strategic alliances, joint ventures and the like, transforming workplaces into hot-house, free market environments. In the short term, this entrepreneurial period improved economic competitiveness in international markets in the countries that embraced it. But as strains began to appear, the concept of "burnout" joined "junk bonds," "software packages" and "e-mail" in the modern business vocabulary (Cooper & Dewe, 2004). Nevertheless, work was carried out essentially the same way as before; it was still business as usual in large or growing medium-sized organizations in U.S. Inc., U.K. Plc., Germany GmBH, and so on (Cooper & Jackson, 1997). By the end of the 1980s and into the early 1990s, a major restructuring of work, as we have never seen since the industrial revolution, was beginning to take place. The effects of recession and efforts to get out of it dominated the early years of the decade. Organizations throughout and the Western world dramatically "downsized," "delayered," "flattened" and "right sized." Whatever euphemism you care to use, the hard reality experienced by many was year-on-year redundancy, constant restructuring, and substantial organizational change. Now many organizations are smaller, with fewer people doing more and feeling much less secure. New technology, rather than being our savior, has added the burden of information overload as well as accelerating the pace of work, as a greater speed of response (e.g., faxes, e-mails) becomes the standard business expectation. And, at the same time, as more and more companies adopt a global perspective, organizations and the individuals they employ are funding that success in the global arena requires fundamental changes in their corporate structures as well as individual competencies. Just as organizations are reengineering themselves to be more flexible and adaptive, individuals are expected to be open to continual change and life-long learning. Workers will be expected to diagnose their abilities, know where to get appropriate training in deficient skills, know how to network, be able to marker themselves to organisations professionally, and tolerate ambiguity and insecurity. (Antoniou & Cooper, 2005)

A Flexible Workforce

As more organizations "outsource," market-test" (in the case of the public sector), utilize "interim management" and the like, many more of us will be selling our services to organizations on a freelance or short-term contract basis. We are creating a corporate culture of blue-collar, white collar, managerial, and professional "temps"—in a phrase, a "contingent workforce." In the United Kingdom, for example, more than 1 in 10 workers are self-employed; part-time work and the perception of people that they are in effect on short-term contracts, are growing faster than permanent full-time work. The number of men in part-time jobs has doubled in the past decade, while the number of people employed by firms of more than 500 employees has slumped to just over one-third of the employed population.

In predicting the look of future corporate life, many experts argue that most organizations will have only a small core of full-time, permanent employees, working from a conventional office. They will buy most of the skills they need on a contract basis, either from individuals working at home and linked to the company by computers and modems (teleworking), or by hiring people on short-term contracts to do specific jobs or to carry out specific projects. In this way companies will be able to maintain the flexibility they need to cope with a rapidly changing world. (Cooper & Jackson, 1997; Sparrow & Cooper, 2003).

This has led to what employers refer to euphemistically as "the flexible workforce," although in family friendly terms it is anything but flexible. The psychological contract between employer and employee in terms of "reasonably permanent employment for work well done" is truly being undermined as more and more employees no longer regard their employment as secure and many more are engaged in part-time work. Indeed, in an ISR (1995) survey of 400 companies in 17 countries employed over 8 million workers throughout Europe, the employment security of workers significantly declined between 1985 and 1995; United Kingdom, from 70% in 1985 to 48% in 1995; Germany, from 83% to 55%; France, from 64% to 50%; the Netherlands, from 73% to 61%; Belgium, from 60% to 54%; and Italy from 62% to 57%.

It could be argued that there is nothing inherently wrong with this trend, but recent Quality of Working Life Surveys by the Chartered Management Institute (CMI) in the United Kingdom (which annually surveys a cohort of 5000 British managers), found some disturbing results (Worrall & Cooper, 2001). It was found that over 60% of this national sample of managers had undergone a major restructuring over the last 12 months involving major downsizing and outsourcing. The consequences of this change, even among an occupational group (i.e., middle and senior managers) supposedly in control of events, were that nearly two out of three experienced increased job insecurity, lowered morale, and the erosion of motivation and loyalty.

Most of these changes involved downsizing, cost reduction, delayering, and outsourcing. Yet the perception was that although inevitably these changes led to an increase in profitability and productivity, decision making was slower and, more importantly, the organization was deemed to have lost the right mix of human resource skills and experience in the process.

In addition, the impact on working patterns was penal, both from a business point of view and in terms of managers' outside lives. This was partly due not only to more work being imposed on the metaphorical "backs of fewer managers," but also to "presenteeism," the need for managers to demonstrate commitment by working longer and unsocial hours —behavior which they feel (possibly falsely) would protect them from the next wave of redundancies.

In the most recent survey, it was found that 77% of executives work over 40 hour weeks, 32% over 50 and nearly 10% over 60 hours, with a substantial minority of them also working frequently on the weekends. In addition, whereas a third of this cohort of executives in 1997 felt that their employer expected them to put in these hours, by 2001 this rose to nearly 60%. What is also disturbing about this trend toward a long hours culture, is the managers' perception of the damage it is inflicting on them and their families: 69% of these executives reported that these hours damaged their health, 77% that it adversely affected their relationship with their children, 72% that it damaged their relationship with their partner, and 60% that long hours reduced their productivity. (These results with managers were also found by DEMOS in society at large). DEMOS's (1995) report Time Squeeze on the U.K. workforce found that 25% of male employees worked more than 48 hours a week; a fifth of all manual workers worked more than 50 hours; one in eight managers worked more than 60 hours per week; and 7 out of 10 British workers want to work a 40-hour week, but only 3 out of 10 do.

This trend toward a long hours culture and intrinsic job insecurity was also having an effect on the family as more and more two-earner families/couples emerged in a climate that was anything but "family friendly." The BT Forum's report, on the Cost of Communication Breakdown (Walker, 1996), found that the proportion of people living in one-parent families in the United Kingdom, for example, increased fourfold between 1961 and 1991, with over 3 million children and young people will grow up in step-families by the year 2000. This is, in no small measure, partly a result of a "long working hours" culture in most public and private sector organisations.

Consequences of Changing Employment Relationships

So what are the consequences of the changing nature of the psychological contract between employer and employee? Sparrow and Cooper (2003) identified four areas that are affected by changing employment relationships at work:

1. What we want out of work and how we maintain individuality in a world where we face a choice between more intense employment or no employment at all.
2. Our relationships with other individuals in a work process that can be altered in terms of social interactions, time patterns and geographical locations.
3. The cooperative and competitive links between different internal and external constituents of the organization in their new more flexible forms.
4. The relationships between key stakeholders and institutions such as governments, unions, and managers.

In addition to the changing relationship at work, there are a number of consequences in the way we work. First, as more and more people work from their home, whether part-time or on a short-term contact, we will be increasingly creating "virtual organizations." The big corporate question here is: How will this virtual organization of the future manage this dispersed workforce, with communication difficulties already apparent in existing organizational structures (Worrall & Cooper, 2001)? Second, with two out of three families/couples two-earner or dual career, how will working from home affect the delicate balance between home and work or indeed the roles between men and women? Indeed, with employers increasingly looking for and recruiting "flexible workers," will not women be preferred to men given their history of flexibility? For example, in the United Kingdom, there are currently five times as many women working part-time as men. Although twice as many men are now working part-time than a decade ago, women are historically more experienced at discontinuous career patterns, flowing in and out of the labor market, working part-time and on short-term contracts (Lewis & Cooper, 2005). Third, since the industrial revolution, many white-collar, managerial and professional workers have not experienced high levels of job insecurity. Even many blue-collar workers who were laid off in heavy manufacturing industries of the past were frequently reemployed when times got better. The question that society has to ask itself is: can human beings cope with permanent job insecurity, without the safety and security of organizational structures, which in the past provided training, development, and careers? The European survey by ISR (1995) provided some cause for concern in this regard, showing the United Kingdom with the worst decline in employee satisfaction in terms of employment security of any of its competitors, from 70% satisfaction levels in 1985 to 47% by 1995 to 2000; at a time when U.K. Plc has been moving faster towards a contingent workforce than all of its European counterparts—a fate soon to be felt by other Europeans.

Will this trend towards stable insecurity, free-lance working and virtual organizations continue?

And, more importantly, can organizations, virtual or otherwise, continue to demand commitment from employees they do not commit to? In comparative terms the U.K. economy is doing remarkably well, but the levels of job insecurity and dissatisfaction are fairly high. Developing and maintaining a "feel good" factor at work and in our economy generally is not just about bottom-line factors (e.g., higher salaries, lowering of income tax, or increased profitability). It is, or should be, in a civilized society, about quality of life issues as well, such as hours of work, family time, manageable workloads, control over one's career, and some sense of job security. As the social anthropologist Studs Terkel (1972) suggested,

> Work is about a search for daily meaning as well as daily bread, for recognition as well as cash, for astonishment rather than torpor, in short, for a sort of life rather, than a Monday through Friday sort of dying.

REFERENCES

Antoniou, A. S., & Cooper, C. L. (2005), *Research companion to organizational health psychology*. Cheltenham, England: Edward Elgar.

Cooper, C. L. (1998). The changing psychological contract at work. *Work and Stress, 12*(2), 97–100.

Cooper, C. L., & Dewe, P. (2004). *Stress: A brief history*. New York: Blackwell.

Cooper, C. L., & Jackson, S. (1997). *Creating tomorrow's organizations: A handbook for future research in organizational behavior*. New York: Wiley.

Demos. (1995). *Time squeeze*. London: Author.

ISR (1995). *Employee satisfaction: Tracking european trends*. London: Author.

Lewis, S., & Cooper, C. L. (2005). *Work-life integration.* New York: Wiley.
Sparrow, P., & Cooper, C. L. (2003). *The employment relationship: Key challenges in HR* London: Elsevier.
Terkel, S. (1972). *Working.* New York: Avon Books.
Walker, J. (1969). *The cost of communication breakdown.* London: BT Forum.
Worrall, L., & Cooper, C. L. (2001). *Quality of working life survey.* London: Chartered Management Institute.

CHAPTER 2

OCCUPATIONAL STRESSORS AND GENDER DIFFERENCES

Ana Maria Rossi

The chapter presents results from a study of occupational stressors among male and female professionals in three large cities in Brazil. A total of 586 usable questionnaires identifying 18 sources of occupational stressors was obtained from four Brazilian nationwide manufacturers. Results indicate that there are some differences between the perception of males and females in terms of sources of occupational stress but there is a general agreement on the most dysfunctional stressors on the job.

OCCUPATIONAL STRESSORS AND GENDER DIFFERENCES

The impact of occupational stress in the organizations has become a major source of concern. Stress is considered one of the most serious hazards to the individual's psychosocial well-being (Bateman & Strasser, 1983). In the past decades several studies on organizational stress have highlighted the complexity of the problem and the need for further research (Bateman & Strasser, 1983; Parker & DeCotiis, 1983). Occupational stress affects the employee's health, with 50% to 80% of all diseases being psychosomatic or of a stress-related nature (Pelletier, 1984). Thus

Stress and Quality of Working Life: Current Perspectives in Occupational Health, 9–17
Copyright © 2006 by Information Age Publishing
All rights of reproduction in any form reserved.

9

far research indicates that the workload, long working hours, and numerous other job/employee interactions contribute to individual stress and strain responses. It results in problems of poor performance, poor morale, high turnover and absenteeism, and workplace violence (Quick, Quick, Nelson, & Hurrell, 1997).

Occupational stress has been shown to be associated with several manifestations of stress. There are numerous behavioral, physiological, and emotional reactions that have been associated with work-related stress (Cooper & Quick, 1999; Fried, Rowland, & Ferris, 1984; Quick et al., 1997; Sauter, 1989). Most of the previous studies have been done with American male professionals. It would be useful to compare and contrast occupational stress between male and female professionals in other cultures to clarify the apparent role of gender perception in influencing physical and psychological health.

A variety of physiological and psychological sysmptoms have been associated with occupational stress. Hoiberg (1982) conducted an 11-year longitudinal study of 184,122 Navy men and found that self-reports of job stress were related to the incidence of 10 different physiological and psychological illnesses. Coronary heart disease and hypertension have been clearly associated with job stress. Several studies have showed a link between coronary heart disease and the amount of stress the individual experiences and his ability to cope with it (Cooper & Marshall, 1976; Rosenman, Brand, Jenkins, Friedman, Straus, & Wurm, 1975).

Past research has also documented that psychological strain and related manifestations of strain (fear, anxiety, depression, etc.) occur in response to environmental overload that imposes a demand on the individual that he perceives to be overwhelming (Ganster, Mayes, Sime, & Tharp, 1982). Basically, an imbalance exists between environmental demands and individual capabilities (Fried et al., 1984). The psychological effects of job stress are also manifested in higher rates of job dissatisfaction and job turnover. Bateman and Strasser (1983) note that job tension leads to an increase in physiological (muscular) tension. D'Arcy, Syrotuick, and Siddique (1984) studied job satisfaction differences between males and females noting that females recorded higher levels of satisfaction than males when job attributions and role distinctions were held constant and that stress on the job can lead to a decrease in job satisfaction (Karasek, 1979).

There is great diversity and disagreement among researchers on the definition of stress. However, researchers agree that there are two types of stress (functional and dysfunctional) that emerged from the "inverted-U research" (Yerkes & Dodson, 1908). This research notes that too much or too little stress can affect the individual's well-being and work performance. That is, at the low end of the scale as stress stimuli increase the performance of the individual also tends to increase. At the midpoint of the scale where stress stimuli are fairly high, there is a change in direction of the scale. As stress stimuli increase, performance tends to decrease because the individual apparently is overloaded and cannot respond to further stimuli.

Most studies in the area of occupational stress focused on the dysfunctional stress as involving "disruptions in the individual's psychological and/or physiological homeostasis that force them to deviate from normal functioning in interactions with their job and work environments" (Allen, Hitt, & Greer, 1982, p. 360).

Davidson and Cooper (1983) among other researchers have investigated some of the primary causes of occupational stressors in the organization as a contributing factor in the development of functional disorders, psychosomatic symptoms, and degenerative disease. This knowledge has encouraged some organizations to offer stress management programs to their employees (Parkinson, 1982; Quick et al., 1997). In spite of this growing awareness, however, there has been a paucity of scientific studies differentiating between men and women regarding occupational stress. It is important to focus on attitudes and practices of the worker that might increase occupational stress and of how the organizational member on the job actually perceives his stressors. Such information provides a communication-based effort to understand occupational stress and how it might affects differently men and women at work.

Morgan and Smircich (1980) note the importance of choosing a method which truly deals with and is sensitive to the phenomena under study. This methodological approach is based, in part, on the belief that it is important to ground the research instrument in the "real world" of day-to-day organizational existence (Browning, 1978). Furthermore, Holmes and Jorgensen (1971) noted that social science research prior to 1971 was strongly biased, preferring to study men instead of women. While stress research since 1971 may not have such a bias, it has also failed to study systematically the differences between men and women. Currently, there is a great need for interdisciplinary and cross-gender research in order to understand the organizational and individual variables that are linked with occupational stress. The primary purpose of this study is to compare and contrast occupational stress that may affect the psychosocial well-being of male and female professionals who were randomly selected for the study.

METHOD

A sample of 900 professionals (450 men and 450 women) was selected from four large nationwide organizations in three large cities in Brazil.

Subjects were chosen randomly from each of the four organizations. The subjects selected answered a questionnaire. In total, 586 were returned (220 men and 366 women).

Procedure

The subjects were asked two questions. The development of the first question followed the work of Rossi, Lubbers, and Di Salvo (1986). Question one listed 18 work situations that may cause stress and asked respondents to identify those situations that caused them the most stress on the job. The 18 work situations were drawn from a review of previous studies of occupational stress. Respondents could identify from 0 to all 18 of the work-related stressors. A follow-up question asked them to rank those they had identified. They were to base their ranking on the number of problems the situations had caused in accomplishing their work. To insure understanding and completeness of the questions, the face validity of the questionnaire was checked through a pilot study of 20 individuals. As a result of the pilot study, some minor changes were made.

Data Analysis

The data generated in this study provides an interesting area of analysis involving the comparison of the responses of the males and females. Few studies have differentiated between males and females in terms of stressors. It is important to look at differences which may exist between the two samples. A good deal of the amount of stress that an individual feels is rooted in his perception of the environment. This study looks for these differences due to males and females different perception of their life and the stressors around them.

Analysis of the data was conducted in two phases. First, the percentage of the total number of times the stressor was chosen by a respondent as causing stress in his life was tabulated for males and females. Second, the rankings of the stressors identified were analyzed. Since an individual respondent could choose any number of stressors, a method was developed to provide a fair tabulation of the rankings. The rankings were inverted (rank 1 became 18, 2 became 17, etc.). The inversion meant that those stressors that were most important to the individual received a higher score. The inverted scores were then tabulated for males and females.

In total, 586 usable surveys were returned, 220 were males and 366 were females. One explanation for the difference in the return rate in the

Table 2.1.   Percentage of Stressors

Rank*	Stressor	Males n = 220 %	Females n = 366 %
1	Uncertainty	58.1%	54.6%
2	Heavy workload	46.3%	59.5%
3	Interpersonal stress	48.1%	54.6%
4	Work demands	47.2%	52.4%
5	Lack of control	48.1%	50.2%
6	Inability to manage your time	34.5%	45.3%
7	Tecnostress	43.6%	38.7%
8	Role conflict	38.1%	37.1%
9	Role ambiguity	30.0%	32.7%
10	Routine jobs	24.5%	34.4%
11	Inadequade resources	33.6%	24.5%
12	Dealing with emotional issues	18.1%	20.7%
13	Preparedness	17.2%	15.3%
14	Workplace bullying	13.6%	16.9%
15	Lack of feedback	10.0%	16.9%
16	Job change	10.9%	15.3%
17	Environmental change	4.5%	14.2%
18	Nonparticipation	11.8%	6.0%
		53.9%	59.0%

* Rank was determined by the row total for each stressor

two groups may be that females who completed the questionnaire were more aware of stress on the job or felt a greater burden due to their stress level. Most of the respondents, both male and female, reported that they held managerial and supervisory positions. Manufacturers were the typical organizations represented regardless of the respondent's sex.

RESULTS

Table 2.1 presents a comparison of the percentages for men and women. The results indicate that there are some differences between men and women in the 18 stressors identified. The percentage totals presented on Table 2.1 indicate that the females identified a larger number of stressors.

Overall there are some important differences between the sexes on what causes them stress on the job. The identification of the relative

importance of the stressors is critical so that the individual may take steps
to alleviate the negative consequences which may result.

Table 2.2 presents the percentage of the inverted rankings received for
each of the 18 stressors. These scores are important because while Table
2.1 made identification of all stressors equal in value, the inverted rankings places greatest value on those stressors that are most dangerous to
the psycho-physiological well-being of the individual.

The inverted rankings presented on Table 2.2 are important because
they allow for the assignment of each stressor as a "high," "moderate-
high," "moderate," or "low" stressor. The scores gradually decrease except
for three places. These natural breaks occur after the 5th, 8th, and 11th
stressors and they provide the division between the stressors levels. Thus,
the first five stressors constitute the "high" stressor category, the next
three make up the "moderate-high" category, the next three make up the
"moderate" category, and the final seven constitute the "low" stressors. It

Table 2.2.   Inverted Rankings

Rank*	Stressor	Males n = 220 %	Females n = 366 %
1	Heavy workload	74.0%	94.3%
2	Uncertainty	91.0%	83.1%
3	Interpersonal stress	75.1%	82.1%
4	Inability to manage your time	72.8%	82.0%
5	Lack of control	76.3%	77.8%
6	Work demands	54.5%	69.7%
7	Role ambiguity	64.2%	57.4%
8	Tecnostress	58.1%	55.4%
9	Role conflict	38.0%	49.7%
10	Routine jobs	44.7%	45.7%
11	Inadequade resources	51.8%	36.9%
12	Dealing with emotional issues	24.5%	29.6%
13	Preparedness	19.0%	24.3%
14	Lack of feedback	23.0%	21.3%
15	Workplace bullying	14.7%	23.9%
16	Job change	15.5%	21.8%
17	Environmental change	6.8%	19.7%
18	Nonparticipation	16.7%	9.0%
		82.1%	88.4%

* RANK was determined by the row total for each stressor

is important to note that these categorizations are generalizations based on the results of the study. Obviously, a particular individual may receive a great deal of stress from a stressor in the low category. These categories may allow researchers and practitioners to begin looking for those occupational stressors which most subjects saw as the most hazardous.

The results of the inverted rankings in Table 2.2 differ from those in Table 2.1. Most notable are the switching of the first and second, and the fourth and sixth stressors. While the number of one and two stressors are very close in effect, it is clear that females are more stressed by the heavy workload and the males receive the greater stress from uncertainty on the job and both affect the employees' perception of how they can manage their own time.

DISCUSSION

This study identifies specific causes of occupational stress and determines whether gender differences exist in terms of males' and females' perception of work-related stress. Overall, this study suggests that males and females experience occupational distress which in turn affects their effectiveness in performing their tasks. These results support the findings of Zappert and Weinstein (1985), Davidson and Cooper (1983), which indicate that occupational stress limits job performance.

Cooper and Marshall (1976) noted that stress is a critical component in determining employee physical and psychological well-being in addition to organizational effectiveness. This study extends the claim that occupational stress impacts on the organizational member's well-being as well as on his performance at work and that every effort should be made to reduce work-related stress. Otherwise, attempts should be made to help employees to develop efficient coping strategies to manage their stress level.

The data revealed that there are some differences between the perception of males and females in terms of occupational stress but there is general agreement on the most dysfunctional stressors on the job. The findings indicate that while the five stressors having the most jeopardizing impact on males and females psychosocial well-being are similar, their ranking is different:

Males	Females
(1) Uncertainty	(1) Heavy Workload
(2) Lack of Control	(2) Uncertainty
(3) Interpersonal Stress	(3) Interpersonal Stress
(4) Heavy Workload	(4) Inability to Manage Your Time
(5) Inability to Manage Your Time	(5) Lack of Control

An interesting finding of this study is that females identify heavy workload as a dysfunctional stressor more than do males. French and Caplan (1972) have identified workload at two levels: being asked to do more than either time or ability permits. This study suggests that females identify workload on both levels. The results indicate that an imbalance exists between the females' needs and abilities and the demands of the job. The imbalance does not appear as critical for males. This result can be explained by the fact that females may try to do more to prove that they belong in the "men's hut" (Ritti & Funkhouser, 1977), and this places demands on them greater than males experience (Zappert & Weinstein, 1985).

Future research is necessary to further investigate these preliminary findings and to develop efficient coping strategies employees can use to reduce the impact of the major occupational stressors. The five stressors identified as "high" deal with the amount of control exercised by an individual. The "control" issue is manifested in their inability to control their workload, the uncertainty individuals face, their inability to control interpersonal relations, and their challenge in managing their own time. Future research should focus on the issue of "control" as a major source of an individual's occupational stress.

REFERENCES

Allen, D. R., Hitt, M. A., & Greer, C. R. (1982). Occupational stress and perceived organizational effectiveness in formal groups: An examination of stress level and stress type. *Personnel Psychology, 35,* 358–369.

Bateman, T. S., & Strasser, S. (1983). A cross-lagged regression test of the relatioships between job tension and employee satisfaction. *Journal of Applied Psychology, 68,* 439–445.

Browning, L. D. (1978). A grounded organizational communication theory derived from qualitative data. *Communication Monographs, 45,* 93–109.

Cooper, C. L., & Marshall, J. (1976). Occupational sources of stress: A review of the literature relating to coronary heart disease and mental ill health. *Journal of Occupational Psychology,* 49, 11–28.

Cooper, C. L., & Quick. J. C. (1999). *Stress and strain.* Oxford, England: Health Press.

D'Arcy, C., Syrotuik, J., & Siddique, C. M. (1984). Perceived job attributes, job satisfaction, and psychological distress: A comparison of working men and women. *Human Relations, 37*(8), 603–611.

Davidson, M., & Cooper, C. (1983). *Stress and the woman manager.* New York: St. Martin's.

French, J. R., & Caplan, R. D. (1972). Organizational stress and individual strain. In A. Morrow (Ed.), *The failure of success.* New York: AMACOM.

Fried, Y., Rowland, K. M., & Ferris, G. R. (1984). The physiological measurement of work stress: A critique. *Personnel Psychology, 37*, 583–615.

Ganster, D., Mayes, B., Sime, W., & Tharp, G. (1982). Managing organizational stress: A field experiment. *Journal of Applied Psychology, 47*, 533–542.

Hoiberg, A. (1982). Occupational stress and illness incidence. *Journal of Occupational Medicine, 24*, 445–451.

Holmes. D. S., & Jorgensen, B. W. (1971). Do personality and social psychologists study men more than women? *Representative Research in Social Psychology, 2*, 71–76.

Karasek, R. A., Jr. (1979). Job demands, job decision latitude and mental strain: Implications for job redesign. *Administrative Science Quarterly, 24*, 285–308.

Morgan, G., & Smircich, L. (1980). The case for qualitative research. *Academy of Management Review, 5*, 491–500.

Parker, D. F., & Decotiis, T. A. (1983). Organizational determinants of job stress. *Organizational Behavior and Human Performance, 32*, 160–177.

Parkinson, R. (1982). *managing health promotion in the workplace: for Implementation and Evaluation*. Palo Alto, CA: Mayfield.

Pelletier, K. R. (1984). *Healthy people in unhealthy places: Stress and fitness at work*. New York: Pelacorte.

Quick, J. C., Quick, J. D., Nelson, D. L., & Hurrell, J. J. (1997). *Preventive stress management in organizations*. Washington, DC: American Psychological Association.

Ritti, W. C., & Funkhouser, D.M. (1977). *The ropes to skip and the ropes to know*. Columbus, OH: Grid.

Rosenman, R. H., Brand, R. J., Jenkins, C. D., Frieman, M., Straus, R., & Wurm, J. (1975). Coronary heart disease in the midwestern collaborative group study. *Journal of the American Medical Association, 233*, 872–877.

Rossi, A. M., Lubbers, C. A., & Di Salvo, V. (1986). Work-related stress: An investigation of gender differences. *Biofeedback and Self-Regulation, 11*(1), 76–77.

Sauter, S. L. (1989). Moderating effects of job control on health complaints in office work. In S. L. Sauter, J. J. Hurrell, & C. L. Cooper (Eds.), *Job control and worker health*. New York: Wiley.

Yerkes, R. M., & Dodson, J. D. (1908). The relation of strength of stimulus to rapidity of habit formation. *Journal of Comparative Neurology and Psychology, 18*, 459–482.

Zappert, L. T., & Weinstein, H. M. (1985). Sex differences in the impact of work on physical and psychological health. *American Journal of Psychiatry, 132*(10), 1174–1178.

CHAPTER 3

TYPE A CORONARY PRONE BEHAVIOR, JOB STRESS, AND HEART DISEASE

Paul J. Rosch

Numerous studies confirm that job stress is far and way the leading source of stress for American adults and that increased job stress is associated with an increased incidence of coronary events and deaths. Type A behavior has also been shown to be as significant a risk factor for coronary heart disease as smoking, hypertension and cholesterol. This chapter will be devoted to clarifying the current confusion about how both job stress and coronary prone behavior should be defined and measured. In addition, we will explore their complex and intricate interrelationships.

EMOTIONS, BEHAVIORAL TRAITS, AND HEART DISEASE: SOME HISTORICAL HIGHLIGHTS

The appreciation that different emotions could have powerful influences on the heart and the recognition of some intimate but poorly understood mind-heart connection is hardly new. Aristotle and Virgil actually taught that the heart rather than the brain was the seat of the mind and soul and

Stress and Quality of Working Life: Current Perspectives in Occupational Health, 19–36
Copyright © 2006 by Information Age Publishing
All rights of reproduction in any form reserved.

similar beliefs can be found in ancient Hindu scriptures and other East-
ern philosophies. Some 2000 years ago, the Roman physician Celsus
unwittingly acknowledged this mind-heart relationship by noting that
"fear and anger, and any other state of the mind may often be apt to
excite the pulse" (Spencer, 1926). Our earliest uses of the word heart
clearly indicate its conceptualization as the seat of one's innermost feelings, temperament, or character. Broken-hearted, heartache, take to
heart, eat your heart out, heart of gold, heart of stone, stouthearted, are
just a few of the words and phrases we still use that vividly symbolize such
beliefs.

William Harvey, who discovered that the circulation of the blood
around the body through vessels was due to the mechanical action of the
heart also recognized that the heart was more than a mere pump. As he
wrote in 1628, "every affection of the mind that is attended either with
pain or pleasure, hope or fear, is the cause of an agitation whose influence
extends to the heart" (Harvey, 1628).

During the 18th century, John Hunter, who elevated surgery from a
mechanical trade to an experimental science, suffered from angina, and
being a keen observer complained, "my life is in the hands of any rascal
who chooses to annoy and tease me" (Home, 1796). He turned out to be
somewhat of a prophet, since it was a heated argument with a colleague
that precipitated his sudden death from a heart attack. Napoleon's favor-
ite physician, Corvisart, wrote that heart disease was due to "the passions
of the mind" (Pedinielli, 1993), among which he included anger, mad-
ness, fear, jealousy, terror, love, despair, joy, avarice, stupidity, and ambition.

With respect to personality and Type A behavioral traits, Von Düsch, a
19th century German physician, first noted that excessive involvement in
work appeared to be the hallmark of people who died from heart attacks.
(Von Düsch, 1868) He did not imply that job stress was the culprit, but
rather that such individuals seemed to be preoccupied with their work
and had few outside interests. Over 100 years ago, Sir William Osler, an
astute clinician, succinctly described the coronary-prone individual as a
"keen, and ambitious man, the indicator of whose engines are set at 'full
speed ahead.'" (Osler, 1892) He later wrote that he could make the pre-
sumptive diagnosis of angina based on the appearance, demeanor, and
mannerisms of the patient in the waiting room and how he entered the
consultation room. (Osler, 1910) In the 1930s, the Menningers suggested
that coronary heart patients tended to be very aggressive. (Menninger &
Menninger, 1936) Flanders Dunbar, who introduced the term "psychosomatic" into American medicine, characterized the coronary prone individual as being authoritarian with an intense drive to achieve unrealistic
goals (Dunbar, 1943). Kemple also emphasized fierce ambition and a

compulsive striving to achieve power and prestige (Kemple, 1945). A half century ago, Stewart Wolf described what he called the "Sisyphus reaction" (Wolf, 1955). In Greek mythology, Sisyphus, the king of Corinth, was doomed by the gods to a life of constant struggle by being condemned to roll a huge marble bolder up a hill, which, as soon as it reached the top, always rolled down again. Wolf characterized people who were coronary prone as constantly striving against real but often self-imposed challenges, and even if successful, not being able to relax or enjoy the satisfaction of achievement (Wolf, 1960).

WHAT IS TYPE A CORONARY PRONE BEHAVIOR?

In 1959, a paper by Meyer (Mike) Friedman and Ray Rosenman appeared in the *Journal of the American Medical Association* titled "Association of specific overt behavior patterns with blood and cardiovascular findings: Blood cholesterol level, blood clotting time, incidence of arcus senilis and clinical coronary artery disease" (Friedman & Rosenman, 1959). The subtitle linking specific behavioral traits with things like blood cholesterol, clotting time, arcus senilis and coronary disease that had no apparent relationship to each other must have seemed strange to many readers. Neither of these two cardiologists had any expertise in psychology, which may have been fortuitous, since they had no preconceived notions. What they did have was an unusual combination of curiosity, diagnostic acumen and a biopsychosocial approach to the patient as a person, rather than someone to be treated in a cookbook fashion based on laboratory tests, symptoms, or signs.

As noted, psychiatrists and others interested in psychosomatic disorders had previously described certain personality characteristics in heart attack patients. However, it was not possible to prove that these had any causal relationship since such idiosyncrasies could have resulted from the illness rather than vice versa. Friedman and Rosenman were the first to explain why specific behaviors could cause heart attacks and contribute to coronary artery disease. The term "Type A" was not mentioned in this initial paper but emerged the following year in an article describing how this type of "overt pattern behavior A" could be detected by a "new psychophysiological procedure" (Friedman & Rosenman, 1960). Rosenman was subsequently able to show the predictive value of this technique so that coronary prone patients could be identified and hopefully treated to prevent future problems (Rosenman et al., 1964).

At the time, animal studies had led to the widespread assumption that heart attacks were due to occlusion of a coronary artery by atherosclerotic deposits resulting from elevated blood cholesterol levels. This, in turn, was primarily the consequence of increased fat and cholesterol intake. Support for this was reinforced by research showing that the significant variation in mortality rates from coronary heart disease in different countries showed a clear correlation with fat consumption. The greater the amount of saturated fat and cholesterol in the average diet the higher the blood cholesterol and death rate from heart disease in that country. However, Friedman and Rosenman could not confirm this close relationship with serum cholesterol and high fat diet in their heart attack patients and looked for other possible contributing factors. They were intrigued by the observation that two-thirds of the heart attacks in the United States occurred in men, while in Mexico the incidence was equal between men and women. The same equal split appeared to exist in southern Italy but not in northern Italy, where the ratio was four men to one woman. This disparity was obviously not due to any difference in diet or other environmental factor, and on further analysis appeared to be related more to social, cultural, and behavioral attitudes that might best come under the heading of "maleness."

Such individuals exhibited certain characteristic activity patterns, including:

1. Self-imposed standards that are often unrealistically ambitious and pursued in an inflexible fashion. Associated with this are a need to maintain productivity in order to be respected, a sense of guilt while on vacation or relaxing, an unrelenting urge for recognition or power, and a competitive attitude that often creates challenges even when none exist.

2. Certain thought and activity styles characterized by persistent vigilance and impulsiveness, usually resulting in the pursuit of several lines of thought or action simultaneously.

3. Hyperactive responsiveness often manifested by a tendency to interrupt or finish a sentence in conversation, usually in dramatic fashion, by varying the speech, volume, and/or pitch, or by alternating rapid bursts of words with long pauses of hesitation for emphasis, indicating intensive thought. Type A persons often nod or mutter agreement or use short bursts of laughter to obliquely indicate to the speaker that the point being made has already been anticipated so that they can take over.

4. Unsatisfactory interpersonal relationships due to the fact that Type As are usually self-centered, poor listeners, often have an attitude of bravado about their own superiority, and are much more easily angered, frustrated, or hostile if their wishes are not respected or their goals are not achieved.

5. Increased muscular activity in the form of gestures, motions, and facial activities such as grimaces, gritting, and grinding of the teeth, or tensing jaw muscles. Often there is frequent clenching of the fist or perhaps pounding with a fist to emphasize a point. Fidgeting, tapping the feet, leg shaking, or playing with a pencil in some rhythmic fashion are also common.

6. Irregular or unusual breathing patterns with frequent sighing, produced by inhaling more air than needed while speaking and then releasing it during the middle or end of a sentence for emphasis.

It was also noted that coronary prone patients tend to be very competitive and often overly aggressive. They are usually in a hurry and consequently eat, talk, walk, and do most other activities at a more rapid pace. Type As are generally more concerned with the quantity rather than the quality of their work, try to do too many things at once, are frequently preoccupied with what they are going to do next, and tend to have few interests outside their work (Rosch, 1983a).

HOW DID THE TYPE A CONCEPT ORIGINATE?

How the Type A coronary prone behavior hypothesis evolved is a fascinating story, especially since it began because of an interest in cholesterol metabolism rather personality characteristics. As Ray Rosenman explained to me in a recent interview (Rosch, 2004),

Mike and I were partners in our San Francisco clinical practice across the street from Mount Zion Hospital and Medical Center. Our Harold Brunn Institute for Cardiovascular Research building adjoined the hospital and following early hospital rounds we spent full mornings in the research lab and afternoons in the office. By 1950, although fat and cholesterol had long been fed to rabbits to produce vascular lesions, little was known about where plasma cholesterol came from or how it was metabolized. We also noted that this type of vascular damage was quite different from that seen in patients with coronary artery disease. We obtained Public Health Service and other grants to begin animal studies and Mike was able to solve many fundamental aspects of cholesterol metabolism. I was later able to delineate the mechanisms underlying low and high plasma cholesterol respectively in hypothyroidism and hyperthyroidism and what caused elevated lipids in patients with nephrosis. Around 1952, because of our growing interest in cholesterol, we obtained blood samples from private patients at every visit for (no-cost) accurate analyses at our research lab. We soon realized that that there were surprising fluctuations in their cholesterol levels that were unrelated to diet or weight, and had little relationship to subsequent coronary events.

We subsequently recognized and reported serious errors and omissions in papers by Keys and others about the contribution of diet to plasma cholesterol. The prevailing dogma, which still persists, was that coronary heart disease was due to elevated cholesterol, which in turn resulted from increased dietary fat intake. Our own and other data that Keys had ignored in reaching his conclusions did not support this and reinforced our belief that socioeconomic influences played a more important role in the increased incidence of coronary disease as well as gender differences.

A discerning secretary in our office practice told us that in contrast to our other patients, those with coronary disease were rarely late for appointments and preferred to sit in hard-upholstered chairs rather than softer ones or sofas. These chairs also had to be reupholstered far more often than others because the front edges quickly became worn out. They looked at their watches frequently and acted impatient when they had to wait, usually sat on the edges of waiting room chairs and tended to leap up when called to be examined. Her astute observations significantly reinforced our own awareness of similar behaviors in our coronary patients, then mainly males, that you summarized so well over two decades ago. (Rosch, 1983a)

Ray also told me that when he asked patients about what they thought had caused their heart problems diet or cholesterol was hardly ever mentioned. Occupational pressures and other sociocultural stresses headed the list. Some spouses had spontaneously volunteered the opinion that their husband's heart attack was directly due to excessive involvement in work related activities. When Rosenman and Friedman subsequently asked the wives, relatives, friends, and coworkers of heart attack patients to list possible contributing factors, they were surprised at how often their assessment similarly ranked job stress right at the top. The cluster of behaviors and activity patterns previously described that also emerged from these sources was far more common in males than female. It was also was evident that the current marked increased incidence of coronary disease had occurred mainly in men without any significant change in their diet, increased prevalence of diabetes, hypertension, or other risk factors. Even when combined, the standard Framingham coronary risk factors of smoking, hypertension, and cholesterol accounted for only about one third of coronary disease patients in prospective studies. It became increasingly clear that these risk factors were merely markers that might predict coronary events but did not cause them. As one authority noted in an extensive review,

The best combinations of the standard risk factors fail to identify most new cases of coronary disease.... And, whereas simultaneous presence of two or more risk factors is associated with extremely high risk of coronary disease, such situations only predict a small minority of cases.... A broad array of recent research studies point with ever increasing certainty to the position that certain psychological, social and behavior conditions do put persons at higher risk of clinically manifest coronary disease. (Jenkins, 1971)

For example, despite the fact that standard risk factor levels were the same, there were striking geographic differences in the prevalence and incidence of coronary disease in diverse populations in Northern versus Southern Europe and the United States versus Mexico. These disparities were not due to any dietary differences and on closer analysis, seemed related more to what might be viewed as a "macho" attitude and personality. I was curious as to why it was decided to label this kind of behavior as "Type A" and Ray explained,

While we were doing prevalence studies in male and female subjects we realized it was necessary to do a prospective study. (Rosenman & Friedman, 1961) I submitted a grant proposal that was twice rejected, and then successfully modified by a suggestion from the Public Health Service Director that we term the two behavior types as "Type A and Type B." After a site visit the grant was approved for two years. The methodology of the Western Collaborative Group Study, including the Structured Interview (SI) for assessing behavior patterns was described in my first follow-up paper. (Rosenman et al., 1966) Later site visits led to grant extensions for long-term follow-up, largely due to the efforts of the remarkable Dr. Stewart Wolf. We became good friends many years later through you, your annual Congress and other activities of the American Institute of Stress."

HOW CAN YOU MEASURE TYPE A CORONARY PRONE BEHAVIOR?

The 1974 best seller *Type A Behavior And Your Heart* (Friedman & Rosenman, 1974) stimulated studies by others and Type A soon became part of vernacular speech. The significant contribution of Type A behavior to coronary heart disease (CHD) was subsequently acknowledged by a committee of authorities assembled by the National Institutes of Health (The Review Panel, 1981), who noted,

The Review Panel accepts the available body of scientific evidence as demonstrating that Type A behavior ... is associated with an increased risk of clinically apparent CHD in employed, middle-aged U.S. citizens. This increased risk is greater than that imposed by age, elevated levels of systolic blood pressure, serum cholesterol, and smoking and appears to be of the same order of magnitude as the relative risk associated with the latter three of these other factors. (p. 1200)

However, the initial support and enthusiasm waned following several studies that failed to confirm the opinion of the NIH expert panel. One problem was that like stress, Type A meant different things to different people. More importantly, researchers also used different assessment or measurement methods so it is not surprising that they reached conflicting conclusions.

It is evident from their initial publications that Friedman and Rosenman were careful to emphasize that Type A was an "overt behavior pattern." What they meant by this were observable traits and characteristics that could be readily detected by others, such as the vocal stylistics, breathing patterns, facial grimaces, body movements, hyperresponsiveness, and accelerated pace of activities previously described. In their extensive study of employees of several large Western corporations, Rosenman and colleagues were able to predict susceptibility to coronary disease by behavioral characteristics such as a tense, alert and confident appearance, strong voice, clipped, rapid and emphatic speech, laconic answers, evidences of hostility, aggressiveness and impatience, and frequent sighing during questioning. As they noted, (Rosenman, et al., 1964):

> Before and during the personal interview, the following observations upon each subject were made and recorded by the interviewer. (1) Degree of mental and emotional alertness (minimal, average, extreme), (2) Speed of locomotion (minimal, average, extreme), (3) Body restlessness (none, average, extreme), (4) Facial grimaces (scowls, teeth-clenching and tic in which teeth are clenched and masseter muscles are tensed, (5) Hand movements (fist-clenching, gestures made with extraordinary vigor, e.g., desk-pounding). (p. 122)

The actual responses to the questions were not particularly important since the major purpose of the interview was to elicit and systematically observe the stress-related body language and speech. In clinical practice, accurate assessment of Type A behavior requires a structured personal interview by a trained investigator using standardized challenges to elicit these tell tale characteristics. For example, one such challenge might be conducted as follows:

The investigator begins the interview by asking the following question in a deliberate and painfully slow, monotonous manner. "Mr. Smith, (2 second pause), most people, when they go to work during the week—that is, Monday through Friday—, get up early (2 second pause),—say around

6:30 to 7 AM. That is probably because it necessary to provide enough time for them to shower, brush their teeth, (2 second pause) and so forth, get dressed, have something to eat, and then they travel by car, bus or train so they can get to work by a certain time (2 second pause), which is often between 8:30 and 9 AM. Now, in your case* (3 second pause), what time do you usually get up (2 second pause) during the week, that is Monday through Friday? How do you travel to work and what time do you usually get there? Unknown to the subject, the interviewer starts a stopwatch as noted by the asterisk above after asking "Now in your case." A flaming Type A would interrupt almost immediately before the question was finished to quickly explain his usual daily routine. In contrast, a Type B would listen to the entire recitation, reflect for a few moments, and then slowly respond with something like "Well, on Mondays, I tend to get up at 6 or a little later but on other days it is usually closer to 7" and continue on with a leisurely narration of possible variations on subsequent weekday habits.

Again, the interviewer is not as interested in the content of the response as much as the manner in which it is conveyed and how the subject acts during the interview with respect to facial expressions, gestures, evidence of impatience, time urgency, and other typical Type A traits. Each of these has a certain value and is rated as to severity to obtain a final assessment. Interviews are videotaped so that several reviewers can carefully review the responses and reach agreement on the significance of each component. These Type A characteristics have been described in detail to emphasize that this complex behavioral pattern can only be accurately assessed by personal observation of the subject by an investigator who has been trained to elicit and evaluate typical responses. Type A behavior is almost impossible to detect in someone who is very sick, bored, depressed, or frightened, such as in a patient recently hospitalized for a heart attack or some other serious medical condition. Reliable ratings therefore require considerable expertise, making large-scale studies quite time consuming and costly.

As a consequence, a variety of questionnaires have been devised to detect such aspects of Type A behavior as competitiveness, ambition, impatience, hostility, preoccupation with work, or a constant sense of time urgency. The Thurstone Temperament Survey's Activity Schedule and Gough Adjective Check List measure only selective Type A behaviors. Others like the Jenkins Activity Survey, Framingham Type A, Vickers and Bortner Scales were designed to duplicate the structured interview. However self-reports fail to capture the stylistics and psychomotor behaviors that are essential to the construct of Type A and its assessment. Self-report questionnaires were rarely validated by those who used them in so many published Type A studies, which also led to considerable confusion in this field. Such questionnaires assess different behavioral characteristics and the subject's perception of attitudes, attributes, and activities and show poor correlation among themselves or with the results of a properly conducted structured interview. The most commonly used instrument, the Jenkins Activity Survey, detects three main behavioral syndromes: (1) hard-driving temperament, (2) job involvement, and (3) speed and impatience (Jenkins, Friedman, & Rosenman, 1965). Although the three scores derived correlate with the total evaluation, they are not necessarily related to one another, and the overall accuracy is only about 70% when compared with a structured personal interview. (Jenkins, Rosenman, & Zyzanski, 1974) It should be emphasized in evaluating any self-administered questionnaire that Type A individuals are often unaware of many of their behavioral patterns or will deny them. No single Type A individual should be expected to exhibit all of the above characteristics, and conversely, some Type A characteristics are often found in Type Bs. Contrary to popular opinion, there is no rating scale for Type B behavior or definition other than the relative absence of Type A traits.

As our understanding and ability to measure Type A improves, it is possible that certain components such as time urgency, latent hostility, aggressiveness, or authoritarianism may be found to have a greater predictive significance for coronary heart disease. In particular, it has been proposed that "hostility" correlates best with coronary disease (Williams, 1984). This conclusion is based on responses to the Minnesota Multiphasic Personality Inventory (MMPI), a 566-item questionnaire developed in 1937 that rapidly became the gold standard for psychological testing of hundreds of thousands of college students and prospective employees. For example, by analyzing responses to various MMPI questions that comprised a subscale, one could screen for tendencies to such undesirable things as schizophrenia, depression, paranoia and introversion. About 50 years ago, two psychologists, Cook and Medley, selected 50 items to group into what they called a hostility (Ho) subscale that could differentiate between teachers who were most likely to have good or poor rapport with students. Redford and colleagues showed that a follow-up of individuals who scored high on Ho scale ratings had significantly higher mortality rates from coronary heart disease. They also reported that the Ho rating scale could be further separated into subscales that measure cynicism and paranoid alienation. However, neither the Ho nor either of its subscales measures anger, irritability or aggression, which are the hallmarks of hostility. Rather, they are more apt to reflect neuroticism and psychopathologic traits that are not predictive of coronary disease.

Like Type A, hostility is best evaluated by observation, rather than self-report questionnaires such as the MMPI and hostility ratings obtained by personal observation do not correlate well with Ho scale measurements.

Subjects with high Ho scores also tend to have high scores on the Jenkins Activity Survey speed and impatience and hard driving temperament subscales. Thus, the Ho scale may simply be measuring certain aspects of Type A coronary-prone behavior but labeling it as something else. I have had occasion to ask both Mike Friedman and Ray Rosenman whether any particular Type A trait was most useful in predicting the likelihood of a coronary event or was it the presence of many that was more important. As emphasized in the original papers, Friedman was most impressed with time urgency, and referred to Type A as "the hurry sickness." Ray Rosenman agreed that there was little doubt that the increased incidence of coronary disease had occurred in association with a faster pace of living, but for him, the cardinal Type A characteristic was constant competitiveness. Even when playing games against children, Type As frequently remain fiercely competitive and hate to lose.

ARE TYPE AS ADDICTED TO THEIR OWN ADRENALINE SECRETION?

As previously proposed, I believe it is quite plausible that Type A is a self-perpetuating behavior due to stress induced adrenaline addiction (Rosch, 1989). It is possible that other stress-related neurohumoral secretions such as serotonin, dopamine or beta-endorphin also have the potential for inducing addiction. Support for this comes from Solomon's "opponent-process theory of acquired motivation," which basically asserts that man is by nature susceptible to various habits and addictions that provide a sense of pleasure (Solomon, 1977). However, when deprived of the thing that is craved, an opposing emotional state often results. The exhilarating feeling of being in love changes to melancholy if one is deprived of any contact with their beloved. People who are hooked on skydiving may become severely depressed if the weather interferes with their activities for a few days. Similarly, withdrawal from cigarettes, alcohol, narcotics, tranquilizers, or recreational drugs often produces an emotional state directly opposite from the pleasurable sensations those substances induce.

Type As who have become addicted to surges of their stress related hormonal secretions might unconsciously seek ways to induce their associated "highs." That could come in the form of constructing contests and challenges, like getting to the airport shortly before takeoff to avoid waiting, turning a car trip into a race by predicting specific times at which check points must be reached, purposely leaving a desk untidy or room untidy, or delaying an assignment to the last minute just so there will be some sort of time urgent, last-minute challenge. When deprived of such stimuli, Type As are apt to be irritable and depressed. Thus, recuperating from a heart attack by spending 2 weeks on a deserted tropical beach might be perfect for many patients but a dangerous prescription for some Type As, who would likely be agitated within an hour if they were unable to get back to their work or contact their office to see what was going on.

STRESS VERSUS CHOLESTEROL AND OTHER "RISK FACTORS" FOR CORONARY HEART DISEASE

It has long been recognized that severe or sudden emotional stress could result in a heart attack or sudden death. Walter Cannon at Harvard first delineated the mechanisms responsible for this in the early part of the last century. (Cannon, 1914) Cannon's studies demonstrated that responses to the stress of acute fear resulted in a marked increase in sympathetic nervous system activity and an outpouring of sympathin (adrenaline) that prepared the animal for lifesaving "fight or flight." His later studies of the mechanism of "bone pointing" or "voodoo" death also implicated excess secretion of hormones from the adrenal medulla into the blood stream as the most likely cause of fatal arrhythmia (Cannon, 1942). Hans Selye's formulation of the stress concept in the late 1940s provided further insight into the role of pituitary and adrenal cortical hormones in mediating damaging cardiovascular responses to stress. His subsequent research included the experimental production of "metabolic cardiac necroses," in which direct biochemical injury to heart muscle rather than occlusion of the coronary vessels was the causative factor (Selye, 1958).

Since then, it has been observed that stress can cause accelerated atherosclerosis and coronary occlusion that is associated with elevated cholesterol, triglycerides, and free fatty acids, increased fibrinogen, haptoglobin, plasma seromucoids, platelet aggregation and adhesiveness, polycythemia, and accelerated blood clotting. We have also become increasingly aware of the important role of stress-induced coronary vasospasm in the production of clinical symptoms and disease (Gersh, Bassendine, Forman, & Walls, 1981) Even more significant has been the identification of myocardial infarction in the absence of significant coronary occlusion due to excessive release of norepinephrine at myocardial nerve endings. This has been shown to produce a specific type of microscopic myocardial damage that appears to be identical in laboratory animals as well as humans who have succumbed to sudden cardiac death as a result of an acutely stressful situation (Cebelin & Hirsch, 1981). There is also abundant evidence that severe and acute emotional stress following an earthquake or other natural disaster or the loss of a loved one can result in hypertension, a heart attack or sudden death (Rosch, 1994a, 1994b).

As emphasized, conventional dogma postulates that heart attacks are due to elevated cholesterol, which in turn is due to a high fat diet, a premise that presumably was proven by Ancel Key's seven-country study that allegedly showed this close correlation (Keys, 1970, 1980). However, we now know that Keys conveniently hand picked these from a list of many more countries in an effort to support the fatty diet →cholesterol→heart attack hypothesis. Had he included all the data available to him he would have confirmed that these associations were weak, absent, and in some instances inverse (Jacobs, et al., 1992). The Framingham study was largely responsible for the belief that cholesterol, cigarettes, and hypertension caused heart attacks but if this was true, then removing these "risk factors" should reduce the incidence of coronary events (Rosch, 1983b)

In 1982, the disappointing results of the 7-year, $115 million MRFIT study were published in the *Journal of the American Medical Association*. MRFIT is an acronym for Multiple Risk Factor Intervention Trail, which was designed to show the beneficial effect of stopping smoking and lowering cholesterol and blood pressure (Multiple Risk Factor Intervention Trial Group, 1982). However, patients in whom these desired results were achieved did not receive any significant protection. In fact, a subset of hypertensives treated with diuretics had a higher incidence of heart attacks than controls, possibly because they caused hypokalemia, which potentiated damaging adrenergic effects and risk for sudden death. (Rosch, 1983b) In contrast, over the same period, two other studies designed to reduce the likelihood of recurrent heart attacks were so successful that they were halted prematurely so that controls would not be denied the benefit of intervention. One was a trial using techniques to reduce Type A coronary prone behavior (Friedman et al., 1982). The other was an NIH sponsored study of almost 4,000 patients in which it was found that after only 2 years the administration of propanolol (Inderal) had reduced mortality by 26% (Beta-Blocker Heart Attack Study Group 1981; Beta-Blocker Heart Attack Study Group, 1982) Both trials strongly suggest that stress-related sympathetic nervous system drive and catecholamine secretion are the major culprits in coronary heart disease. Behavioral modification is aimed at turning off the epinephrine-norepinephrine spigot, and propanolol and other beta-blockers blunt the damaging effects of such agents on the cardiovascular system. These cardioprotective effects have been so well documented that it has been suggested that beta-blockers be administered to all heart-attack patients provided there are no contraindications (Khan, 1983).

TYPE A BEHAVIOR, JOB STRESS, AND CORONARY HEART DISEASE

Numerous surveys confirm that occupational pressures are far and away the leading source of stress for American adults and that job stress has escalated progressively over the past 4 decades (Rosch, 2001). While the causes for this vary with occupations and positions, most contributors fall into the following categories:

- How Work And Tasks Are Designed—Heavy workload; infrequent rest breaks; long work hours and shift work; hectic and routine tasks that: have little inherent meaning, do not allow workers to utilize their skills, and most importantly, provide little sense of control.

- Management Style—Lack of participation by workers in decision-making; poor communication in the organization; lack of company policies that take employees' family and personal obligations into consideration.

- Interpersonal Relationships—Poor social environment and lack of support or help from coworkers and supervisors.

- Vague Or Changing Job Description—Conflicting or uncertain job expectations; too much responsibility; too many hats to wear; too many superiors, coworkers or customers making very different demands.

- Concerns About Employment Or Career—Job insecurity and lack of opportunity for advancement, or promotion; rapid changes for which workers are unprepared due to unanticipated downsizing, mergers and hostile acquisitions.

- Environmental Concerns—Unpleasant or dangerous physical conditions in the workplace such as crowding, noise, air pollution, or failure to address ergonomic problems.

- Discrimination—Lack of opportunity for advancement or promotion because of age, gender, race, religion, or disability despite legislation designed to prevent this.

- Violence, Physical And Verbal Abuse—An average of 20 workers a week are murdered and 18,000 are physically abused in the United States but the number may be higher since many such crimes are not reported. Homicide has become the second leading cause of workplace deaths overall and ranks first for females.

The relationship between job stress and illness was recognized 300 years ago by Bernardo Ramazzini, who described in detail the diseases of people engaged in 40 different kinds of work and urged his fellow physicians to question their patients about their occupations (Ramazzini, 1713). While the major focus was on physical hazards such as "sharp and acid particles" in the air at certain work environments, he was well aware of the role of personal habits, behavior and psychosocial factors in causing illness and emphasized the importance of prevention. The clear link between job stress and cardiovascular disease was scientifically demonstrated 15 years ago by Karasek and Theorell (Karasek & Theorell, 1990) and has since been confirmed by numerous other investigators using their demand/control model and it is essential to emphasize the importance of this approach.

While there are numerous claims that certain occupations are extremely stressful and therefore more likely to cause heart disease, these are usually self-serving and designed to obtain higher wages or more benefits for members by unions and organizations and are based on anecdotal self-report questionnaires rather than objective scientific studies. Various rankings of the "most" and "least" stressful jobs are also misleading since job stress is entirely dependent on the person/environment fit as assessed by the perception of having little control but significant demands. Some Type As thrive in the pressure cooker of life in the fast lane, having numerous responsibilities and doing several things at once provided they feel in control. This would overwhelm others who are content to do dull, dead end assembly line duties that present no challenge since they are well within their capabilities. Conversely, this could be very stressful for a Type A because of the perception of having no control over what is going on. Although Type As tend to be preoccupied with work-related activities it is a common misconception that they are under more stress than others or that their exaggerated cardiovascular reactivity to challenges leads to sustained hypertension and coronary disease. In point of fact, Type As rarely perceive stress and never admit to being stressed although they are notorious for causing stress in others (Rosenman, 1990, 1993).

Stress is difficult for scientists to define since it is a subjective phenomenon that differs for each of us and we all respond to stress differently. Things that are distressful for some people can be pleasurable for others or have little significance either way, as can be readily illustrated by observing passengers on a steep roller coaster ride. Some are crouched down in the back seats with their eyes shut, jaws clenched, white knuckled as they clench the retaining bar. They cannot wait for the ride in the torture chamber to end and get on solid ground to scamper away. But up front are the thrill seekers, yelling and relishing every abrupt plunge, and who race to get on the very next ride! And in between, you may find a few with an air of nonchalance that seems to border on boredom. So, was the roller coaster ride stressful?

The roller coaster is a useful analogy that helps to explain stress. What distinguished the riders in the back from those up front was the sense of control they had over the event. While neither group had any more or less control their perceptions and expectations were quite different. Although stress is difficult to define, all of our clinical and experimental research confirms that the perception of having no control is always distressful—and that is what stress is all about. Many times we create our own stress because of faulty perceptions. You can teach people to move from the back of the roller coaster to the front and nobody can make you feel inferior unless you allow them to. Stress is an unavoidable consequence of life but there are some stresses you can do something about and others that you can't hope to avoid or control. The trick is in learning to distinguish between the two so that you do not waste your time and talent, like Don Quixote, tilting at windmills you can never conquer. The best way to accomplish this is in learning how to correct faulty perceptions and develop a better sense of control over your activities at work as well as at home. This will not only improve your quality of life but also help protect you from coronary heart disease and other stress-related disorders.

REFERENCES

Beta-Blocker Heart Attack Study Group (1981). Beta-blocker heart attack trial. *JAMA, 246,* 2073–2074.

Beta-Blocker Heart Attack Study Group (1982). Beta-blocker heart attack trial. *JAMA, 247,*1701–1714.

Cannon, W. J. (1914) The emergency function of the adrenal medulla in pain and the major emotions. *Am J Physiol, 33,* 356–372.

Cannon, W. J. (1942) "Voodoo" death. *Am Anthropol, 44,* 169–181.

Cebelin, M. S., & Hirsch, C. S. (1981). Human stress cardiomyopathy: Myocardial lesions in victims of homicidal assaults without internal injuries. *Hum Pathol, 2,* 123–132.

Dunbar, H. F. (1943). *Psychosomatic diagnosis.* New York: Hoeber and Harper.

Friedman, M., & Rosenman, R. H. (1959). Association of specific overt behavior patterns with blood and cardiovascular findings: Blood cholesterol level, blood clotting time, incidence of arcus senilis and clinical coronary artery disease. *JAMA, 169,* 1286–1296.

Friedman, M., & Rosenman, R. H. (1960) Overt behavior pattern in coronary artery disease: Detection of overt pattern behavior A in patients with coronary artery disease by a new psycho-physiological procedure. *JAMA, 173,* 1320–1325.

Friedman, M., & Rosenman, R. H. (1974). *Type A behavior and your heart.* New York: Knopf.

Friedman M., Thoresen, C. E., Gill, J. J., Ulmer, D., Thompson, L., Powell, L., et al. (1982). Feasibility of altering Type A behavior pattern after myocardial infarction. Recurrent coronary prevention project study: Methods, baseline results and preliminary findings. *Circulation, 66,* 83–92.

Gersh, B. J., Bassendine, M. F., Forman, R., & Walls, R. S. (1981). Case report: Coronary artery spasm and myocardial infarction in the absence of angiographically demonstrable obstructive coronary disease. *Mayo Clin Proc, 56,* 700–708.

Harvey, W. (1628). *Anatomica de Motu Cordis* [On the movement of the heart and blood in animals]. Cited in Willius & Keyes (1941) Classics in cardiology, p. 15. New York: Dover.

Home, E. (1796). "A short account of the Author's Life." *A Treatise on the Blood, Inflammation and Gunshot Wounds,* by J. Hunter. Philadelphia: T. Bradfors.

Jacobs, D., Blackburn, H., Higgins, M., Reed, D., Iso, H., McMillan, G., Neaton, J., et al. (1992) Report of the conference on low blood cholesterol: Mortality associations. *Circulation, 86,* 1046–1060.

Jenkins, C. D., Friedman, M., & Rosenman, R. H. (1965). *The Jenkins activity survey for health prediction,* Chapel Hill: University of North Carolina.

Jenkins, C. D., Rosenman, R. H., & Zysanski, S. J. (1974) Prediction of clinical coronary heart disease by a test for the coronary-prone behavior pattern. *NEJM, 290,* 1272–1275.

Jenkins, C. D. (1971). Psychological and social precursors of coronary disease (PT. 1). *NEJM, 282,* 244–254.

Karasek, R. A., & Theorell, T. (1990) *Healthy work: Stress, productivity, and the reconstruction of working life.* New York: Basic Books.

Khan, A. H. (1983). Beta-adrenoceptor blocking agents: Their role in reducing chances of recurrent infarction and death. *Arch Intern Med, 143,*1759–1762.

Kemple, C. (1945). Rorschach method and psychosomatic diagnosis: Personality traits in patients with rheumatic disease, hypertensive cardiovascular disease, coronary occlusion and fracture. *Psychosomatic Medicine, 7,* 85–89.

Keys, A. (1970). Coronary heart disease in seven countries. *Circulation, 41*(Suppl. 1), 1–211.

Keys, A. (1980). *Seven countries: A multivariate analysis of death and coronary heart disease.* London: Harvard University Press.

Menninger, K. A., & Menninger, W. C. (1936). Psychoanalytic observations in cardiac disorders. *American Heart Journal, 11,* 10–21.

Multiple Risk Factor Intervention Trial Research Group. (1982). Multiple risk factor intervention trial: Risk factor changes and mortality results. *JAMA, 248,* 1465–1477.

Osler, W. (1892). *Lecture on angina pectoris and allied states.* New York. Appleton.

Osler, W. (1910). The Lumleian lectures on angina pectoris. *Lancet, 1,* 839–844.

Pedinielli, L. (1993). Jean Nicolas Corvisart, Physician-in-chief at the court of Emperor Napoleon. *J Chir, 12,* 548-550.

Ramazzini, B. (1713). *Translation of the Latin text of De Morbus Artificum Diatriba of 1713,* published under the auspices of the NY Academy of Medicine 1964. New York: Havner Press.

The Review Panel on Coronary-Prone Behavior and Coronary Heart Disease. (1981). A critical review. *Circulation, 63,* 1199–1215.

Rosch, P. J. (1983a). Stress and cardiovascular disease. *Comprehensive Therapy, 9*, 6–13.

Rosch, P. J. (1983b). Stress, cholesterol and coronary heart disease. *Lancet, 2*, 851-852.

Rosch, P. J. (1989) "Stress Addiction": Causes, consequences, and cures. In F. Flach (Ed.), *Stress and its management* (pp. 189–202) New York: Norton.

Rosch, P. J. (1994a). Does stress cause hypertension? *Stress Medicine, 10*, 141–143.

Rosch, P. J. (1994b). Can stress cause coronary heart disease? *Stress Medicine, 10*, 207–210.

Rosch, P. J. (2001). *Health and stress: The newsletter of the American Institute of Stress. 3*, 1-3.

Rosch, P. J. (2004) *Health And Stress: The newsletter of the American Institute of Stress.* No. 10.

Rosenman, R. H. (1990). Cardiovascular reactivity: Physiological or psychological? In R. Schmidt (Ed.), *Theoretical and applied aspects of health psychology* (pp. 78–94). London: Harwood.

Rosenman, R. H. (1993). Relationships of Type A behavior pattern with coronary heart disease. In J. Goldberger & S. Breznitz (Eds.), *Handbook of stress-theoretical and clinical aspects* (pp. 185–204). New York: Free Press

Rosenman, R. H., & Friedman M. (1961). Association of a specific overt behavior pattern in females with blood and cardiovascular findings. *Circ., 24*, 1173-84

Rosenman, R. H., Friedman, M., Strauss, R., Wurm, M., Kositchek, R., Hahn, W., & Werthessen, N. T. (1964). A predictive study of coronary heart disease. *JAMA, 189*, 15–22

Rosenman, R. H., Friedman, M., Straus, R., Wurm, M., Jenkins, C. D., Messinger, H. B., et al. (1966). Coronary heart disease in the western collaborative group study: A follow-up experience of two years. *JAMA, 195*, 86–92.

Selye, H. (1958). *The chemical prevention of cardiac necroses.* New York: Ronald Press.

Solomon, R. L. (1977). An opponent-process theory of acquired motivation. The affective dynamics of addiction. In J. D. Maser & M. Seligman (Eds.), *Psychopathology: Experimental models* (pp. 66–103). San Francisco: W. H. Freeman.

Spencer, W. G. (1926). Celsus *De Medicina. Proceeding of the Royal Society of Medicine, 19*, 129.

Thoresen, C. E. Friedman, M. Gill, J. J., & Ulmer, D. (1982). The recurrent coronary prevention project: Some preliminary findings. *Acta Med Scandinav, 660*(Suppl.), 172–192.

Von Düsch, T. (1868). *Lehrbuch der Herzkrankheiten* [Textbook of the heart diseases]. Leipzig, Germany: Verlag von Wilhelm Engelman

Williams, R. (1989). *The trusting heart: Great news about Type A behavior.* New York: Random House.

Wolf, S. (1955). Psychosomatic aspects of industrial medicine. *South Med J, 4*, 79.

CHAPTER 4

UNDERSTANDING
JOB BURNOUT

Christina Maslach

In recent years, "burnout" has become a popular way to describe the personal agony of job stress. The evocative imagery of a flame being reduced to ashes seems to resonate with people's own experience of a psychological erosion over time. The initial "fire" of enthusiasm, dedication, and commitment to success has "burned out," leaving behind the smoldering embers of exhaustion, cynicism, and ineffectiveness. The literary model for this phenomenon, as portrayed in Graham Greene's *A Burnt-Out Case* (1961), is the spiritually tormented and disillusioned architect who quits his job and withdraws into the African jungle. But much research over the past 25 years has established that this phenomenon is not merely a fictional one, and that it is not reserved for rare cases. Rather, burnout is a fairly common and widespread job experience, which serves as an indicator of a major disruption in people's relationship with their work.

WHAT IS BURNOUT?

Job burnout is a psychological syndrome that involves a prolonged response to chronic interpersonal stressors on the job. The three key

Stress and Quality of Working Life: Current Perspectives in Occupational Health, 37–51
Copyright © 2006 by Information Age Publishing
All rights of reproduction in any form reserved.

dimensions of this response are an overwhelming exhaustion, feelings of cynicism and detachment from the job, and a sense of ineffectiveness and lack of accomplishment. This definition is a broader statement of the multidimensional model that has been predominant in the burnout field (Maslach, 1993).

The *exhaustion* dimension represents the basic individual stress component of burnout. It refers to feelings of being overextended and depleted of one's emotional and physical resources. Workers feel drained and used up, without any source of replenishment. They lack enough energy to face another day or another problem, and a common complaint is "I'm overwhelmed, overloaded, and overworked – it's just too much." The major sources of this exhaustion are work overload and personal conflict on the job.

The *cynicism* dimension represents the interpersonal context component of burnout. It refers to a negative, callous, or excessively detached response to various aspects of the job. It usually develops in response to the overload of emotional exhaustion, and is self-protective at first—an emotional buffer of "detached concern." If people are working too hard and doing too much, they will begin to back off, to cut down, to reduce what they are doing. But the risk is that the detachment can result in the loss of idealism and the dehumanization of others. Over time workers are not simply creating a buffer and cutting back on the quantity of work but are also developing a negative reaction to people and to the job. As cynicism develops, people shift from trying to do their very best to doing the bare minimum. Their performance on the job can amount to "How do I get through, still get my paycheck, and get out of here?" Cynical workers cut back on the amount of time spent at the office or the job site and the amount of energy they devote to their job. They are still performing, but doing it at the bare minimum, so the quality of that performance declines.

The *inefficacy* dimension represents the self-evaluation component of burnout. It refers to feelings of incompetence and a lack of achievement and productivity in work. This lowered sense of self-efficacy is exacerbated by a lack of job resources, as well as by a lack of social support and of opportunities to develop professionally. People experiencing this dimension of burnout ask themselves, "What am I doing? Why am I here? Maybe this is the wrong job for me." This sense of inefficacy may make burned-out workers feel that they have made a mistake in choosing their career path and often makes them dislike the kind of person they think they have become. Thus, they come to have a negative regard for themselves, as well as for others.

Unlike acute stress reactions, which develop in response to specific critical incidents, burnout is a cumulative reaction to ongoing occupational stressors. With burnout, the emphasis has been more on the process of psychological erosion, and the psychological and social outcomes of this chronic exposure, rather than just the physical ones. Because burnout is a prolonged response to chronic interpersonal stressors on the job, it tends to be fairly stable over time. Different factors in the workplace are predictive of the different dimensions of burnout, but all three dimensions should be examined to get a good sense of what's going on when workers experience this phenomenon.

The problem of burnout first surfaced in caregiving and human service occupations, such as health care, mental health, social services, the criminal justice system, religious professions, counseling, and education (Maslach, 1982/2003). All of these occupations share a focus on providing aid and service to people in need—in other words, the core of the job is the relationship between provider and recipient. This interpersonal context of the job meant that, from the beginning, burnout was studied not so much as an individual stress response, but in terms of an individual's relational transactions in the workplace. Moreover, this interpersonal context focused attention on the individual's emotions, and on the motives and values underlying his or her work with recipients. The therapeutic or service relationships that caregivers or providers develop with recipients require an ongoing and intense level of personal, emotional contact. Although such relationships can be rewarding and engaging, they can also be quite stressful. Within such occupations, the prevailing norms are to be selfless and to put others' needs first; to work long hours and do whatever it takes to help a client or patient or student; to go the extra mile and to give one's all. Moreover, the organizational environments for these jobs are shaped by various social, political, and economic factors (such as funding cutbacks or policy restrictions) that result in work settings that are high in demands and low in resources.

Recently, as other occupations have become more oriented to "high-touch" customer service, the phenomenon of burnout has become relevant for these jobs as well (Maslach & Leiter, 1997). New research has been done with participant samples in this wider range of occupations, but the bulk of the research findings on burnout are still based on samples in health care, education, and human services (Maslach, Jackson, & Leiter, 1996; Schaufeli & Enzmann, 1998).

Although burnout has been identified primarily as a phenomenon in the world of work, the significance of the social context and interpersonal relationships for burnout suggests that burnout might be relevant to other domains of life. Indeed, several authors have applied the concept of burnout to the family. Burnout has been used to analyze the relationship between parents and children (Procaccini & Kiefaber,

1983), and to the relationship between members of a marital couple (Pines, 1996).

THE IMPACT OF JOB BURNOUT

Why should we care about job burnout? It is not uncommon for senior managers in organizations to downplay the importance of employees feeling stressed and burned out (Maslach & Leiter, 1997). The general view is that if workers are having a bad day, then that is their own personal problem—it is not a major concern for the organization. However, the kinds of issues identified by both researchers and practitioners suggest that burnout should indeed be considered a major concern because it can have many costs, both for the organization and for the individual employee. Research has found that job stress is predictive of lowered job performance, problems with family relationships, and poor health, and studies have shown parallel findings with job burnout.

Of primary concern to any organization should be the poor quality of work that a burned-out employee can produce. When employees shift to minimum performance, minimum standards of working, and minimum production quality, rather than performing at their best, they make more errors, become less thorough, and have less creativity for solving problems. For example, one study found that nurses experiencing higher levels of burnout were judged by their patients to be providing a lower level of patient care (Leiter, Harvie, & Frizzell, 1998), while another study found that burned-out police officers reported more use of violence against civilians (Kop, Euwema, & Schaufeli, 1999).

Burnout has been associated with various forms of negative responses to the job, including job dissatisfaction, low organizational commitment, absenteeism, intention to leave the job, and turnover (see Schaufeli & Enzmann, 1998, for a review). People who are experiencing burnout can have a negative impact on their colleagues, both by causing greater personal conflict and by disrupting job tasks. Thus, burnout can be "contagious" and perpetuate itself through informal interactions on the job. When burnout reaches the high cynicism stage, it can result in higher absenteeism and increased turnover. Employees suffering from burnout do the bare minimum, do not show up regularly, leave work early, and quit their jobs at higher rates than engaged employees.

The relationship of personal health to human stress has always been at the core of stress research. Stress has been shown to have a negative impact on both physical health (especially cardiovascular problems) and psychological well being. The individual stress dimension of burnout is exhaustion, and, as one would predict, that dimension has been correlated with various physical symptoms of stress: headaches, gastrointestinal disorders, muscle tension, hypertension, cold/flu episodes, and sleep disturbances (see Leiter & Maslach, 2000a, for a review).

Burnout has also been linked to depression, and there has been much debate about the meaning of that link (see Maslach & Leiter, 2005). A common assumption has been that burnout causes mental dysfunction— that is, it precipitates negative effects in terms of mental health, such as depression, anxiety, and drops in self-esteem. An alternative argument is that burnout is not a precursor to depression but is itself a form of mental illness. The most recent research on this issue indicates that burnout is indeed distinguishable from clinical depression, but that it seems to fit the diagnostic criteria for job-related neurasthenia (Schaufeli, Bakker, Hoogduin, Schaap, & Kladler, 2001). The implication of all of this research is that burnout is an important risk factor for mental ill health, and this can have a significant impact on both the family and work life of the affected employee.

Given that most research on burnout has focused on the job environment of the workplace, there has been relatively less attention devoted to how burnout affects home life. However, the research studies on this topic have found a fairly consistent pattern of a negative "spillover" effect. Workers who experienced burnout were rated by their spouses in more negative ways, and they themselves reported that their job had a negative impact on their family and that their marriage was unsatisfactory (e.g., Burke & Greenglass, 2001).

UNDERSTANDING THE PERSON WHO BURNS OUT

Some of the popular "wisdom" about burnout is that it is due to particular characteristics of the individual. One common belief is that it is the most high-striving people—the high-achievers, the workaholics—who are so highly motivated that they work too hard and do too much. The presumed paradox is that it is the best who burn out. However, an even more common view is that it is the worst who burn out. The people who "can't take the heat" are people who are incompetent or unmotivated slackers. From this perspective, burnout is beneficial because it weeds out the weak workers—leading them to either quit or be fired. Although this belief can be common among administrators and managers, it is not well supported by research evidence.

But can we identify the people who are most likely to experience burnout? Are they distinctive in terms of their personality? Several personality traits have been studied in an attempt to answer this question, and while there is not a large body of consistent findings, there are some suggestive trends (see Schaufeli & Enzmann, 1998, for a review). Burnout tends to be higher among people who have low self-esteem, an external locus of control, low levels of hardiness, and a Type A behavior style. Those who are burned-out cope with stressful events in a rather passive, defensive way, whereas active and confronting coping styles are associated with less burnout. In particular, confronting coping is associated with the dimension of efficacy. A more consistent trend has emerged from studies on the Big Five personality dimensions, which have found that burnout is linked to the dimension of neuroticism. Neuroticism includes trait anxiety, hostility, depression, self-consciousness, and vulnerability. People who score highly on neuroticism are emotionally unstable and prone to psychological distress; thus, it makes sense that such people would be more at risk for burnout.

Are there other personal characteristics that characterize the burnout-prone individual? Several demographic variables have been studied in relation to burnout, but the studies are relatively few and the findings are not that consistent (see Schaufeli & Enzmann, 1998, for a review). Age is the one variable that tends to show a correlation with burnout. Among younger employees the level of burnout is reported to be higher than it is among those aged over 30 or 40 years. Age is clearly confounded with work experience, so burnout appears to be more of a risk earlier in one's career, rather than later. The reasons for such an interpretation have not been studied very thoroughly. However, these findings should be viewed with caution because of the problem of "survival bias"—i.e., those who burn out early in their careers are likely to quit their jobs, leaving behind the survivors who have lower levels of burnout.

Do men and women differ with regard to burnout? According to popular opinion, the answer should be "yes" (e.g., women should be more stressed by the "double shift" of job and family responsibilities), but the empirical evidence tends to say "no." In general, the demographic variable of sex has not been a strong predictor of burnout. The one small but consistent sex difference is that males often score slightly higher on the dimension of cynicism. There is also a tendency in a few studies for women to score slightly higher on exhaustion. These results could be related to gender role stereotypes, but they may also reflect the confounding of sex with occupation (e.g., police officers are more likely to be male, nurses are more likely to be female). With regard to marital status, those who are unmarried seem to be more prone to burnout compared to those who are married. Singles seem to experience even higher burnout levels than those who are divorced. As for ethnicity, very few studies have assessed this demographic variable, so it is not possible to summarize any empirical trends.

UNDERSTANDING THE SITUATIONS THAT CAUSE BURNOUT

Although there is some evidence for individual risk factors for burnout, there is far more research evidence for the importance of situational variables. Over 2 decades of research on burnout have identified a plethora of organizational risk factors across many occupations in various countries (see the reviews by Maslach, Schaufeli, & Leiter, 2001; Schaufeli & Enzmann, 1998). The conclusion of all these studies is that burnout is due largely to the nature of the job, rather than to the characteristics of the individual employee.

However, this conclusion is responding to an "either/or" question ("is it the person *or* is it the job"), and it may well be that an "and" question is the better way to frame the issue. That is, there are both personal *and* situational variables that determine burnout, and the key issue is how best to conceptualize the combination or interaction of them. Building on earlier models of job-person fit (e.g., French, Rodgers, & Cobb, 1974), in which better fit was assumed to predict better adjustment and less stress, Maslach and Leiter (1997) formulated a burnout model that focuses on the degree of match, or mismatch, between the individual and key aspects of his or her organizational environment. The greater the gap, or mismatch, between the person and the job, the greater the likelihood of burnout; conversely, the greater the match (or fit), the greater the likelihood of engagement with work.

What are these key aspects of the organizational environment? An analysis of the research literature on organizational risk factors for burnout has led to the identification of six major domains: workload, control, reward, community, fairness, and values (Maslach & Leiter, 1997). The first two areas are reflected in the demand-control model of job stress (Karasek & Theorell, 1990), and reward refers to the power of reinforcements to shape behavior. Community captures all of the work on social support and interpersonal conflict, while fairness emerges from the literature on equity and social justice. Finally, the area of values picks up the cognitive-emotional power of job goals and expectations.

Work Overload

The first of these six areas is the one that everybody thinks of first: work overload. With work overload, employees feel that they have too much to do, not enough time to perform required tasks, and not enough resources to do the work well. There clearly is an imbalance, or mismatch, between the demands of the job and the individual's capacity to meet those demands. Not surprisingly, work overload is the single best predictor of the exhaustion dimension of burnout. People experiencing work overload are often experiencing an imbalance in the load between their job and their home life as well. For example, they may have to sacrifice family time or vacation time in order to finish their work.

Lack of Control

The second key area is a sense of lack of control. Research has identified a clear link between a lack of control and high levels of stress. Lack of control on the job can result from a number of factors. Employees who are micromanaged, and who are not allowed to use their own wisdom or experience to make decisions, will feel that they do not have much personal discretion and autonomy in their work. They may feel they are being held accountable, and yet they do not have the ability to control what it is they are being held accountable for. In other cases, employees will feel a lack of control because working life has become more chaotic and ambiguous as a result of economic downturns. Many employees find themselves worrying about mergers, downsizing, layoffs, and changes in management. They will also feel out of control if they are in a situation where they might be called in to work, told to leave early, or sent off on a trip with little or no notice. These kinds of situations are very disruptive to personal relationships. In all of these instances, the lack of control has an important impact on levels of stress and burnout.

Insufficient Rewards

The third critical area is insufficient rewards. This occurs when employees believe they are not getting rewarded appropriately for their performance. The standard rewards that most people think of are salary or benefits or special "perks." However, in many cases the more important rewards involve recognition. It matters a great deal to people that somebody else notices what they do, and that somebody cares about the quality of their work. When employees are working hard and feel that they are doing their best, they want to get some feedback on their efforts. The value of such concepts as "walk-around" management lies in its power to reward: there is explicit interest in what employees are doing, and the direct acknowledgement and appreciation of their accomplishments. Employee morale is heavily dependent on rewards and recognition.

As mentioned earlier, many of the jobs in which burnout was first identified were in the human service professions. These jobs are often ones where positive feedback is almost designed out of the process. People come to the employee because they are in trouble, sick, having difficulties, or have broken the law. When the clients (or patients, or customers) are no longer in trouble, or are healthy or feeling happy, they go away—and are then replaced by somebody else who has problems, or is sick, or is in trouble with the law. In this scenario for human service workers, their "successes" always leave, and they have less of an opportunity to see the effect of their hard work. Human service professions deal with negative emotions and negative feedback on a regular basis; indeed, a "good day" is often one in which nothing bad happens. In other words, there is no positive reinforcement, just a lack of negative reinforcement. Positive recognition in this type of situation is very important in preventing burnout because it does not occur as a routine part of the job.

Breakdown in Community

The fourth area has to do with the ongoing relationships that employees have with other people on the job. When these relationships are characterized by a lack of support and trust, and by unresolved conflict, then there is a breakdown in the sense of community. Work relationships include the full range of people that employees deal with on a regular basis, such as the recipients of their services, their coworkers, their boss, the people they supervise, outside vendors or salespeople, or people in the larger community outside the organization.

If work-related relationships are working well, then there is a great deal of social support, and employees have effective means of working out disagreements. But when there is a breakdown in community and there is not much support, there is real hostility and competition, which makes conflicts difficult to resolve. Under such conditions, stress and burnout are high, and work becomes difficult.

Absence of Fairness

The fifth area, an absence of fairness in the workplace, seems to be quite important for burnout, although it is a relatively new area of burnout research. The perception that the workplace is unfair and inequitable is probably the best predictor of the cynicism dimension of burnout. Anger and hostility are likely to arise when people feel they are not being treated with the respect that comes from being treated fairly. Even incidents that appear to be insignificant or trivial can, if they signal unfair treatment, generate intense emotions and have great psychological significance.

According to equity theories (Walster, Berscheid, & Walster, 1973; Siegrist, 1996), when people are experiencing the imbalance of inequity, they will take various actions to try to restore equity. Some actions might involve standard organizational procedures (e.g., for resolving grievances), but if employees do not believe there is any hope of a fair resolution, they may take other actions in areas that they can control. For instance, if employees think they are not being paid as well as they deserve, they may leave work early or take company supplies home with them, because "they owe it to me." It is possible that, in some extreme instances, employees might take action against the person (or persons) whom they may consider responsible for the inequity. Workplace violence often occurs around issues of perceived unfairness, but there has not been sufficient research on this topic.

Value Conflicts

Although there has not been a lot of research on the impact of values, current work suggests that it may play a key role in predicting levels of burnout (Leiter & Maslach, 2004). Values are the ideals and goals that originally attracted people to their job, and thus they are the motivating connection between the worker and the workplace (beyond the utilitarian exchange of time and labor for salary). Value conflicts arise when people are working in a situation where there is a conflict between personal and organizational values. Under these conditions, employees may have to grapple with the conflict between what they want to do and what they have to do. For example, people whose personal values dictate that it is wrong to lie may find themselves in a job where lying becomes necessary for success. Successful job performance may require a bold lie, or perhaps just a shading of the truth (e.g., to get the necessary authorization, or to get the sale). People who experience such a value conflict will give the following kinds of comments: "This job is eroding my soul," or "I cannot look at myself in the mirror anymore knowing what I'm doing. I can't live with myself. I don't like this." If workers are experiencing this kind of mismatch in values on a chronic basis, then burnout is likely to arise.

To reiterate an earlier point, the key issue here is the fit, or match, between the person and the job, and not the specific type of person or type of job environment per se. For example, a Machiavellian individual, who believes that the end justifies the means, will have a better fit with a job in which lying is essential for success, and will probably not experience value conflict.

Other kinds of value conflicts may arise between conflicting values within the organization. For example, the organization may insist that the highest priority is the customer, and will encourage employees to go to any length to make customers happy. However, at the same time the company may judge employee performance on sales, which encourages the employee to sell at any cost, regardless of whether the customer wants it or not. Employees often feel they are caught between conflicting values in this common scenario.

A Mediation Model

This framework of the six areas of person-job match or mismatch has identified the key causal sources of the burnout-engagement continuum. Given that burnout is also linked to important personal and situational effects, there is sufficient evidence to suggest that burnout mediates the impact of organizational stressors on stress outcomes. In other words, stressors (mismatches) in the six areas do not cause the outcome (such as poor performance), but they do cause an experience of burnout or engagement, and this in turn leads to both personal and organizational consequences (Leiter & Maslach, 2004). This mediation model is depicted in Figure 4.1.

WHAT CAN BE DONE ABOUT BURNOUT?

Finding solutions to the problem of burnout has been a key driver of much of the research in this area. Unlike other research on the workplace, which used a top-down approach derived from a scholarly theory, burnout research initially utilized a bottom-up, or "grass roots" approach derived from people's actual workplace experiences. The potential benefit of this applied framework is that the empirical findings can be more easily translated into actual interventions. Even though there is still much to be learned about burnout, what have we learned so far that can be used to deal with the problem?

THE MEDIATION ROLE OF BURNOUT

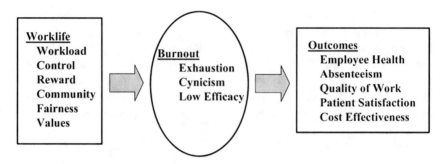

Figure 4..1.   A mediation model of burnout and engagement.

The Positive Goal of Engagement

When faced with a negative experience like burnout, people are likely to frame the problem as "how do we get rid of it?" The response to this question is likely to focus on strategies for eliminating the stressors that lead to burnout or for reducing the negative impact of burnout by helping people cope more effectively. These are standard strategies within the stress management literature, and they can have great value within any program to deal with burnout.

However, getting rid of a negative problem is not the same thing as achieving a positive alternative. To be truly effective, interventions to reduce burnout need to also identify a desired goal state. A goal that is framed as the absence of something negative, like burnout, is not going to be as motivating as a goal that involves the presence of something positive. Thus, there has been a recent research focus on the positive antithesis of burnout, namely job engagement.

As indicated at the beginning of this article, burnout can be conceptualized as an erosion of engagement with the job. Energy turns into exhaustion, involvement turns into cynicism, and efficacy turns into ineffectiveness. According to this analysis, engagement is the direct opposite of burnout and thus is defined (and measured) in terms of the three dimensions of energy, involvement, and efficacy. Research has found that positive scores on engagement are related to more positive matches in the six areas (Maslach & Leiter, 1997, 1999). An alternative approach to engagement has assumed that it is indeed a positive state, but not necessarily the exact opposite of burnout. According to this approach, engagement is defined as a persistent, positive affective-motivational state of fulfillment in employees that is characterized by vigor, dedication, and absorption (see Maslach, Schaufeli, & Leiter, 2001, for a description of these two approaches to engagement).

Regardless of how this positive state of engagement is defined, the important implication is that it represents a desired goal for any burnout interventions. A work setting that is designed to support the development of these characteristics of engagement should be successful in promoting the well being and productivity of its employees. Thus, any plans for intervention should be framed as "how do we promote job engagement?" and not simply "how do we get rid of burnout?" Such a framework will lead people to consider what factors in the workplace are likely to enhance employees' energy, vigor and resilience; to promote their involvement and absorption with the work tasks; and to ensure their dedication and sense of efficacy and success on the job. The answers to "how do we promote engagement?" can provide new possibilities for intervention strategies, which might not have been considered if the focus was only on burnout. In addition, because the goal of engagement is to "make things better in the workplace," it can have a more powerful motivating effect on employees than the goal to reduce some of the bad things about the job.

The Diagnostic Value of the Six Areas

The framework of the six areas of worklife was developed originally as a way of organizing the vast research literature on organizational factors in burnout (Maslach & Leiter, 1997). However, subsequent work revealed that the six areas could be used as a diagnostic tool to identify those areas that were especially problematic, whether for an individual or for an organization. The scores in these six areas yielded a "profile" of the areas of strength and weakness, thus pointing to more specific targets of intervention. For example, if a profile showed that workload was not a problem but that there was a serious mismatch in community, then an intervention that was designed to reduce overtime would not be as effective as an intervention that dealt with support among team members.

The six-area framework has now been incorporated into assessment programs developed for organizations (Leiter & Maslach, 2000b) and for individuals (Leiter & Maslach, 2005). This framework provides guidelines for a more customized strategy to reduce burnout and promote engagement. Rather than focusing on the latest fads, or on "one-size-fits-all" strategies, this framework helps direct any proposed interventions to the specific problems in this particular situation.

CONCLUSION

Burnout is not a problem of people but of the social environment in which they work. The structure and functioning of the workplace shape how people interact with one another and how they carry out their jobs. And when that workplace does not recognize the human side of work, and there are major mismatches between the nature of the job and the nature of people, then there will be a greater risk of burnout. Future progress in dealing effectively with burnout requires a focus on the positive goal of promoting engagement, and not simply of reducing burnout. The mediation model of burnout, with its framework of six areas of person-job match, provides an important diagnostic tool for tailoring solutions to the actual problems.

AUTHOR'S NOTE

This chapter is adapted from Maslach, C. (2005). Understanding burnout: Work and family issues. In D. F. Halpern & S. E Murphy (Eds.), *From work-family balance to work-family interaction: Changing the metaphor* (pp. 99-114). Mahwah, NJ: Erlbaum.

REFERENCES

Burke, R. J., & Greenglass, E. R. (2001). Hospital restructuring, work-family conflict and psychological burnout among nursing staff. *Psychology and Health, 16,* 83–94.

French, J. R. P. Jr., Rodgers, W., & Cobb, S. (1974). Adjustment as person-environment fit. In G. V. Coelho, D. A. Hamburg, & J. E. Adams (Eds.), *Coping and adjustment* (pp. 316–333). New York: Basic Books.

Greene, G. (1961). *A burnt-out case.* New York: Viking Press.

Karasek, R., & Theorell, T. (1990). *Stress, productivity, and the reconstruction of working life.* New York: Basic Books.

Kop, N., Euwema, M., & Schaufeli, W. (1999). Burnout, job stress, and violent behaviour among Dutch police officers. *Work & Stress, 13,* 326–340.

Leiter, M. P., Harvie, P., & Frizzell, C. (1998). The correspondence of patient satisfaction and nurse burnout. *Social Science & Medicine, 47,* 1611–1617.

Leiter, M. P., & Maslach, C. (2000a). Burnout and health. In A. Baum, T. Revenson, & J. Singer (Eds.), *Handbook of health psychology* (pp. 415–426). Hillsdale, NJ: Erlbaum.

Leiter, M. P., & Maslach, C. (2000b). *Preventing burnout and building engagement: A complete program for organizational renewal.* San Francisco: Jossey-Bass.

Leiter, M. P., & Maslach, C. (2004). Areas of worklife: A structured approach to organizational predictors of job burnout. In P. L. Perrewe & D. C. Ganster (Eds.), *Research in occupational stress and well-being* (Vol. 3, pp. 91–134). Oxford, England: Elsevier.

Leiter, M. P., & Maslach, C. (2005). *Banishing burnout: Six strategies for improving your relationship with work.* San Francisco: Jossey-Bass.

Maslach, C. (1993). Burnout: A multidimensional perspective. In W. B. Schaufeli, C. Maslach, & T. Marek (Eds.), *Professional burnout: Recent developments in theory and research* (pp. 19–32). Washington, DC: Taylor & Francis.

Maslach, C. (2003). *Burnout: The cost of caring.* Englewood Cliffs, NJ: Prentice-Hall. (Original work published 1982)

Maslach, C. (2005). Understanding burnout: Work and family issues. In D. F. Halpern & S. E. Murphy (Eds.), *From work-family balance to work-family interaction: Changing the metaphor* (pp. 99–114). Mahwah, NJ: Erlbaum.

Maslach, C., Jackson, S. E., & Leiter, M. P. (1996). *The Maslach Burnout Inventory* (3rd ed.). Palo Alto, CA: Consulting Psychologists Press.

Maslach, C., & Leiter, M. P. (1997). *The truth about burnout.* San Francisco: Jossey-Bass.

Maslach, C., & Leiter, M. P. (1999). Burnout and engagement in the workplace: A contextual analysis. *Advances in Motivation and Achievement, 11,* 275–302.

Maslach, C., & Leiter, M. P. (2005). Stress and burnout: The critical research. In C. L. Cooper (Ed.), *Handbook of stress medicine and health* (2nd ed., pp. 153–170). Boca Raton, FL: CRC Press.

Maslach, D., Schaufeli, W. B., & Leiter, M. P. (2001). Job burnout. In S. T. Fiske, D. L. Schacter, & C. Zahn-Waxler (Eds.), *Annual review of psychology, 52,* 397–422.

Pines, A. M. (1996). *Couple burnout.* New York: Routledge.

Procaccini, J., & Kiefaber, M. W. (1983). *Parent burnout.* New York: Doubleday.

Schaufeli, W. B., Bakker, A. B., Hoogduin, K., Schaap, C., & Kladler, A. (2001). The clinical validity of the Maslach Burnout Inventory and the Burnout Measure. *Psychology and Health, 16,* 565–582.

Schaufeli, W. B., & Enzmann, D. (1998). *The burnout companion to study and practice: A critical analysis.* London: Taylor & Francis.

Siegrist, J. (1996). Adverse health effects of high-effort/low-reward conditions. *Journal of Occupational Health Psychology, 1,* 27–41.

Walster, E., Berscheid, E., & Walster, G. W. (1973). New directions in equity research. *Journal of Personality and Social Psychology, 25,* 151–176.

CHAPTER 5

STRESS AND THE
WORK-FAMILY INTERFACE

Jonathon R. B. Halbesleben and Kelly L. Zellars

In this chapter, we discuss the role of the work-family interface in the experience of stress and strain. We note that work and family roles can have both negative (e.g., work-family conflict) and positive (e.g., work-family facilitation) implications for stress. We briefly review literature on the positive and negative outcomes of the work-family interface and suggest interesting new contexts within which to study the work-family interface. We conclude the chapter by discussing techniques to manage the work-family interface.

STRESS AND THE WORK-FAMILY INTERFACE

Over the past decade, research focusing on the relationships between work and family roles in the context of job strain has increased dramatically. This has been triggered, in part, because demographic changes have increased the number of dual-earner families and led to a shift in the ways that we think about work and family roles (Bond, Galinsky, & Swanberg, 1998; Frone, 2003; Gilbert, 1993). As the number of females in the workplace soars and family arrangements deviate from the traditional gender based roles, work and family role are no longer independent but

Stress and Quality of Working Life: Current Perspectives in Occupational Health, 53–68
Copyright © 2006 by Information Age Publishing
All rights of reproduction in any form reserved.

rather closely interconnected (Burke & Greenglass, 1987; Edwards & Rothbard, 2000). Tensions surfacing from the work-family interface have generated research examining the positive and negative effects resulting from simultaneously occupying roles. For example, the interface between work and family is a source of stress (e.g., work-family conflict) but is also a source of social support. Using role theory, researchers have suggested that the divergent roles compete for finite employee resources such as time and energy (Greenhaus & Beutell, 1985; Kahn, Wolfe, Quinn, Snoek, & Rosenthal, 1964). However, multiple roles can also provide greater access to resources that support well-being of employees (Ruderman, Ohlott, Panzer, & King, 2002).

In this chapter we address the often paradoxical role of work and family roles in both adding to and reducing stress. We begin with a brief discussion of how work and family roles are linked. We then discuss the negative effects of the work-family interface, including issues of work-family conflict and spillover of stress and strain. We also briefly discuss the positive side of the work-family interface, discussing such issues as work-family facilitation and social support. We offer a number of interesting, yet understudied, contexts within which to study the work-family interface and conclude with a discussion of more practical techniques to manage the interface.

Linking Work and Family

To fully understand the implications for the work-family interface and stress, we must begin by considering the manner in which work and family are linked. In their recent work, Edwards and Rothbard (2000) organized work-family linkages into six categories: spillover, compensation, segmentation, resource drain, congruence, and work-family conflict. These mechanisms help us to understand how one domain can either support or impair the other domain; as such, these mechanisms highlight how the work-family interface can have both positive and negative effects in terms of stress. For example, the "compensation" mechanism suggests that an individual dissatisfied with the manner in which their career is proceeding may turn to family activities to experience more positive feelings or satisfaction. Alternatively, positive effects can emerge via "spillover" in that skills that allow one to effectively navigate one domain may also positively influence the other domain. A more direct linkage emerges with work-family conflict where competing demands in the two domains are frequently incompatible. In this chapter, we first focus on those mechanisms which tend to operate as a negative linkage, particularly work-family conflict and the negative side of spillover. We then discuss the positive side of work-family linkages, or how one may facilitate the other, and conclude with a brief discussion of managing the interface.

THE NEGATIVE SIDE OF THE WORK-FAMILY INTERFACE

Work-Family Conflict

In their seminal work, Greenhaus and Beutell (1985) defined work-family conflict as "a form of interrole conflict in which the role pressures from the work and family domains are mutually incompatible in some respect" (p. 77). For example, time spent on family activities is time unavailable for work obligations. Research has revealed that the conflict between work and family roles is bidirectional; that is, one can experience work-family conflict where work interferes with family and family-work conflict where family interferes with work (Frone, Russell, & Cooper, 1992a, 1992b). A significant number of studies in this area have attempted to determine the causes of work-family conflict with the majority exploring issues emerging at least in part from Greenhaus and Beutell's (1985) original conceptualization of work-family conflict. Specifically, researchers have focused predominantly on three different role strains (time-based, strain-based, and behavior-based).

A significant characteristic of the role environment is the amount of time spent at work versus that spent with family. Researchers have argued that when more time is spent in one role (e.g., at work), less time is left for other roles, increasing the likelihood of work-family conflict (Frone, 2003). Recently, Voydanoff (2004), using data reported in the 1997 National Study of the Changing Workforce, found that time based work demands were strongly and positively related to work-family conflict. Such results are consistent with earlier research (Major, Klein, & Erhart, 2002) that found among 513 employees in a Fortune 500 company that work time was significantly and positively related to work interfering with family. Interestingly, Wallace (1997) reported that hours worked influenced feelings of spillover, although many of the factors related to number of hours worked (e.g., importance of work to personal identity, organizational pressures) did not necessarily translate into feelings of work. Exploring the issue further, some researchers have suggested that psychological involvement in a role may be more important than actual time spent in the role. Studies testing this assumption generally report that greater involvement in one role is associated with higher conflict between roles (e.g., Carlson & Kacmar, 2000; Meyer, Stanley, Herscovitch, & Topolnytsky, 2002; Parasuraman & Simmers, 2001). Thus, involvement (whether in terms of time or psychological commitment) can be a source of tension within the work-family interface.

Researchers have attempted to dissect relationships underlying work-family conflict in order to clarify the nature of the relationships between the conflict and various strains, but clarity has been elusive (Demerouti, Bakker, & Bulters, 2004). For example, some studies have found that work-family conflict is a mediator such that stressors lead to conflict, which in turn leads to strain (e.g., Geurts & Demerouti, 2003; Wallace, 1997). Over time, conflicts between work and family roles take a toll on employees and become a source of work-related strain, which may explain why a growing body of research suggests work-family conflict leads to burnout (cf., Bacharach, Bamberger, & Conley, 1991; Montgomery, Peeters, Schaufeli, & Den Ouden, 2003). More specifically, conservation of resources (COR) theory (Hobfoll, 1998) argues individuals strive to acquire, retain, and protect what they value. "Major life stressors are likely to have a significant impact on resource acquisition and protection, but even minor hassles may collectively act to diminish people's capacity to cultivate and guard their resources" (p. 55). Thus, COR theory argues that the repeated demand on work and family resources occurs at a pace that cannot be replenished fast enough, leading to burnout (Hobfoll & Shirom, 2000).

Alternatively, other researchers have argued the opposite pattern, where strain causes work-family conflict, which subsequently leads to more stress (e.g., Zapf, Dormann, & Frese, 1996). They argue that working individuals experiencing strain (e.g., exhaustion) are more likely to repeatedly fall behind in their work, creating more pressure for themselves. Kelloway, Gottlieb, and Barham (1999) provide some support for this relationship among healthcare and retail grocery workers; they found that strain led to higher work-family conflict over a six month period.

Considering these perspectives simultaneously suggests that work-family conflict leads to strain, but strain also leads to a greater likelihood of work-family conflict. Indeed, Demerouti et al. (2004) recently argued that we must carefully consider the reciprocal relationships between work-family conflict and burnout to truly understand their relationships. In a longitudinal study of workers from a Dutch employment agency, they found support for the notion of a "loss spiral" whereby work pressure and emotional exhaustion were associated with later work-family conflict and work-family conflict was associated with subsequent work pressure and exhaustion. Their work underscores the need to consider more complex models of the relationships between stress constructs and work-family conflict.

Spillover and Crossover of Stress

Another key linkage between work and family is spillover. Most often characterized as negative, work spillover is a subjective perception of the degree to which workers feel their work is invading their nonwork life (Wallace, 1997). More generally, spillover reflects situations where one domain has an influence (positive or negative) on the other domain. Stress researchers have been particularly interested in two issues where stress in one area of work-family life influences another: the manner in which stress from work spills over to family life (and vice versa) and, to a lesser degree, the extent to which stress crosses over from one spouse to the other.

Spillover between work and family can emerge in affect (e.g., mood, satisfaction), values (the priority of work and family activities as part of identity), and skills or behaviors. Some researchers (e.g., Judge & Watanabe, 1994; Zedeck, 1992) approach spillover as a similarity between a construct in the work domain and a distinct but related construct in the family domain. Others (e.g, Eckenrode & Gore, 1990) approach spillover as a transferring of experiences (e.g, fatigue) between domains such that the experience in one domain is influenced by the experience in the other domain. For example, an individual who experiences a negative mood arising from an argument with one's spouse prior to leaving home may carry the negative mood throughout the day, leading to a negative perception of one's job duties.

A more dramatic example of spillover occurs when a spouse exhibits strains displayed by the other spouse. For example, Westman and Etzion (1995) investigated the manner in which burnout can crossover from husbands to wives and vice versa. They proposed that crossover could occur between spouses due to a variety of processes: demands on one spouse creating new demands on the other, demands on one spouse influencing the mood of the other, the mood of one spouse creating demands for the other, or the mood of one spouse influencing the mood of the other. In their sample of 101 couples, they found evidence that burnout in one spouse crossed over to impact the other spouse, in that burnout scores of one spouse were associated with later burnout scores of the other spouse. While they were unable to specify the exact process that caused the crossover within their sample, their findings provide compelling evidence that the work and family interface can be influenced through contagion processes across family members. However, the news is not all bad. In the same study, Westman and Etzion (1995) also found that sense of control was a key factor in reducing burnout and crossover of burnout. This suggests that not only can stress effects crossover from one spouse to another, but resources that help to deal with stress (in this case, sense of control) can also crossover. It is with these findings in mind that we turn to the more positive outcomes of work-family interface.

THE POSITIVE SIDE OF THE WORK-FAMILY INTERFACE

Although the preponderance of research examining the work-family interface has focused on the conflicts and strains that emerge, researchers have begun to explore how an individual's work and family roles can positively influence each other. We now briefly summarize the emerging literature in this area.

Work-Family Facilitation

In an attempt to more clearly define the balance between work and family, a number of authors (e.g., Grzywacz & Marks, 2000; Kirchmeyer, 1992) have proposed that work and family roles can be mutually supportive. In other words, there are situations where experiences in the family facilitate work experiences (or vice versa) because of development of skills in one setting that transfer to another situation. For example, an individual may develop conflict management skills at work that facilitate the manner in which he or she addresses conflict at home or in other settings away from work. Similar positive spillover may emerge in areas of improved communication and goal setting, which may mitigate the occurrence of work-family conflict. Indeed, one could argue that such an effect is a positive form of spillover between work and family.

In related research, findings suggest that family resources may be mobilized to address strain at work (specifically, burnout). In contrast to resource drain, where an individual transfers personal resources (e.g., energy) from the family domain to the work domain, mobilizing family resources refers to utilizing family members to address work-related problems. In a longitudinal study of staff at a Canadian hospital, Leiter (1990) found an inverse relationship between family resource mobilization and burnout. Just as an action coping style and utilization of professional skills were associated with reduced burnout over the 6-month timeframe of the study, the mobilization of family resources also reduced burnout. More recently, Grzywacz & Marks (2000), using data from employed adults participating in the National Survey of Midlife Development in the United States, found that more positive affective support from the family domain was associated with positive spillover.

The most frequent form of facilitation studied by researchers is social support. Measures of social support capture an employee's perception

that an individual or group cares about the employee's anxiety and difficulties and is available and willing to offer assistance. Theory suggests several means by which social support can operate, including preventive
effects (i.e., reducing stressors), therapeutic effects (i.e., lessening strains),
and moderating effects (i.e., alleviating effects of stressors on strains and
the effects of strains on outcomes) (Pinneau, 1975). Empirical studies
have examined the structure of the relationship with social support acting
as a moderator of felt stress in influencing the emergence of strain, where
the social support helps to address the felt stress before it generates
strains (Beehr, 1985; Etzion, 1984; Ganster, Fusilier, & Mayes, 1986).
More recently, researchers have found that family support is associated
with lower work-related stress and strain (e.g., Baruch-Feldman, Brondolo, Ben-Dayan, & Schwartz, 2002). However, family support as a moderator of work-related stressors is not the only source of support. Indeed,
the majority of studies examining job stress and burnout have focused on
sources of support within the workplace. Overall, the data suggest the
perceived quality of workplace support is positively linked to important
work outcomes such as satisfaction and stress and burnout.

In sum, reviews of the literature suggest the relationship between support and outcomes is complex and depends on the source of support (cf.,
Baruch-Feldman et al., 2002; Halbesleben, in press). For example, Thomas and Ganster (1995) found that supervisor support can reduce work-
family conflict. Carlson and Perrewé (1999) explored this issue further,
finding that social support (both family support and work support) helps
to alleviate stressors that cause work-family conflict. This work suggests
that social support may have a number of possible effects when considering work and family contexts. While more research is needed to understand the specific nature of the effect (e.g., direct vs. moderator; effect on
strain vs. effect on stressors), the key finding is that the research concerning social support consistently finds that it is beneficial in reducing the
negative effects of stress, strain, and work-family conflict. With this need
for further research in mind, we turn now to a discussion of unique contexts in which we might engage in further study of the work-family interface.

UNIQUE CONTEXTS IN WHICH TO STUDY THE
WORK-FAMILY INTERFACE

While research examining the positive and negative sides of the work-
family interface has proliferated rapidly over the past few years, there
remain a number of questions that have not been addressed. In this section, we will offer two unique contexts within which to study the rela-

tionship between the work-family interface and stress that have been not been fully capitalized on, with the hope that these contexts might push forward the field by providing unique perspectives on work and family roles.

Same-Career Couples

Recent work by Halbesleben, Zellars, Carlson, Perrewé, and Rotondo (2005) provides a unique opportunity to understand the differences in the effect of work and nonwork sources of social support. They studied a unique population of working adults—those who work in the same occupation or at the same workplace as their spouse, terming those individuals same-career couples (as opposed to the notion of a dual-career couple, where both spouses work, but in different occupations and workplaces; the experience of dual career couples in the context of stress and work-family conflict has been wide studied; see for example, Aryee, 1993; Izraeli, 1988; Parasuraman, Greenhaus, & Granrose, 1992; Rosenbaum & Cohen, 1999). They proposed that same-career couples may have a unique advantage, whereby the spouses can provide each other with the types of support, specifically instrumental support, typically more commonly available from coworkers or supervisors. Indeed, in their study of about 150 members of same-career couples and 450 members of dual-career couples, they found that those participants in a same-career relationship reported higher instrumental support from their spouse, which was associated with lower burnout among the same-career couples. Their study provided an interesting means by which to understand the ways that family roles can further support work roles through social support.

However, the work of Halbesleben et al. (2005) did not consider the effects of work-family conflict among same-career couples, who are in a unique situation in that the separation of and identification with work and family roles may be blurred. In other words, the mechanisms for linking work and family as described by Edwards and Rothbard (2000) are likely experienced quite differently in same career couples. As such, more research is needed to understand, for example, how spillover occurs in same-career couples (e.g., is it facilitated by less clear boundaries between work and family roles?) or how whether compensation becomes less of a factor because the roles are so closely intertwined. Future studies of same-career couples offer an opportunity to better understand this unique marital arrangement, but also allow for interesting studies of the underlying dynamics of work and family.

Family Business

The family business provides another context in which distinctions between work and family roles become blurred. Family businesses are those in which the owner and at least one other family member work (Ward, 1987; Ward & Aronoff, 1990). People working in family business are believed to be especially susceptible to role conflict (Beehr, Drexler, & Faulkner, 1997), in large part because family members overlap in their involvement with multiple roles, each generating a specific set of expected behaviors, which may conflict. Simultaneously filling multiple roles increases the likelihood of work-related roles to influence (either negatively or positively) the nonwork roles of these workers (Gupta & Beehr, 1981; Kanter, 1989; Schmitt & Bedeian, 1982). As such, workers in family business are likely to be susceptible to role-related stress and experience a disruption in harmony among family members (Beehr, Drexler, & Faulkner, 1997) at work or at home. Moreover, research (Tetrick, Slack, DeSilva, & Sinclair, 2000) suggests that owners perceive less social support from work-related sources than nonowners.

While family businesses provide a clear opportunity to better understand the nature of interrole conflict in generating stress and strain, they may also be a good context within which to study the positive components of the work-family interface. Beehr, Drexler, and Faulkner (1997) compared family members to nonfamily members of the same firms and to members of similar nonfamily-owned businesses and found more advantages than disadvantages. Instrumental support provided by coworkers has been shown to mitigate job stress and strain. In family businesses, perhaps instrumental support is more available and utilized since success of the individual is clearly tied to the success of the family business. In fact, the greater expectations on family members may include greater pressure to provide such support to other family members. Indeed, this may provide a particularly interesting paradox to study: does the pressure to provide support to a family member increase stress (as it puts greater expectations on the worker) or does it reduce stress (knowing that the other family member has similar pressures put on them to reciprocate support)?

Thus far, there is a paucity of published empirical research on these topics, with few studies that go beyond a description of a single case study. The Beehr, Drexler, and Faulkner (1997) study referred to above is one of the few large scale studies of these issues (sample size of over 200). While they found that work-family conflict was associated with a greater likelihood of psychological strain at work, they also found few differences between family members working in family businesses, nonfamily members working in family businesses, and workers in nonfamily businesses on other negative outcomes (conflict, strain). However, they did not specifically explore resources, such as social support, leaving a need for future research to further address these issues.

MANAGING THE WORK-FAMILY INTERFACE

The complexity of the work-family interface leads to significant challenges for managers as they seek to reduce work-family conflict and support work-family facilitation. For example, research has tended to find that personal coping strategies, where employees are essentially asked to consider their own strategies for dealing with work and family role stressors, tend not to be effective in reducing stress, strain (e.g., burnout), or work-family conflict (Frone, 2003; Halbesleben & Buckley, 2004). This suggests that organizations need to consider more systemic options when attempting to deal with stress associated with the interface between work and family.

One suggested route to the reduction of work-family conflict and its associated negative influence on stress and strain has been to design policies that help to integrate work and family roles; such programs often fall under the title of family-friendly policies (e.g., permitting teleworking, developing more family-based activities at work, on-site day care programs). Only a handful of studies have explored the efficacy of such programs in reducing work-family and family-work conflict; their findings have tended to be mixed (Kossek & Ozeki, 1999). For example, studies by Thompson, Beauvais, and Lyness (1999) and Judge, Boudreau, and Bretz (1994) found a negative relationship between the availability of work-family policies and work-family conflict. However, a number of other researchers have found that family-friendly policies have had limited effect on reducing work-family conflict (e.g., Barling, 1994; Goff, Mount, & Jamison, 1990; Solomon, 1994; Thomas & Ganster, 1995). The number of family-friendly initiatives

> don't show the frantic early-morning rush as parents whisk kids out of bed ... all the while worrying that a tardy child will make them late for work. Statistics don't show the split-second timing that workers live with daily ... mothers and fathers who fidget in late afternoon meetings because they can't get to phone to be sure their school-age child arrived safely ... or the ones the who lie to their supervisor because the babysitter is late. (Solomon, 1994. p. 75)

In understanding these studies, Frone (2003) has suggested that improvements must be made to future research efforts aimed at understanding the effect of family-friendly initiatives. First, Frone notes that most studies have either examined only work-family conflict or used a measure of conflict that confounded work-family and family-work conflict (Judge et al., 1994, is an exception). This is a key criticism because, as Frone and Yardley have suggested, much of the effect of family-friendly initiatives should be on family-work conflict (though interestingly, the study by Judge et al. found no effect of such programs on family-work conflict). Moreover, Frone argued that the research designs of many of the studies of interventions to improve the work-family interface have significant limitations, such as the failure to assess pretest measures of work-family conflict. Finally, Frone notes that availability of family-friendly benefits may not be as important as utilization of those benefits. One relatively large study (Thompson, Beauvais, & Lyness, 1999) of 276 managers and professionals provided empirical verification that perceptions of a supportive work-family culture were associated with greater utilization of family friendly benefits and programs. The researchers defined and measured three dimensions of work-family culture: perceived managerial support, negative career outcomes for devoting time to family responsibilities, and organizational time demands and expectations that interfere with family responsibilities. The findings indicate that managerial support dimension was significantly related to utilization of family friendly programs. More studies are needed to more fully explore benefit utilization and its relationship with conflict. Initial evidence suggests utilization of benefits is likely to be a better predictor than availability.

So where does this leave us? The literature suggests that providing employees with resources, both work and family-based, will help to alleviate burnout (cf., Leiter, 1990). However, the literature has been far less clear on how organizations can design interventions to provide such resources. Boles, Johnston, and Hair (1997) provided some guidance in the context of sales jobs; they suggested that realistic scheduling and greater autonomy (allowing the sales people to set their own schedule) might help to reduce work-family conflict. Moreover, they suggested that care be taken in setting expectations, particularly the utilization of role models of performance. For example, companies often acclaim the "superstar" salesperson that works many more hours than average, noting that setting such an example puts pressure on workers to sacrifice time with their family in order to meet the expectations of their employers. Perhaps providing training to improve sales techniques could increase sales without increasing hours (and also costs), thus reducing the infringement on hours devoted to family obligations.

Another option may be to develop social support networks. Carlson and Perrewé (1999) suggested mentoring programs as one way to develop social support at work. They argue that mentoring relationships offer an opportunity for both mentors and protégés to develop social support that would help to avoid work-family conflict. However, despite these useful suggestions by Boles et al. (1997) and Carlson and Perrewé (1999), collaboration between organizations and researchers to develop strategies that can reduce stress that specifically occurs as a result of conflict between work and family would be particularly valuable as we seek to address this concern in organizations.

CONCLUSION

While research concerning the interface between work and family roles has seen a dramatic increase over the past few decades, there is still a great deal that we need to understand about the manner in which work and family roles conflict and support each other and their relationship to stress and strain. The vast majority of research has been dedicated to the notion of work-family conflict; however, as we have noted, the interface between work and family can lead to conflict but can also have supportive outcomes such as social support and work-family facilitation. More research is needed to understand the positive aspects of the work-family interface and how they might reduce the likelihood of stress and strain. Moreover, there is a very practical need to develop and evaluate strategies for organizations as they seek to develop an environment characterized by work-family balance.

Additionally, there is a need for more cross-cultural research in work and family issues and their relationship to stress. While some initial research suggests that work-family conflict and other work-family issues generalize to other cultures (e.g., Yang, Chen, Choi, & Zou, 2000), the vast majority of the research in this area has been limited to investigations in the United States. A more comprehensive view of the work-family that is integrates notions of national culture would be particularly valuable as we seek to fully understand the role of the work-family interface in the stress literature.

REFERENCES

Aryee, S. (1993). Dual-earner couples in Singapore: An examination of work and nonwork sources of their experienced burnout. *Human Relations, 46,* 1441–1468.

Bacharach, S. B., Bamberger, P., & Conley, S. (1991). Work-home conflict among nurses and engineers: Mediating the impact of role stress on burnout and satisfaction at work. *Journal of Organizational Behavior, 12,* 39–53.

Barling, J. (1994). Work and family: In search of more effective workplace interventions. In C. Cooper & D. M. Rousseau (Eds.), *Trends in organizational behaviour* (pp. 63-73). Chichester, England: Wiley.

Baruch-Feldman, C., Brondolo, E., Ben-Dayan, D., & Schwartz, J. (2002). Sources of social support and burnout, job satisfaction, and productivity. *Journal of Occupational Health Psychology, 7*, 84–93.

Beehr, T. A. (1985). The role of social support in coping with organizational stress. In T. A. Beehr & R. S. Bhagat (Eds.), *Human stress and cognition in organizations: An integrated perspective* (pp. 375–398). New York: Wiley.

Beehr, T. A., Drexler, J. A., & Faulkner, S. (1997). Working in small family businesses: Empirical comparisons to non-family businesses. *Journal of Organizational Behavior, 18*, 297–312.

Boles, J. S., Johnston, M. W., & Hair, J. F. (1997). Role stress, work-family conflict, and emotional exhaustion: Inter-relationships and effects on some work-related consequences. *Journal of Personal Selling & Sales Management, 17*, 17–28.

Bond, J. T., Galinsky, E., & Swanberg, J. E. (1998). *The 1997 national study of the changing workforce*. New York: Families and Work Institute.

Burke, R. J., & Greenglass, E. (1987). Work and family. In C. L. Cooper & I .T. Robertson (Eds.), *International review of industrial and organizational psychology* (273-320). New York: Wiley.

Carlson, D. S., & Kacmar, K. M. (2000). Work-family conflict in the organization: Do life role values make a difference? *Journal of Management, 26*, 1031–1054.

Carlson, D. S., & Perrewé, P. L. (1999). The role of social support in the stressor-strain relationship: An examination of work-family conflict. *Journal of Management, 25*, 513–540.

Demerouti, E., Bakker, A. B., & Bulters, A. J. (2004). The loss spiral of work pressure, work-home interference, and exhaustion: Reciprocal relations in a three-wave study. *Journal of Vocational Behavior, 64*, 131–149.

Eckenrode, J., & Gore, S. (1990). *Stress between work and family*. New York: Plenum.

Edwards, J. R., & Rothbard, N. P. (2000). Mechanisms linking work and family: Clarifying the relationship between work and family constructs. *Academy of Management Review, 25*, 178–199.

Etzion, D. (1984). Moderating effect of social support on the stress-burnout relationship. *Journal of Applied Psychology, 69*, 615–622.

Frone, M. R. (2003). Work-family balance. In J. C. Quick & L. E. Tetrick (Eds.), *Handbook of occupational health psychology* (pp. 143–162). Washington, DC: American Psychological Association.

Frone, M. R., Russell, M., & Cooper, M. L. (1992a). Antecedents and outcomes of work-family conflict: Testing a model of the work-family interface. *Journal of Applied Psychology, 77*, 65–78.

Frone, M. R., Russell, M., & Cooper, M. L. (1992b). Prevalence of work-family conflict: Are work and family boundaries asymmetrically permeable? *Journal of Organizational Behavior, 13*, 723–729.

Ganster, D. C., Fusilier, M. P., & Mayes, B. T. (1986). Role of social support in the experience of stress at work. *Journal of Applied Psychology, 71*, 102–110.

Geurts, S. A. E., & Demerouti, E. (2003). Work/non-work interface: A review of theories and findings. In M. J. Schabracq, J. A. M. Winnubst, & C. L. Cooper (Eds.), *Handbook of work and health psychology* (pp. 279–312). Chichester, England: Wiley.

Gilbert, L. A. (1993). *Two careers/one family.* Newbury Park, CA: Sage.

Goff, S. J., Mount, M. K., & Jamison, R. L. (1990). Employer supported child care, work-family conflict, and absenteeism: A field study. *Personnel Psychology, 43,* 793–809.

Greenhaus, J. H., & Beutell, N. J. (1985). Sources of conflict between work and family roles. *Academy of Management Review, 10,* 76–88.

Grzywacz, J. G., & Marks, N. F. (2000). Reconceptualizing the work-family interface: An ecological perspective on the correlates of positive and negative spillover between work and family. *Journal of Occupational Health Psychology, 5,* 111–126.

Gupta, N., & Beehr, T. A. (1981). Relationships among employees' work and nonwork responses. *Journal of Occupational Behavior, 2,* 203–209.

Halbesleben, J. R. B. (in press). Sources of social support and burnout: A meta-analytic test of the conservation of resources model. *Journal of Applied Psychology.*

Halbesleben, J. R. B., & Buckley, M. R. (2004). Burnout in organizational life. *Journal of Management, 30,* 859–880.

Halbesleben, J. R. B., Zellars, K., Carlson, D. S., Perrewé, P. L., & Rotondo, D. (2005, November). *When your spouse is (like) a coworker: Marital working status, social support, & burnout.* Paper presented at the annual meeting of the Southern Management Association, Charleston, SC.

Hobfoll, S. E. (1998). *Stress, culture, and community. The psychology and philosophy of stress.* New York: Plenum Press.

Hobfoll, S. E., & Shirom, A. (2000). Conservation of resources: Applications to stress and management in the workplace. In R. T. Golembiewski (Ed.), *Handbook of organizational behavior* (2nd ed., pp. 57–81). New York: Dekker.

Izraeli, D. N. (1988). Burning out in medicine: A comparison of husbands and wives in dual-career couples. *Journal of Social Behavior and Personality, 3,* 329–346.

Judge, T. A., Boudreau, J. W., & Bretz, R. D. (1994). Job and life attitudes of male executives. *Journal of Applied Psychology, 79,* 767–782.

Judge, T. A., & Wantanabe, S. (1994). Individual differences in the nature of the relationship between job and life satisfaction. *Journal of Occupational and Organizational Psychology, 67,* 101–107.

Kahn, R. L., Wolfe, D. M., Snoek, J. D., & Rosenthal, R. A. (1964). *Organizational stress: Studies in role conflict and ambiguity.* New York: Wiley.

Kanter, R. M. (1989). Work and family in the United States: A critical review and agenda for research and policy. *Family Business Review, 2,* 77–114.

Kelloway, E. K., Gottlieb, B. H., & Barham, L. (1999). The source, nature and direction of work family conflict: A longitudinal investigation. *Journal of Occupational Health Psychology, 4,* 337–346.

Kirchmeyer, C. (1992). Perceptions of nonwork-to-work spillover: Challenging the common view of conflict-ridden domain relationships. *Basic and Applied Social Psychology, 13,* 231–249.

Kossek, E. E., & Ozeki, C. (1999). Bridging the work-family policy and productivity gap: A literature review. *Community, Work, & Family, 2,* 7–32.

Leiter, M. P. (1990). The impact of family resources, control coping, and skill utilization on the development of burnout: A longitudinal study. *Human Relations, 43,* 1067–1083.

Major, V. S., Klein, K. J., & Ehrhart, M. G. (2002). Work time, work interference with family, and psychological distress. *Journal of Applied Psychology, 87,* 427–436.

Meyer, J. P., Stanley, D. J., Herscovitch, L., & Topolnytsky, L. (2002). Affective, continuance, and normative commitment to the organization: A meta-analysis of antecedents, correlates, and consequences. *Journal of Vocational Behavior, 61,* 20–52.

Montgomery, A. J., Peeters, M. C. W., Schaufeli, W. B., & Den Ouden, M. (2003). Work-home interference among newspaper managers: Its relationship with burnout and engagement. *Anxiety, Stress, & Coping, 16,* 195–211.

Parasuraman, S., Greenhaus, J. H., & Granrose, C. K. (1992). Role stressors, social support, and well-being among two-career couples. *Journal of Organizational Behavior, 13,* 339–356.

Parasuraman, S., & Simmers, C. (2001). Type of employment, work-family conflict and well-being: A comparative study. *Journal of Organizational Behavior, 22,* 551–568.

Pinneau, S. R., Jr. (1975). *Effects of social support on psychological and physiological strains.* Unpublished doctoral dissertation, University of Michigan.

Rosenbaum, M., & Cohen, E. (1999). Equalitarian marriages, spousal support, resourcefulness, and psychological distress among Israeli working women. *Journal of Vocational Behavior, 54,* 102–113.

Ruderman, M. N., Ohlott, P. J., Panzer, K., & King, S. N. (2002). Benefits of multiple roles for managerial women. *Academy of Management Journal, 45,* 369–386.

Schmitt, M., & Bedeian, A. G. (1982). A comparison of LISREL and two-stage least squares analysis of a hypothesized life-job satisfaction reciprocal relationship. *Journal of Applied Psychology, 67,* 806–817.

Solomon, C. (1994). Work-family's failing grade: Why today's initiatives aren't enough. *Personnel Journal, 73,* 72–87.

Tetrick, L. E., Slack, K. J., DaSilva, N., & Sinclair, R. R. (2000). A comparison of the stress-strain process for business owners and nonowners: Differences in job demands, emotional exhaustion, satisfaction, and social support. *Journal of Occupational Health Psychology, 5,* 464–476.

Thomas, L. T., & Ganster, C. D. (1995). Impact of family-supportive work variables on work-family conflict and strain: A control perspective. *Journal of Applied Psychology, 80,* 6–15.

Thompson, C. A., Beauvais, L. L., & Lyness, K. S. (1999). When work-family benefits are not enough: The influence of work-family culture on benefit utilization, organizational attachment, and work-family conflict. *Journal of Vocational Behavior, 54,* 392–415.

Voydanoff, P. (2004). The effects of work demands and resources on work-to-family conflict and facilitation. *Journal of Marriage and Family, 66,* 398–412.

Wallace, J. E. (1997). It's about time: A study of hours worked and work spillover among law firm lawyers. *Journal of Vocational Behavior, 50,* 227–248.

Ward, J. L. (1987). *Keeping the family business healthy.* San Francisco: Jossey-Bass.

Ward, J. L., & Aronoff, C. E. (1990). Just what is a family business? *Nation's Business, 78*(2), 54–55.

Westman, M., & Etzion, D. (1995). Crossover of stress, strain, and resources from one spouse to another. *Journal of Organizational Behavior, 16,* 169–181.

Yang, N., Chen, C. C., Choi, J., & Zou, Y. (2000). Sources of work-family conflict: A Sino-U.S. comparison of the effects of work and family demands. *Academy of Management Journal, 43,* 113–123.

Zapf, D., Dormann, C., & Frese, M. (1996). Longitudinal studies in organizational stress research: A review of the literature with reference to methodological issues. *Journal of Occupational Health Psychology, 1,* 145–169.

Zedeck, S. (1992). *Work, families, and organizations.* San Francisco: Jossey-Bass.

CHAPTER 6

NEGATIVE AND POSITIVE CROSSOVER IN THE FAMILY AND AMONG TEAM MEMBERS

Mina Westman

There is ample evidence supporting the crossover hypothesis; job demands are transmitted from employees to their partners, affecting their psychological and physical health. This chapter delineates possible mechanisms that underlie the crossover process. The chapter relates to several gaps in crossover research: The role of gender, positive crossover, and crossover and emotional contagion among team members. The chapter concludes with recommendations for future research and the implications for management theory and practice.

There is ample evidence that job stress has an impact on workers' mental and physical well-being (Kahn & Byosiere, 1992). However, little attention has been paid to reactions of the workers' partners to their stress and well-being. It is only recently that researchers have turned their attention to the phenomenon of stress and strain crossover, namely, the reaction of

Stress and Quality of Working Life: Current Perspectives in Occupational Health, 69–86

individuals to the job stress experienced by those with whom they interact regularly. Bolger, DeLongis, Kessler, and Wethington (1989) differentiate between two situations in which stress is contagious: *spillover*—stress experienced in one domain of life results in stress in the other domain for the same individual; and *crossover*—stress experienced in the workplace by the individual leads to stress being experienced by the individual's spouse at home. Whereas spillover is an intraindividual, interdomain contagion of stress, crossover is a dyadic, interindividual, interdomain contagion, generating similar reactions in another individual. In other words, spillover occurs from home to work and from work to home, for the same individual, whereas crossover is conceptualized as a process occurring from one individual at the work place to his/her spouse at home. This indicates that whereas spillover affects only the individual, crossover can affect the dyad and the group. Spillover research has been conducted at the individual level of analysis, under the assumption that the role behavior of one spouse in the two spheres is unaffected by that of the other. Crossover research is based on the propositions of the spillover model, recognizing the fluid boundaries between work and family life, and noting that spillover is a necessary, but not a sufficient condition for crossover (Westman, 2006). The crossover model adds another level of analysis to previous approaches by considering the interindividual level and the dyad as an additional focus of research.

In sum, the interpersonal process that occurs when a stress or strain experienced by one person affects the level of strain of another person in the same social environment is referred to as crossover. Findings suggest that one partner's strain affects the well being of the other so that one's strain is often a stressor to the other (see Westman, 2001; Westman, 2006), for an overview).

Westman (2006) stated that

> Most crossover research does not rely on a systematic theoretical approach that distinguishes between the possible explanations of crossover effects.... Furthermore, a better understanding of these processes will enable identification of effective strategies for coping with the stress crossover effectively. (pp. 167–168)

In an effort to deal with this issue, Westman and Vinokur (1998) specified three main mechanisms to account for the experience of crossover. These mechanisms involve a direct crossover based on empathic reactions, an indirect mediating interaction process, and the impact of common stressors.

Direct empathic crossover implies that stress and strain are transmitted from one partner to another directly as a result of empathic reactions. The basis for this view is the finding that crossover effects appear between closely related partners who care for each other and share the greater part of their lives together. According to Lazarus (1991, p. 287), empathy is "sharing another's feelings by placing oneself psychologically in that person's circumstances." The core relational theme for empathy involves a sharing of another person's emotional state, mainly strain. Accordingly, strain in one partner produces an empathic reaction in the other that increases his or her strain.

Indirect crossover of strain is a transmission of strain mediated by personal attributes and the interaction between the partners. The explanation of crossover as an indirect process focuses on specific coping strategies and interpersonal transactions, such as social support, social undermining, and the communication style.

Researchers have rarely looked into personality attributes that might help explain the crossover process. This lack is noteworthy, considering the importance of personality in stress research (Spector & O'Connell, 1994). Future crossover research should include personal attributes such as the Big Five (Digman, 1990), Type A behavior pattern (TABP), (Edwards & Baglioni, 1991), negative affectivity (NA), (Watson & Clark, 1984) and workaholism (Burke, 2004). These attributes may play a role in moderating the crossover relationship. Including such variables in crossover models would help to understand the crossover process.

Communication Characteristics, what people say to each other or how they react to events in which they are involved, affect the crossover process. The literature supporting this explanation implies the need to focus on the couple's communication pattern in terms of the kinds of interaction likely to enhance the partners' experience of stress or strain. Jones and Fletcher (1993) have addressed the nature of information communicated between the partners as mediating the crossover process, suggesting that the communication may mediate the relationship between the partners' mood. They found that the woman's mood was affected by her partner's communication pattern: it was more positive when her husband offloaded worries and frustrations, but more negative when he became withdrawn or distracted. Jones and Fletcher suggested that the frequency and nature of couples' work-related discussion is likely to be a mediator in the transmission process.

The interaction; social undermining is referred to in the literature as social hindrance, social conflict, and negative social support. According to Vinokur and van Ryn (1993), social undermining consists of behaviors directed toward the target person that express negative affect, convey negative evaluation or criticism, or hinder the attainment of instrumental goals. Researchers have shown that social conflict is symptomatic of the stress and strain of cohabiting partners (Abbey, Abramis, & Caplan, 1985; Vinokur & van Ryn, 1993). The explanation that the crossover process is mediated by negative social interactions is supported by empirical find-ings from two lines of research. First, research documents that frustration is often an outcome of stressful conditions that trigger aggression (Berkowitz, 1989). Second, the literature on family processes also reports that stressed couples exhibit high levels of negative conflictual interac-tions (Schaefer, Coyne, & Lazarus, 1981). The increased distress and its accompanying frustration lead to aggressive behavior (Berkowitz, 1989) or otherwise lead an individual to initiate or exacerbate a negative inter-action sequence with the partner, as shown in studies on social undermin-ing (Duffy, Ganster, & Pagon, 2002; Vinokur & van Ryn, 1993).

Thus, indirect crossover occurs when an increase in the strain of one partner triggers a provocative behavior or exacerbates a negative interac-tion sequence with the other partner, often expressed as social undermin-ing behavior toward the other person and perceived as such by the partner (Vinokur & van Ryn, 1993). The strain of one person that leads to his or her social undermining behavior toward the other acts as a stressor for the recipient of this behavior, and this stressor causes the recipient's strain level to increase. Here we witness crossover in the sense that one's strain results in an increase in the strain of the other, but the crossover does not occur unless it is bridged or mediated by another intermediate process of negative social interactions.

Finally, *common stressors* impact the strain of both partners and the posi-tive correlation detected between the strains of the two spouses will *appear* as being due to a crossover effect. Thus, Westman and Vinokur (1998) have suggested that common stressors in a shared environment (e.g., the death of a friend, economic problems) that increase both partners' strain need to be considered as a spurious case of crossover. However, common stressors may affect each spouse's strain and still cause crossover through the other two suggested mechanisms: empathy and the interaction pro-cess.

Westman (2006) suggests that the three mechanisms of crossover can operate independently of one another and are not mutually exclusive. Therefore, it is quite possible that some of the proposed mechanisms operate jointly. To illustrate, Vinokur, Price, & Caplan (1996) found that financial strain, representing common stressors, increased depression in the job seeker and in the spouse. These depressive symptoms increased the partner's undermining behavior, which increased depressive symp-toms in the job seeker, indicating an indirect crossover effect via social interaction. Similarly, Westman and Vinokur (1998) found both direct and indirect crossover between spouses as well as effects due to common stres-sors. Westman, Vinokur, Hamilton, and Roziner (2004) studying Russian officers and their spouses found both direct crossover of marital dissatis-faction and indirect crossover operating together. However, strong evidence was also provided for gender asymmetry in the crossover process in this sample of primarily dual earner couples, but with traditional gender ideologies. Marital dissatisfaction crossed over from husbands to wives but not vice versa and social undermining behavior played a role in the process of crossover of marital dissatisfaction for husbands, but not for wives. The possibility that several mechanisms may operate simultaneously requires an analytical model that takes into account all the potential contributors to crossover.

Researchers have focused on various variables to demonstrate the crossover process. Studies have focused on different variables in the crossover process. Some have focused on the crossover of *job stress* from the individual to the spouse (e.g., Burke, Weir, & DuWors, 1980) and some have examined the process whereby *job stress* of the individual affects the *strain* of the spouse (Jones & Fletcher, 1993, 1996; Long & Voges, 1987). However, most of them have studied how psychological *strain* of one partner affects the *strain* of the other (Barnett, Raudenbush, Brennan, Pleck, & Marshall, 1995; Demerouti, Bakker, & Schaufeli, 2005; Mitchell, Cronkite, & Moos, 1983; Westman & Etzion, 1995; Westman, Etzion, & Danon, 2001; Westman, Etzion, & Horovitz, 2004; Westman, Vinokur, et al., 2004). Crossover effects have mainly been found for psychological strains such as anxiety, burnout, depression, distress, marital and life dissatisfaction, and work-family conflict.

Some crossover studies have examined heterogeneous samples (e.g., Bakker, Demerouti, & Schaufeli, 2005; Barnett et al., 1995; Rook Dooley, & Catalano, 1991), though most of them have examined specific occupational groups. Samples cover the range of police officers (Beehr, Johnson, & Nieva, 1995; Jackson & Maslach, 1982), prison officers (Long & Voges, 1987), administrators of correctional institutes (Burke et al., 1980), career officers (Westman & Etzion, 1995; Westman & Etzion, in press; Westman, Vinokur, et al., 2004); plant operators (Jackson, Zedeck, & Summers, 1985), expatriates (Takeuchi, Yun, & Teslu, 2002; Van der Zee & Salome, 2005), and bank employees (Hammer, Allen, & Grigsby, 1997). To illustrate, Burke et al. (1980) found that specific occupational demands experienced by male administrators of "correctional institutions" were correlated with higher levels of dissatisfaction and distress in their spouses. Long and Voges (1987) found that wives of prison officers could accurately perceive the sources of their husbands' stress and that both husband and wife had reduced psychological well-being compared to norms. Westman and Etzion (1995) have examined the crossover of burnout between career officers and their spouses. They have demonstrated a bidirectional crossover of burnout between male and female partners (i.e., burnout in one partner was positively related to burnout in the other, after controlling their own job stress and resources. Similarly, Westman and Etzion (2005) found a bidirectional crossover of work-family conflict in a sample of 220 women serving in the U.S. Air Force and their spouses. Similarly, Hammer et al. (1997) found a bidirectional crossover of work family conflict from husbands to wives and vice versa in a sample of bank employees. Van der Zee and Salome (2005) found a crossover of subjective well-being from expatriates to their partners. Replicating these findings in various occupational groups augments external validity and extends the generalizability of these findings.

THE ROLE OF GENDER IN THE CROSSOVER PROCESS

A review of crossover research demonstrates that crossover may be unidirectional or bidirectional. Reviewing the directionality of crossover of stress and strain raises the issue of the role of gender in the crossover process. Gender is certainly a potential moderator of the impact of one's stress on the spouse's strain, because of differences in the traditional role demands and expectations for men and women (Lambert, 1990). There is some indication that women are more susceptible than men to the impact of stressors affecting their partners (Kessler, 1979). Kessler and McLeod (1984) suggested that because of their greater involvement in family affairs, women become more sensitive not only to the stressful events that they themselves experience but also to those that affect other family members. Johnson and Jackson (1998) demonstrated that whereas men's levels of stress dropped after reentering the work force, their wives' strain remained high. They suggest that women may act as "shock absorbers," taking on the men's stress. Similarly, Haviland and Malatesta (1981) found that women were more vulnerable to emotional contagion than men.

Some researchers detected only uni-directional crossover from husbands to wives. To illustrate, Jones and Fletcher (1993) found transmission of husbands' job demands on wives' anxiety and depression after controlling wives' job stress. However, they did not find such an effect from wives to husbands, perhaps because the women in their sample did not experience high levels of stress. Similarly, Westman et al. (2001), and Westman, Vinokur, et al. (2004) found crossover of burnout and marital dissatisfaction only from husbands to wives. The study of Russian officers and their wives (Westman, Vinokur, et al., 2004) demonstrating a strong crossover of marital dissatisfaction from husband to wives but no crossover from wives to husbands exemplifies the dual-career family with a relatively traditional gender-role ideology (Olson & Matkovsky, 1994). Conversely, Mauno and Kinnunen (1999) found no gender differences in their study of couples and related this finding to the fact that in Finland the roles of women and men are relatively equal compared to other countries. This among other findings indicates that culture should be considered in research on cohabiting couples. Thus, evidence concerning gender differences in the crossover process is mixed. Considering the inconsistency of the results of the role of gender in the crossover process, the role of gender needs to be reexamined in terms of traditional versus modern gender-role ideology, and on cross-cultural differences.

Recent studies of dual-career families found bidirectional crossover effects of stress or strain of similar magnitude from husbands to wives and from wives to husbands (Barnett et al., 1995; Demerouti et al., 2005; Hammer et al., 1997; Hammer, Bauer, & Grandey, 2003; Mauno & Kinnunen, 2002; Westman & Etzion, 1995; Westman & Etzion, 2005; Westman & Vinokur, 1998). To illustrate, Westman and Etzion (1995) demonstrated a crossover of burnout from career officers to their spouses and vice versa, after controlling husbands' and wives' own job stress and resources. Hammer et al. (1997) also found a bidirectional crossover of work family conflict from husbands to wives and vice versa. Similarly, Westman and Etzion (2005) found a bidirectional crossover of work-family conflict between air force women and their spouses. These were cross-sectional studies, but the bidirectional nature of the crossover effect has also been demonstrated in studies using longitudinal designs. Barnett et al. (1995), Westman and Vinokur (1998), and Westman, Etzion, and Horovitz (2004) found bidirectional crossover of distress, depression, and anxiety from husbands to wives and from wives to husbands using longitudinal designs.

The study of crossover thus far was limited to the transmission of strain between spouses. Westman (2001) has suggested adding new topics to crossover research specifying (a) crossover at the workplace and (b) positive crossover. This chapter elaborates on these issues.

CROSSOVER AT THE WORKPLACE

Previous crossover research was based on the work-family interface, thus, researchers focused only on the family as the "victim" of the employee's stress. However, as the crossover framework is based on role theory we can broaden the scope of research and investigate the crossover of stress and strain among role senders in the work environment. What happens to one member of a dyad, whether a family member or a work group member, affects the other. We can broaden the conceptualization of the unit of study from the couple to the work team. This approach is consistent with Moos's (1984) theory that people are part of a social system and have to be understood in these systems. The family is one such system and the workgroup is another. Each member is linked to other members and change in one will effect change in others. Thus, a person's stress generated at the workplace can transmit to others in the work team. Team members who share the same environment may start a crossover chain of stress and strain among themselves whether the source of stress is in the family or at the workplace. The shared environment that is crucial to the crossover process characterizes workplaces where employees work in close cooperation. Bolger et al. (1989) suggested that conflicts with persons in ongoing, nonfamily relationships might be particularly distressing because they have continuity and usually lack sufficient intimacy and understanding to prevent arguments from being perceived as a major threat. Clearly, the study of crossover should be extended to investigate it in the workplace.

The review of the literature shows that Westman and Etzion (1999) conducted the first crossover field study in the workplace. The respondents were 47 school principals and 183 teachers in Israeli elementary schools. The main goal of the study was to examine whether the crossover effect found among couples also occurs in the workplace. They found a crossover of work-induced strain from school principals to teachers and vice versa after controlling for their job stress. Furthermore, being undermined by their principals elevated teachers' job-induced tension. Thus crossover of strain was evident in the workplace and the two suggested crossover mechanisms, direct and indiret crossover were supported.

CROSSOVER OF BURNOUT AMONG TEAM MEMBERS

Edelwich and Brodsky (1980) were the first to relate to the possibility of crossover of burnout at work.

> If burnout only affected individuals in isolation, it would be far less important and far less devastating in its impact than it is. Burnout in Human Services Agencies is like an infection in hospitals; it gets around. It spreads from clients to staff, from one staff member to another, and from staff back to clients. (p. 25)

Thus, a person's stress generated at the workplace can transmit to others in the work team. Individuals in the work team who share the same environment may start a crossover chain of stress and strain among themselves. The shared environment which is crucial to the crossover process characterizes workplaces where job incumbents work in close cooperation.

Changing the traditional unit of analysis from the couple to the work team, Westman, Roziner, and Bakker (2005) focused on the crossover of job stress and exhaustion among 310 employees of an employment agency, working in 100 teams. The multilevel analysis used in the study confirmed the existence of a meaningful team-level exhaustion construct. Whereas the crossover hypothesis was not supported in the whole sample two significant moderator were detected; team cohesion and colleague social support. Both variables which represent the interpersonal relationship in the team moderated the crossover process. Accordingly, crossover of job stress and exhaustion from the team to the individual was detected in teams who were high in team cohesion and teams who were high in colleagues' social support. These results extend previous crossover research by demonstrating that crossover processes operate within teams as well as within dyads. Thus, individuals' mood can be affected by the collective moods of team to which they belong, but only in teams which are characterized by good interpersonal relationships.

CROSSOVER OF BURNOUT AMONG TEAM MEMBERS: EMOTIONAL CONTAGION

Another similar approach demonstrated and developed by a group of Dutch researchers looked at crossover at the workplace from a different angle. Buunk and Schaufeli (1993) have suggested that colleagues may act as role models, whose symptoms are imitated through a process of "emotional contagion." That is, employees may perceive symptoms of burnout in their colleagues and automatically take on these symptoms. This process is labeled emotional contagion: "The tendency to automatically mimic and synchronize facial expressions, vocalizations, postures, and movements with those of another person and, consequently, to converge emotionally" (Hatfield, Cacioppo, & Rapson, 1994, p. 5). The emphasis in this definition is clearly on a nonconscious process. Research has indeed shown that, in conversations, people automatically mimic the facial expressions, voices, postures, and behaviors of others (e.g., Bavelas, Black, Lemery, & Mullett, 1987; Bernieri, Reznick, & Rosenthal, 1988), and that individuals' conscious experience may be shaped by such facial feedback (Laird, 1984; Siegman & Reynolds, 1982). Thus, several researchers focused on emotional contagion of burnout at the workplace. They view contagion as a reciprocal emotional reaction toward the other person in a close relationship (see e.g., Bakker & Schaufeli, 2000; Bakker, Schaufeli, Sixma, & Bosweld, 2001). Accordingly, being exposed to the burnout of one's team members brings out in the individual a reciprocal emotional contagious reaction of burnout.

Bakker and Schaufeli (2000) examined a burnout contagion process among Dutch high school teachers. They examined two conditions that may increase contagion: frequency of exposure to other teachers who talk about their work-related problems and personal susceptibility to emotional contagion. They found that burnout contagion was most pronounced under high risk conditions; the prevalence of perceived burnout among collegues was most strongly related to individual teachers' burnout when teachers communicated frequently with their colleagues about their work-related problems and when they were highly susceptible to emotional contagion.

In a similar vein, Bakker et al. (2001) have investigated burnout contagion in a sample of 507 general practitioners. Their findings supported the burnout contagion model. Furthermore, burnout contagion was most pronounced among general practitioners who were highly susceptible to emotional contagion. This suggests that general practitioners who are particularly sensitive to the emotions expressed by their colleagues (e.g., depression, cynicism, black humor) are most likely to "catch" the burnout symptoms of the people with whom they interact (possibly also their patients).

Finally, Bakker, Demerouti, and Schaufeli (2003) investigated socially induced burnout among a sample of 490 employees of a large banking and insurance company working in 47 teams. The focus was on direct and indirect transference of burnout from the team to individual team members, using structural equation modeling analyses. Their results revealed that team exhaustion and team efficacy explained a unique proportion of the variance in individual employees' exhaustion and efficacy, even after controlling for the impact of job demands, job control, and social support. Furthermore, *indirect* transference of burnout was hypothesized to take place, because team burnout would change the working conditions for individual team members in an unfavorable way.

Taken together, the reviewed literature supports the existence of crossover at the workplace. The findings suggest that job burnout can cross over among employees who are members of the same work team, and that situational (e.g., frequency of exposure, changing working conditions) as well as personality factors (e.g., susceptibility to emotional contagion) play a role in the crossover process at the work place.

POSITIVE CROSSOVER

As evident from the literature review, most crossover research focused on crossover of *negative* emotions (stress and strain). To illustrate, crossover studies to date have investigated crossover of negative emotions and states, including job stress, depression, dissatisfaction, burnout, anxiety, and work-family conflict (for a review see Westman, 2001; Westman,

2006). One possible reason for the neglect of the possibility of positive crossover is that stress research relies heavily on medical models, with their emphasis on negative effects, just as negative affectivity was investigated for many years before researchers broadened their interest to positive affectivity.

In accordance with the trend of positive psychology, Westman (2001) has suggested broadening the definition of crossover into contagion of positive as well as negative events. The empathy definitions mentioned before allow for the sharing of both positive and negative emotions. If the crossover process operates via empathy, one would expect to find not only negative crossover but positive crossover as well. Thus, empathy could just as easily involve the sharing of another's positive emotions and the conditions that bring them about. Positive events and emotions may also cross over to the partner and have a positive impact on his or her well-being.

Investigating the issue of positive crossover, Etzion and Westman (2001) examined the effect of an organized tour abroad on the crossover of burnout between spouses. They collected data from couples who took a two-week vacation abroad, before (chronic stress) and after the vacation (positive event). Though they did not detect positive crossover, they did find an ameliorating impact of the vacation on the crossover of burnout. Whereas they demonstrated a bidirectional crossover of burnout before the vacation, no significant crossover effect was found after the vacation. These findings indicate that positive events such as vacations, or a change from a stressful environment to a tranquil one, may stop the vicious circle of crossover of strain from one spouse to another.

A few studies found positive group emotional contagion. Totterdel, Kellet, Briner, and Teuchmann (1998) studied 65 community nurses in 13 teams daily for 3 weeks. They found an association between nurses' mood and the collective mood of their team members over time, after controlling for daily hassles. Next they studied a team of accountants who rated their own moods and their team members' mood 3 times a day for 4 weeks. They found that the accountants' mood and their judgment of their teammate's mood were associated with the collective mood of their teammates. Thus they demonstrated that there is an association between people's mood and the collective mood of their teammates at work over time; also, and apparently, accountants' mood was clearly observable, suggesting the possibility of automatic contagion of positive emotions (cheerfulness, happiness, etc.). Similarly, Barsade (2002) conducted an experiment with a trained confederate enacting mood conditions. She demonstrated an influence of emotional contagion on individual-level mood and attitudes. Furthermore, the positive emotional contagion group members demonstrated improved cooperation, decreased conflict, and increased subjective task performance.

Whereas the former were experiments, Bakker and his colleagues found evidence for positive crossover in three different field studies. Bakker, Demerouti, and Schaufeli (2005) detected crossover of work engagement (vigor and dedication) in a field setting among partners in a study of 323 couples working in a variety of occupations. The crossover relationships were significant, after controlling for characteristics of the work and home environment of both partners. Similarly, Demerouti et al. (2005), found a bidirectional crossover of life satisfaction between 191 couples of dual earner couples. These findings expand previous crossover research, particularly by showing that positive experiences at work may be transferred to the home domain.

Bakker, Van Emmerik, and Euwema (2004) investigated the crossover of burnout and work engagement among 2,229 Dutch constabulary officers, working in one of 85 teams. On the basis of theories on crossover and emotional contagion, they hypothesized that both types of work-related feelings and attitudes may transfer from teams to individual team members. The results of multilevel analyses confirmed this crossover phenomenon by showing that team level burnout and work engagement are related to individual team members' burnout (i.e., exhaustion, cynicism, and reduced professional efficacy) and work engagement (vigor, dedication, and absorption), after controlling for individual members' job demands and resources.

Finally, in a study among 178 music teachers and 605 students from 16 different music schools Bakker (2005) examined the crossover of peak experiences (Csikszentmihalyi, 1990). He hypothesized that job resources, including autonomy, performance feedback, social support and supervisory coaching have a positive influence on the balance between teachers' challenges and skills, which, in turn, contributes to their experience of flow (absorption, work enjoyment, and intrinsic work motivation). In addition, using emotional contagion theory, he hypothesized that flow may crossover from teachers to their students. The results based on structural equation modelling analyses offered support for both hypotheses.

Following these results, one can think of many instances of positive crossover, such as enjoyable experiences at one's job leading to the crossover of job satisfaction and engagement, eliciting a good mood in the partner at home. Similarly, supportive family relationships and attitudes can create positive crossover to the work setting. Altogether, positive crossover appears to be a fertile field for enhancing theoretical thinking and making practical contributions to the literature.

THEORETICAL AND PRACTICAL IMPLICATIONS

Findings support the theoretical and practical relevance of the crossover model (Westman, 2001; Westman, 2006). Overall, it seems feasible based on the existing evidence, though additional research is needed to test it more directly, particularly with regard to certain moderators and additional underlying mechanisms. The crossover model is proposed as an exploratory tool that can help to close the gap in our knowledge of the ways in which work influences family life, and vice versa and better understand processes among team members. The effect of job demands or life events may be multiple, affecting the individual, a spouse, family members, friends, managers, and coworkers. Furthermore, findings of crossover reinforce the idea that a more complete understanding of the relationship between family and work stress may be achieved by changing the unit of study from the individual to the family and the work team.

Furthermore, whereas crossover is usually defined and studied as a transmission of stress or strain, it is suggested that the scope of its definition and investigation should be broadened to include the transmission of positive events and feelings as well. In the past few years there has been growing interest in the field of positive psychology, which includes topics such as optimism, happiness, love, support, and so forth. Future crossover studies should incorporate the crossover processes of positive affect and related experiences. The investigation of positive crossover can add to theoretical thinking and broaden the current boundaries of crossover models. It also carries many practical implications, as suggested by Westman (2001): for example, positive actions taken by management may contribute to additional positive outcomes that have not been originally planned, including eliciting good mood and satisfaction in the employee's team members and spouse.

The focus of crossover research should be extended from the family milieu where the vast majority of crossover studies have been conducted, to the workplace. As suggested by Westman (2001), the work team is a venue eminently conducive to the development of relations characterized by crossover, and the identification of both positive and negative crossover in the workplace has crucial theoretical and practical implications. So far, only a few studies have examined crossover in the work setting (Bakker & Schaufeli, 2000; Bakker et al., 2001; Westman & Etzion, 1999; Westman et al., 2005) and this new research domain needs further investigation.

Sandler, Wolchik, MacKinnon, Ayers, and Roosa (1997) suggest that the first step in developing interventions for preventing the adverse consequences of stress is to evaluate conceptual models of the explanatory pathways. The findings of some crossover studies are based on a conceptual model with explicit pathways and therefore offer an important direction for the design of future interventions for couples experiencing stress and strain. Some of these findings suggest that such interventions should focus on the reduction of social undermining as it is found to be a powerful mediator of the adverse impact of stress on strain. From the organizational perspective, the ripple effect of stress and strain has far-reaching implications. Because of the important role of coping in the crossover process, special attention should be paid to the appropriate coping strategies to buffer crossover. The result of such attention might be more effective employees and happier families.

Findings also suggest that efforts to reduce the stress and strain of employees should target their spouses too. It would be advisable for management to provide assistance programs to individuals working in stressful conditions and their spouses. It appears that if a distressed spouse is not part of the solution, he or she is likely to become a big part of the problem. Thus, what is needed are programs that train and counsel couples in developing skills for reducing negative interactions and enhancing their relationships (Markman, Renick, Floyd, & Stanley, 1994). The same applies to interventions aimed at the team level. The primary objective of such programs is prevention and improved functioning, achieved by focusing on techniques designed to help couples and teams manage negative affect and handle conflict situations constructively.

REFERENCES

Abbey, A., Abramis, D. J., & Caplan, R. D. (1985). Effects of different sources of social support and social conflict on well-being. *Basic and Applied Social Psychology, 6,* 111–129.

Bakker, A. B. (2005). Flow among music teachers and their students: The crossover of peak experience. *Journal of Vocational Behavior, 66,* 1–25.

Bakker, A. B., Demerouti, E., & Schaufeli, W. B, (2003). The socially induced burnout model. In S. P. Shohov (Ed.), *Advances in psychology research* (Vol. 25, pp. 13–30). New York: Nova Science.

Bakker, A .B., Demerouti, E., & Schaufeli, W. B. (2005). The crossover of burnout and work engagement among working couples. *Human Relations, 58,* 661–689.

Bakker, A. B, & Schaufeli, W. B. (2000). Burnout contagion process among teachers. *Journal of Applied Social Psychology, 30,* 2289–2308.

Bakker, A. B., Schaufeli, W. B., Sixma, H. J., & Bosweld, D. (2001). Burnout contagion among general practitioners. *Journal of Social and Clinical Psychology, 20,* 82–98.

Bakker, A. B., Van Emmerik, H., & Euwema, M. C. (2004). *Crossover of burnout and engagement in work teams.* Manuscript submitted for publication.

Barsade, S. G. (2002). The ripple effect: Emotional contagion and its influence on work behavior. *Administrative Science Quarterly, 47,* 644–675.

Barnett, R, C., Raudenbush, S. W., Brennan, R. T., Pleck, J. H., & Marshall, N. L. (1995). Changes in job and marital experience and change in psychological distress: A longitudinal study of dual-earner couples. *Journal of Personality and Social Psychology, 69,* 839–850.

Bavelas, J. B., Black, A., Lemery, C. R., & Mullett, J. (1987). Motor mimicry as primitive empathy. In N. Eisenberg & J. Strayer (Eds.), *Empathy and its development* (pp. 317–338). New York: Cambridge University Press.

Beehr, T. A., Johnson, L. B., & Nieva, R. (1995). Occupational stress: Coping of police and their spouses. *Journal of OrganizationalBehavior, 16,* 3–25.

Berkowitz, L. (1989). Frustration-aggression hypothesis: Examination and reformulation. *Psychological Bulletin, 106,* 59–73.

Bernieri, F. J., Reznick, J. S., & Rosenthal, R. (1988). Synchrony, pseudosynchrony, and dissynchrony: Measuring the entrainment process in mother-infant interactions. *Journal of Personality and Social Psychology, 54,* 1242–1253.

Bolger, N., DeLongis, A., Kessler, R., & Wethington, E. (1989). The contagion of stress across multiple roles. *Journal of Marriage and the Family, 51,* 175–183.

Burke, R. J. (2004). Workaholism, self-esteem, and motives for money. *Psychological Reports, 94,* 457–463.

Burke, R. J., Weir, T., & DuWors, R. E. (1980). Work demands on administrators and spouse well-being. *Human Relations, 33,* 253–278.

Buunk, B. P., & Schaufeli, W. B. (1993). Burnout: A perspective from social comparison theory. In W. B. Schaufeli, C. Maslach, & T. Marek (Eds.), *Professional burnout. Recent developments in theory and research* (pp. 53–69). Washington, DC: Taylor & Francis.

Csikszentmihalyi, M. (1990). *Flow: The psychology of optimal experience.* New York: Harper Collins.

Demerouti, E., Bakker, A., & Schufeli, W. (2005). Spillover and crossover of exhaustion and life satisfaction among dual-earner parents. *Journal of Vocational Behavior, 67,* 266–289.

Digman, J. M. (1990). Personality structure: Emergence of the five-factor model. *Psychological Assessment, 41,* 417–440.

Duffy, M., Ganster, D., & Pagon, M. (2002). Social undermining in the workplace. *Academy of Management Journal, 45,* 331–351.

Edelwich, J., & Brodsky, A. (1980). *Burnout: Stages of disillusionment in the helping professions.* New York: Human Sciences Press.

Edwards, J. R., & Baglioni, A. J. (1991). Relationship between Type A behavior pattern and mental and physical symptoms: A comparison of global and component measures. *Journal of Applied Psychology, 76,* 276–290.

Etzion, D., & Westman, M. (2001). Vacation and the crossover of strain between spouses—Stopping the vicious cycle. *Man and Work, 11,* 106–118.

Hammer, L. B., Allen, E., & Grigsby, T. D. (1997). Work-family conflict in dual-earner couples: Within individual and crossover effects of work and family. *Journal of Vocational Behavior, 50,* 185–203.

Hammer, L. B., Bauer, T., & Grandey, A. (2003). Work-family conflict and work-related withdrawal behaviors. *Journal of Business and Psychology, 17,* 419–436.

Hatfield, E., Cacioppo, J. T., & Rapson, R. L. (1994). *Emotional contagion.* New York: Cambridge University Press.

Haviland, J. M., & Malatesta, C. Z. (1981). The development of sex differences in nonverbal signals: Fallacies, facts and fantasies. In C. Mayo & N. M. Henley (Eds.), *Gender and nonverbal behavior* (pp. 183–208). New York: Springer-Verlag.

Jackson, S. E., & Maslach, C. (1982). After-effects of job-related stress: Families as victims. *Journal of Occupational Behavior, 3,* 63–77.

Jackson, S. E., Zedeck, S., & Summers, E. (1985). Family life disruptions: Effects of job-induced structural and emotional interference. *Academy of Management Journal, 28,* 574–586.

Johnson, A., & Jackson, P. (1998, July). A longitudinal investigation into the experience of male managers who have re-entered the workforce after redundancy, and their families. *Proceedings of the International Work Psychology Conference,* Sheffield, England.

Jones, F., & Fletcher, B. (1993). An empirical study of occupational stress transmission in working couples. *Human Relations, 46,* 881–902.

Jones, F., & Fletcher, B. (1996). Taking work home: A study of daily fluctuations in work stressors, effects on mood and impact on marital partners. *Journal of Occupational Psychology, 69,* 89-106.

Kahn, R. L., & Byosiere, P. (1992). Stress in organizations. In D. Dunnette & L. M. Hough (Eds.), *Handbook of industrial and organizational psychology* (pp. 571–651). Palo Alto, CA: Consulting Psychology Press.

Kessler, R. C. (1979). A strategy for studying differential vulnerability to the psychological consequences of stress. *Journal of Health and Social Behavior, 20,* 100–108.

Kessler, R. C., & McLeod, J.D. (1984). Sex differences in vulnerability to undesirable life events. *American Sociological Review, 49,* 620–631.

Laird, J. D. (1984). The real role of facial response in the experience of emotion: A reply to Tourangeau and Ellsworth, and others. *Journal of Personality and Social Psychology, 47,* 909–917

Lambert, S. J. (1990). Processing linking work and family: A critical review and research agenda. *Human Relations, 43,* 239–257.

Lazarus, R. S. (1991). *Emotion & adaptation.* New York: Oxford.

Long, N. R., & Voges, K. E. (1987). Can wives perceive the source of their husbands' occupational stress? *Journal of Occupational Psychology, 60,* 235–242.

Markman, H. J., Renick, M. J., Floyd, F., & Stanley, S. M. (1994). Preventing marital distress through effective communication and conflict management: A four- and five-year follow-up. *Journal of Consulting and Clinical Psychology, 61,* 70–77.

Mauno, S., & Kinnunen, U. (1999). The effects of job stressors on marital satisfaction among Finnish dual-earner couples. *Journal of Organizational Behavior, 20,* 879–895.

Mauno, S., & Kinnunen, U. (2002). Perceived job insecurity among dual-earner couples: Do its antecedents vary according to gender, economic sector and measure used? *Journal of Occupational and Organizational Psychology, 75,* 295–314

Mitchell, R., Cronkite, R., & Moos, R. (1983). Stress, coping and depression among married couples. *Journal of Abnormal Psychology, 92*, 433–448.

Moos, R. (1984). Context and coping: Toward a unifying conceptual framework. *American Journal of Community Psychology, 12*, 5–25.

Olson, D. H., & Matskovsky, M. S. (1994). Soviet and American families: A comparative overview. In J. W. Maddock, M. J. Hogan, A. I. Anatolyi, & M. S. Matskovsky (Eds.), *Families before and after perestroika: Russian and U.S. perspectives* (pp. 9–35). New York: Guilford.

Rook, S. K., Dooley, D., & Catalano, R. (1991). Stress transmission: The effects of husbands' job stressors on emotional health of their wives. *Journal of Marriage and the Family, 53*, 165–177.

Sandler, I. N., Wolchik, S. A., MacKinnon, D., Ayers, T. S., & Roosa, M. W. (1997). Developing linkages between theory and intervention in stress and coping processes. In S. A. Wolchik & I. N. Sandler (Eds.), *Handbook of children's coping: Linking theory and intervention* (pp. 3–40). New York: Plenum.

Schaefer, C., Coyne, J. C., & Lazarus, R. S. (1981). The health-related functions of social support. *Journal of Behavioral Medicine, 4*, 381–406.

Siegman, A. W., & Reynolds, M. (1982). Interviewer-interviewee nonverbal communications: An interactional approach. In M. Davis (Ed.), *Interaction rhythms: Periodicity in communicative behavior* (pp. 249–278). New York: Human Sciences Press.

Spector, P. E., & O'Connell, B. J. (1994). The contribution of personality traits, negative affectivity, locus of control and Type A to the subsequent reports of job stressors and job strains. *Journal of Occupational and Organizational Psychology, 67*, 1–12.

Takeuchi, R., Yun, S., & Teslu, P. T. (2002). An examination of crossover and spillover effects of spouse and expatriate cross-cultural adjustment on expatriate outcomes. *Journal of Applied Psychology, 85*, 655–666.

Totterdel, P., Kellet, S., Briner, R., & Teuchman, K. (1998). Evidence of mood linkage on work group. *Journal of personality and Social Psychology, 74*, 1504–1515.

Van der Zee, K., & Salome, E. (2005). Role interference and subjective well-being among expatriate families. *European Journal of Work and Organizational Psychology, 24*, 239–262.

Vinokur, A., Price, R. H., & Caplan, R. D. (1996). Hard times and hurtful partners: How financial strain affects depression and relationship satisfaction of unemployed persons and their spouses. *Journal of Personality and Social Psychology, 71*, 166-179.

Vinokur, A., & van Ryn, M. (1993). Social support and undermining in close relationships: Their independent effects on mental health of unemployed persons. *Journal of Personality and Social Psychology, 65*, 350–359.

Watson, D., & Clark, L. E. (1984). Negative affectivity: The disposition to experience aversive emotional states. *Psychological Bulletin, 96*, 465–498.

Westman, M. (2001). Stress and strain crossover, *Human Relations, 54*, 717–751.

Westman, M. (2006). Crossover of stress and strain in the work--family context. In F. Jones, R, Burke, & M. Westman (Eds.), *Work—Life balance: A psychological perspective* (pp. 163–184). New York: Psychology Press.

Westman, M., Bakker, A., & Roziner, I. (2005, August). *Crossover of exhaustion within teams: The role of the quality of interpersonal relationships.* Conference on Teams, Technion, Haifa.

Westman, M., & Etzion, D. (1995). Crossover of stress, strain and resources from one spouse to another. *Journal of Organizational Behavior, 16,* 169–181.

Westman, M., & Etzion D. (1999). The crossover of strain from school principals to teachers and vice versa. *Journal of Occupational Health Psychology, 4,* 269–278.

Westman, M., & Etzion, D. (2005). The crossover of work-family conflict. *Journal of Applied Social Behavior, 35,* 1936-1957.

Westman, M., Etzion, D., & Danon, E. (2001). Job insecurity and crossover of burnout in married couples. *Journal of Organizational Behavior, 22,* 467–481.

Westman, M., Etzion, D., & Horovitz, S. (2004). The toll of unemployment does not stop with the unemployed. *Human Relations, 57,* 823–844.

Westman, M., & Vinokur, A. (1998). Unraveling the relationship of distress levels within couples: Common stressors, emphatic reactions, or crossover via social interactions? *Human Relations, 51,* 137–156.

Westman, M., Vinokur, A., Hamilton, L., & Roziner, I. (2004). Crossover of marital dissatisfaction during downsizing: A study of Russian army officers and their spouses. *Journal of Applied Psychology, 89,* 769–779.

CHAPTER 7

CONSEQUENCES OF DEPRESSED MOOD AT WORK

The Importance of Supportive Superiors

Jason Stoner and Pamela L. Perrewé

We examine the consequences of experiencing a depressed mood while at work. Depressed mood can lead to detrimental organizational consequences such as a lack of organizational commitment, lower performance, fewer extra-role behaviors (i.e., organizational citizenship behaviors), an increased tendency to leave the organization and even burnout. We also examine the importance of having supportive supervisors to help reduce the negative consequences associated with having a depressed mood at work.

CONSEQUENCES OF DEPRESSED MOOD AT WORK: THE IMPORTANCE OF SUPPORTIVE SUPERIORS

A bad day at work—everyone has had one. A day when nothing seems to go the right way. A day when every aspect of work is shadowed by an unexplainable dark cloud. Work tasks are unpleasant and attempted with little enthusiasm. Some may even classify work on "bad days" as down-

Stress and Quality of Working Life: Current Perspectives in Occupational Health, 87–99
Copyright © 2006 by Information Age Publishing

right unbearable. Yet, after a night's rest or a few days, work attitudes seem to rebound, returning to the status quo (some may even say they enjoy work). However, what happens when a bad day at work turns into several bad weeks at work, which, in turn, leads to a general negative and unenthusiastic work attitude? This state, known as depressed mood at work, is the focus of this paper.

Depressed mood at work (DMW) is a concept that is usually thought of as a consequence of some organizational stressor such as role conflict (e.g., Heinisch & Jex, 1997) or role ambiguity (e.g., Beehr, 1976). Depressed mood at work refers to a general disheartened, disenchanted, down and blue feelings individuals experience while at work (Quinn & Sheppard, 1974). Research has concluded that depressed mood at work could result from a variety of organizational stressors such as a lack of job control (Evans & Fischer, 1992), role overload (Beehr, 1981), and inter-personal conflict (Heinisch & Jex, 1997). To date, however, little research in the organizational sciences has examined the outcomes of depressed mood at work. It is proposed in this paper that depressed mood at work could lead to serious negative organizational outcomes such as increases in turnover intentions and burnout, and decreases in performance and organizational citizenship behaviors. Furthermore, this paper proposes that the negative consequences of depressed mood at work could be buff-ered by supervisor support. That is, supervisors, who are perceived to be supportive of their employees, may be able to mitigate the negative con-sequences (we propose) employees experience as a result of depressed mood at work, such that employees will not have increased turnover intentions and burnout, nor decreases in performance and organizational citizenship behavior. Supervisor support may serve as an antidote for the negative consequences of depressed mood at work.

This chapter proposes a model that examines the consequences of depressed mood at work as well as a work factor (i.e., supervisor sup-port) that may moderate that relationship. In explaining the model (see Figure 7.1), we will first define the concept of depressed mood at work. In this section, depressed mood at work will be conceptually differenti-ated from depression and burnout. Following, a brief discussion will be provided as to why depressed mood at work is an important concept to study. A review of the causes of depressed mood at work will also be provided. To spell out the model, propositions are offered about the consequences of depressed mood at work. Furthermore, it is proposed that supervisor support will minimize the negative consequences of depressed mood at work. Concluding this chapter, managerial implica-tions are discussed.

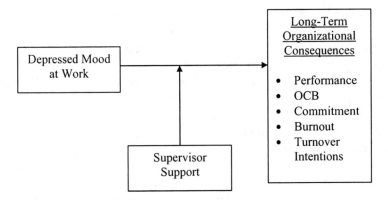

Figure 7.1.   Model of proposed interaction of variables.

DEPRESSED MOOD AT WORK

What is Depressed Mood at Work?

Depressed mood at work is a general despairing feeling towards work (Quinn & Sheppard, 1974). It is characterized by irritability, decreased energy, decreased work interest, and a decreased sense of usefulness that persists over a period of time (Quinn & Sheppard, 1974). Some researchers (e.g., Beehr, 1976; Evans & Fischer, 1992) have conceptualized depressed mood at work as a component of psychological strain and health. However, there is little precedent for the boundaries of what constitutes depressed mood at work. By examining the term, depressed mood at work, we arrive at a conceptual definition.

Depressed mood at work is a unique concept in that it contains elements of depression with contextual limitations. The American Heritage College Dictionary (1993) defines depressed as "low in spirits; dejected" (p. 374). Mood describes a general feeling state that is more stable than emotions, yet less stable than personality (Elsbach & Barr, 1999). Moods are relatively generic and temporary yet could linger for a period of time (Fiske & Taylor, 1991). By adding the contextual constraint of work, depressed mood at work refers to a negative feeling state that is very specific; that is, negative (depressed) feelings that are relatively temporary (mood) and are manifested and emerge while on the job (work). To this end, the relatively temporary aspect of mood has two uses. First, the negative feelings, themselves, can be temporary in nature, and second, the depressed mood could be relatively temporary in that it only is present while at work.

In regard to the first use of the word mood, the temporary nature of moods notes that depressed mood at work is less fatalistic than burnout or depression. Although some researchers (e.g., Burke, Greenglass, & Schwarzer, 1996; Ogus, Greenglass, & Burke, 1990) have viewed work-related depression in the context of burnout (Baba, Jamal, & Tourigny, 1998), depressed mood at work is unique in that it is a relatively mild form of poor psychological well-being. Burnout, for example, is characterized by "emotional exhaustion, depersonalization, and decreased personal accomplishment" (Baba, Jamal, & Tourigny, 1998, p. 96). Zellars, Perrewé, and Hochwarter (2000) noted that burnout is "cognitive defeat, or hopelesness" (p. 1,570). Since depressed mood at work is temporary in nature, it is more likely to be considered a cognitive set-back rather than implying cognitive defeat.

Depressed mood at work can be differentiated from general depression by the second use of mood (e.g., feelings that only emerge at work). General depression is noted as being global "negative feelings, self-destructive thoughts, emotional fatigue, and social withdrawal" (Baba et al., 1998, p. 97) that is not specific to an organizational setting (Leiter & Durup, 1994). Furthermore, Hobfoll, Lomranz, Eyal, Bridges, and Tzemach (1989) noted depressed mood should not "be interpreted as representing clinical depression so much as general psychological malaise" (p. 1005). Thus, general depression is different from depressed mood at work in the latter is specific to the workplace. Therefore, both burnout and depression are distinctly different from depressed mood at work.

Specifically, we conceptualize that depressed at work as a precursor to more severe long-term outcomes such as burnout and voluntary turnover. That is, depressed mood at work mediates the relationship between organizational stressors and negative, long-term outcomes. Depressed mood at work is part of the transition stage from stressors to negative, long-term consequences; a mild form of ill psychological health. This assertion is supported by the affective events theory (Weiss & Cropanzano, 1996) and the conservation of resources theory (Hobfoll, 1989). The affective events theory notes that stimuli that are mild are more likely to lead to emotion driven moods rather then emotion driven behaviors. Consequently, the emotion driven moods influence cognitive processes and behaviors (Weiss & Cropanzano, 1996). Hobfoll (1989) asserted that when individuals lack the ability to offset resource loss, a loss spiral could develop. As such, it is implied that individuals will go through a varying degree of levels of resource depletion that range from completely healthy to burnout. Thus, individuals experiencing a depressed mood at work may have their resources depleted and be on a spiraling decent toward burnout.

WHY IS DEPRESSED MOOD AT WORK IMPORTANT TO STUDY AS AN INDEPENDENT VARIABLE?

Although the term depressed mood at work has appeared in the organizational sciences for almost 30 years, it has not been a popular variable to study. For instance, Kahn and Byosiere's (1992) review of the literature on stressors and strains referenced 60 studies that investigated psychological responses to work stress such as burnout and depression. However, depressed mood at work is not once mentioned as a construct of interest. Although Kahn and Byosiere's (1992) list is by no means exhaustive of the research on organizational stress, it does illustrate that depressed mood at work is often overlooked in stress research.

Depressed mood at work should be of interest to organizational scientists and practitioners alike. Specifically, if depressed mood at work is conceptualized as a mild form of ill psychological outcomes, it is perhaps a better construct to study as an independent/mediator variable so that moderating variables can be investigated. In doing so, we are able to examine what happens when employees experience depressed moods at work and what organizations can do to help. Organizations may be in a better position to help employees who are experiencing a depressed mood at work rather than other concepts such as general depression. For instance, Lucas (2004) asserted that individuals who suffer from depression range from those who may be treated with analytic psychotherapy to those who may require medication for treatment. As such, organizations may not be able to quickly and readily assist employees experiencing depression. Given all of this, it is useful to study depressed mood at work because it provides an opportunity for managers to have a greater impact on helping employees prior to a depressed mood at work leading to long-term negative outcomes.

WHAT ARE THE CAUSES AND OUTCOMES OF DEPRESSED MOOD AT WORK?

As stated earlier, although the concept of depressed mood at work has appeared in the organizational sciences for over thirty years (i.e., Quinn & Sheppard, 1974), it has been relatively understudied. The concept of depressed mood at work has not been abundantly researched, as noted earlier. Thus, theoretical and empirical work on the causes and consequences of depressed mood at work is sparse. Further, little research has been conducted on the consequences of depressed mood at work, presumably due to researchers considering depressed mood at work as a result of stressors instead of a precursor to more intense strain.

Causes of Depressed Mood at Work

In some of the early work on role strain, Beehr (1976) examined role strain as a consequence of role ambiguity. One of the components of role strain he studied was depressed mood at work. In that study, Beehr (1976) found that role ambiguity did lead to depressed mood at work but was moderated by job autonomy and group cohesiveness. In a later study, Beehr (1981) confirmed his findings of role ambiguity leading to depressed mood at work. Here, Beehr (1981) also found that role over-load and under utilization of skill were related to depressed mood at work. Other researchers (e.g., Heinisch & Jex, 1997) have validated the role ambiguity—depressed mood at work relationship. These researchers also found that role conflict, workload, and interpersonal conflict were correlated with depressed mood at work (Heinisch & Jex, 1997). Heinisch and Jex (1997) also examined the moderating effects of negative affect and gender and found that females and individuals high in negative affect experienced higher levels of depressed mood at work in the adverse conditions reported above.

Other variables such as job control (Erickson & Wharton, 1997; Evans & Fischer, 1992) and interrole conflict (Stewart & Barling, 1996) have been shown to correlate with depressed mood at work. Erickson and Wharton (1997) also showed depressed mood at work to be correlated with income level, time spent with coworkers, time spent at work, and not being authentic. Higgins, Duxbury, and Johnson (2000) implied that depressed mood at work could be a result of person-environment fit. In their study, Higgins et al. (2000) found that career women (i.e., those who desired to have a career of their own) had lower levels of depressed mood at work than women who were pursuing careers but would prefer to not work outside of the home. Hobfoll et al. (1989) found that depressed mood could be found at the population level of analysis as a reaction to war. Finally, Stoner and Hochwarter (2003) found that, after controlling for several dispositional (i.e., positive affect, negative affect, and emotional labor) and situational (i.e., age, gender, and organizational tenure) variables, psychological contract violation, perceptions of organizational politics, job tension, and job dissatisfaction were related to depressed mood at work.

Consequence of Depressed Mood at Work

As noted earlier, depressed mood at work has not been investigated as an antecedent to long-term personal and organizational outcomes. However, several streams of research seem to give credence that depressed mood at work may be a "step" that links organizational conditions (e.g., role conflict, role ambiguity, etc.) and long-term organizational outcomes (e.g., burnout, performance, turnover, etc.). Specifically, we turn to the literature on the affective events theory (Weiss & Cropanzano, 1996) and the conservation of resources theory (e.g., Hobfoll, 1989). Both of these research streams imply that long-term consequences could be a result of a process, or many stimuli over time, rather than one stimulus at one point in time.

The affective events theory notes that stimuli, which do not elicit initial strong emotional reactions, are likely to influence one's mood (Weiss & Cropanzano, 1996). Consequently, it is one's mood that will influence attitudes, which dictates one's behaviors (Weiss & Cropozano, 1996). In this theory, depressed mood at work would be the result of weak emotion-evoking stimuli that would aid attitude formation. For instance, according to the affective events theory, employees who perceive their increase in workload as a workplace stressor will have one of two reactions to the stressor: (1) strong emotional reaction, or (2) a weak emotional reaction. If the increase in workload results in a strong emotional reaction (e.g., get extremely anger with job when told about work increase), employees will behave quickly based on their emotions (e.g., quit their job). However, if the increase in workload only elicits a weak or moderate emotional reaction (e.g., slightly perturbed with job when told about work increase), employees will experience a general mood that is constant with their emotional reaction (e.g., depressed mood at work). The emotional reaction will influence employees' attitudes (e.g., a negative attitude toward work); which will, in turn, drive behaviors (e.g., intentions to quit). In the latter scenario, depressed mood at work would mediate the process of weak or moderate emotion-evoking stimuli leading to behaviors.

Furthermore, the conservation of resources theory (e.g., Hobfoll, 1989) notes that individuals have a limited amount of resources (e.g., energy) that they are able to use at any one period of time. Individuals will begin to use resources when they begin to feel stress; and, if they do not replenish their resources, the drain will make them susceptible to even more resource loss. That is, when a resource is used, individuals must replenish the resource (or a substitutable one) to prevent a downward spiral of resource loss. For the current discussion, individuals who perceive workplace stressors as excessively taxing and lack the opportunity to replenish resources a downward spiral begins toward resource depletion (e.g., burnout). In this theory, depressed mood at work could be an intermediate state between observing stressors and complete resource exhaustion.

It is proposed in this paper that depressed mood at work could be an antecedent to many negative, long-term consequences. Specifically, we argue that depressed mood at work will be negatively correlated with organizational outcomes such as self-perceptions of performance, organizational citizenship behaviors, and organizational commitment. That is, as individuals experience high levels of depressed mood at work, they are likely to put forth less effort toward in-role behaviors (performing job tasks) and citizenship behaviors (performing extra tasks that are not required by one's job), and are less likely to feel emotionally attached and committed to their organization. Conversely, we expect that there will be a positive correlation between depressed mood at work and several negative, long-term organizational consequences. Specifically, we argue that depressed mood at work will lead to burnout and/or turnover intentions. In sum, and as illustrated in Figure 7.1, we propose that depressed mood at work will be negatively related to performance, organizational citizenship behaviors, and organizational commitment, yet positively related to burnout and intentions leave.

Depressed mood at work and performance.   A negative relationship is anticipated between depressed mood at work and performance because individuals who are experiencing high amounts of depressed mood at work are likely to feel as though they are not able to focus their energy on performing their job. This assertion is supported by the tenants of goal-setting theory (e.g., Locke & Latham, 1990; Locke, Shaw, Saari, & Latham, 1981). Specifically, goal setting theory notes that performance is influenced by goal-directed effort (Locke & Latham, 2002). One of the characteristics of depressed mood at work is a decrease in effort while at work. Thus, as one decreases their effort (as those high in depressed mood at work do), we expect decreases in performance.

Depressed mood at work and organizational citizenship behaviors.   Likewise, it is possible that individuals high in depressed mood at work will perform fewer organizational citizenship behaviors. Organizational citizenship behaviors (OCBs) help the organization but are not necessarily required by the employees' job description (Van Dyne, Graham, & Dienesch, 1994). For example, employees who straighten up a mutual supply closet or those who arrive early to work and stay late without expectations of compensation are displaying organizational citizenship behaviors. However, individuals who are experiencing depressed mood at work probably do not feel mentally motivated to be "company do-gooders." That is, individuals who are experiencing feelings of downheartedness are less likely to want to do extra tasks while at work.

Depressed mood at work and organizational commitment.   We also argue that depressed mood at work will lead to low organizational commitment. Organizational commitment is best described as "a strong attachment to an organization" (Allen & Meyer, 1990; Hochwarter, Perrewé, Ferris, & Guerico, 1999, p. 280; O'Reilly & Chapman, 1986). Organizational commitment has been shown to correlate with motivation, job involvement, and job satisfaction (Mathieu & Zajac, 1990). When individuals are experiencing distaste for their workplace, as excepted with depressed mood at work, they are not likely to have feelings of commitment to their organization.

Depressed mood at work and burnout.   The burnout literature suggests that depressed mood at work may be a viable antecedent to organizational outcomes. Generally, burnout has three characteristics: emotional exhaustion, depersonalization, and reduced feelings of personal accomplishment (Maslach, 1982). Individuals who feel as though they are disenchanted with work (i.e., high depressed mood at work) for a period of time are likely to begin to feel a sense of emotional exhaustion and depersonalization. Halbesleben and Buckley (2004) noted depersonalization is a "response to the aforementioned emotional exhaustion and describes a process whereby employees detach from their job and begin to develop callous or uncaring attitudes toward their job" (pp. 859–860). This suggests that burnout is not a phenomenon that occurs at one point in time, but rather is a result of a process. It is likely that depressed mood at work is at the beginning of the process.

Furthermore, the works of Hobfoll (1989) imply that burnout is a result of a depletion of resources. This depletion of resources happens because individuals encounter a downward spiral of resource decline when their resources are taxed and not replenished. It is likely, as stated earlier, that depressed mood at work is a intermediate state between psychological health and burnout.

Depressed mood at work and turnover.   Furthermore, individuals who experience depressed mood at work will also be more likely to leave their job than individuals who do not experience depressed mood at work. Griffeth and Hom (1995) offered an integrated model of the employee turnover process. In their model, intentions to quit (i.e., withdrawal cognitions) are directly related to turnover. It stands to reason that depressed mood at work would lead to withdrawal cognitions because individuals would have a decreased sense of work interest and usefulness while at work.

> **Proposition 1:**   Depressed mood at work will be associated with long-term organizational outcomes. Specifically, depressed mood at work will be negatively associated with performance, OCBs, and commitment and positively associated with burnout and intentions to turnover.

What Can Managers Do?

Research in the area of social support has been extensive, revealing, yet, inconclusive (for complete reviews see Beehr, 1994; Viswesvaran, Sanchez, & Fisher, 1999). Generally speaking, social support is conceptualized as friendly, respectful, and helpful people (Beehr, 1995). Social support researchers (e.g., Caplan, Cobb, French, Harrison, & Pinneau, 1975; Cohen & Willis, 1985) have proposed several different ways in which to classify social support systems and how they work. For the purposes of this paper, we are concerned with functional social support systems; which could be either emotional based or instrumental based (Beehr & Glazer, 2001). Emotional based functional social support systems attempt to put individuals in positive moods whereas instrumental based functional social support systems attempt to reduce strain by giving tangible assistance (Beehr & Glazer, 2001).

The sources of social support are frequently classified as being either supervisor-based, coworker support, or outside support (Beehr & Glazer, 2001). Which social support provides the most relief is probably best represented by the matching hypothesis (Cohen & Wills, 1985). The matching hypothesis calls for the need to match the type of social support and the stressor. From the perspective of practicing managers, the application of supervisor support is of particular interest. That is, it is appropriate to examine the interaction of supervisor support and depressed mood at work because (1) supervisors are able to address work issues, and (2) supervisors are able to control their use of social support, but not coworker social support or outside social support.

It is proposed that supervisor support will moderate the relationship between depressed mood at work and the long-term negative consequences discussed above. Specifically, it is posited that individuals who perceive high amounts of supervisor support will have higher performance, perform more organizational citizenship behaviors, and be more committed to their organization than those who perceive low amounts of supervisor support when the level of depressed mood at work is high. Furthermore, it is posited that individuals who perceive high amounts of supervisor support will be less likely to burnout and less likely to leave the organization than those who perceive low amounts of supervisor support when the level of depressed mood at work is high. Thus,

> Proposition 2:   Supervisor support will moderate the relationship between depressed mood at work and long-term organizational consequences such that those high in supervisor support will have higher performance, OCBs, and commitment, and less burnout and fewer turnover

intentions than those low in supervisor support under conditions of high depressed mood at work.

CONCLUSION

The purpose of this paper was to explore some of the consequences of an understudied concept known as depressed mood at work. In doing so, we have provided a theoretical context in which depressed mood at work can be examined empirically. Specifically, depressed mood at work is illustrated to be a mood state that mediates the relationship between exposure to long-term stressors and long-term organizational consequences. Furthermore, this paper describes what practicing managers can do to reduce the negative long-term organizational consequences of experienced depressed mood at work. Specifically, it is proposed that supervisor support will diminish the negative outcomes the result from depressed mood at work.

REFERENCES

Allen, N. J., & Meyer, J. P. (1990). Organizational socialization tactics: A longitudinal analysis of links to newcomers commitment and role orientation. *Academy of Management Journal, 33*, 847–858.

American Heritage college dictionary (3rd ed.). (1993). Boston: Houghton Mifflin.

Baba, V. V., Jamal, M., & Tourigny, L. (1998). Work and mental health: A decade in Canadian research. *Canadian Psychology, 39*, 94–107.

Beehr, T. A. (1976). Perceived situational moderators of the relationship between subjective role ambiguity and role strain. *Journal of Applied Psychology, 61*, 35–40.

Beehr. T. A. (1981). Work-role stress and attitudes toward co-workers. *Group and Organization Studies, 6*, 201–210.

Beehr, T. A. (1994). *Meta-analysis of occupational stress and social support.* Paper presented at the annual meeting of the Midwestern Psychological Association, Chicago, Il.

Beehr, T. A. (1995). Psychological Stress in the Workplace. London, England: Routledge.

Beehr, T. A., & Glazer, S. (2001). A cultural perspective of social support in relation to occupational stress. In P. L. Perrewé & D. C. Ganster (Eds.), *Research in occupational stress and well being* (Vol. 1, pp. 97–102) Oxford, England: Elsevier.

Burke, R. J., Greenglass, E. R., & Schwarzer, R. (1996). Predicting teacher burnout over time: Effects of work stress, social support, and self-doubts on burnout and its consequences. *Anxiety, Stress, and Coping, 9*, 261–275.

Caplan, R. D., Cobb, S., French, J. R. P. Jr., Harrison, R. V., & Pinneau, S. R. (1975). *Job demands and worker health: Main effects and occupational differences.* Washington, DC: U.S. Government Printing Office.

Cohen, S., & Wills, T. A. (1985). Stress, social support, and buffering hypothesis, *Psychological Review, 98,* 310–357.

Elsbach, K. D., & Barr, P. S. (1999). The effects of mood on individuals' use of structured decision protocols. *Organization Science, 10,* 181–198.

Erickson, R. J., & Wharton, A. S. (1997). Inauthenticity and depression: Assessing the consequences of interactive service work. *Work and Occupations, 24,* 188–213.

Evans, B. K., & Fischer, D. G. (1992). A hierarchical model of participatory decision-making, job autonomy, and perceived control. *Human Relations, 45,* 1169–1189.

Fiske, S. T., & Taylor, S. E. (1991). *Social cognition.* New York: McGraw-Hill.

Griffeth, R. W., & Hom, P. W. (1995). The employee turnover process. In G. R. Ferris (Ed.), *Research in personnel and human resources management* (Vol. 13, pp. 245–293). Greenwich, CT: JAI Press.

Halbesleben, J. R. B., & Buckley, M. R. (2004). Burnout in organization life. *Journal of Management, 30,* 859–879.

Heinisch, D. A., & Jex, S. M. (1997). NA and gender as moderators of the relationship between work related stressors and depressed mood at work. *Work and Stress, 11,* 146–157.

Higgins, C., Duxbury, L., & Johnson, K.L. (2000). Part-time work for women: Does it really help balance work and family. *Human Resource Management, 39,* 17–32.

Hobfoll, S. E. (1989). Conservation of resources: A new attempt at conceptualizing stress. *American Psychologist, 44,* 513–524.

Hobfoll, S. E., Lomranz, J., Eyal, N., Bridges, A., Tzemach, M. (1989). Pulse of a nation: Depressed mood reactions of Isralis to the Israel-Lebanon War. *Journal of Personality and Social Psychology, 56,* 1002–1012.

Hochwarter, W. A., Perrewé, P. L., Ferris, G. R., & Guerico, R. (1999). Commitment as an antidote to the tension and turnover consequences of organizational politics. *Journal of Vocational Behavior, 55,* 277–297.

Kahn, R. L., & Byosiere, P. (1992). Stress in organizations. In M. D. Dunnette & L. M. Hough (Eds.), *Handbook of industrial and organizational psychology* (pp. 571–650). Palo Alto, CA: Consulting Psychologists Press.

Leiter, M. P., & Durup, J. (1994). The discriminant validity of burnout and depression: A confirmatory factor analytic study. *Anxiety, Stress, and Coping, 7,* 357–373.

Locke, E. A., & Latham, G. P. (1990), Work motivation and satisfaction: Light at the end of the tunnel. *Psychological Science, 1,* 240–246.

Locke, E. A., & Latham, G. P. (2002). Building a practically useful theory of goal setting and task motivation: A 35-year odyssey. *American Psychologist, 57,* 705–717.

Locke, E. A., Shaw, K. N., Saari, L. M., Latham, G. P. (1981). Goal setting and task performance: 1969–1980. *Psychological Bulletin, 90,* 125–152.

Lucas, R. (2004). The management of depression—Analytic, antidepressants or both? *Psychoanalytic Psychotherapy, 18*, 268–284.

Maslach, C. (1982). Understanding burnout: Definitional issues in anlyzing a complex phenomenon. In W. S. Paine (Ed.), *Job stress and burnout* (pp. 29–41). Beverly Hills, CA: Sage.

Mathieu, J. E., & Zajac, D. M. (1990). A review and meta-analysis of antecedents, correlates, and consequences of organizational commitment. *Psychological Bulletin, 108*, 171–194.

Ogus, E. D., Greenglass, E. R., & Burke, R. J. (1990). Gender-role differences, work stress and depersonalization. *Journal of Social Behavior and Personality, 5*, 387–398.

O'Reilly, C. A., & Chatman, J. (1986). Organizational commitment and psychological attachment: The effects of compliance, identification, and internalization on prosocial behavior. *Journal of Applied Psychology, 71*, 492–499.

Quinn, R., & Shepard, L. (1974). *The 1972–1973 quality of employment survey.* Ann Arbor, MI: Institute for Social Research, University of Michigan.

Stewart, W., & Barling, J. (1996). Father's work and children's behavior. *Journal of Organizational Behavior, 17*, 221–232.

Stoner, J., & Hochwarter, W. (2003, November). *The contextual determinants of depressed mood at work.* Paper presented at the 2003 Southern Management Association conference, Clearwater, FL.

Van Dyne, L., Graham, J. W., & Dienesch, R. M. (1994). Organizational citizenship behavior: Construct redefinition, measurement, and validation. *The Academy of Management Journal, 37*, 765–802.

Viswesvaran, C., Sanchez, J. I., & Fisher, J. (1999). The role of social support in the process of work stress: A meta-analysis. *Journal of Vocational Behavior, 54*, 314–334.

Weiss, H. M., & Crapanzano, R. (1996). Affective events theory: A theoretical discussion of the structure, causes, and consequences of affective experiences at work. In B. M. Staw, & L. L. Cummings (Eds.), *Research in organizational behavior: An annual series of analytical essays and critical reviews* (Vol. 18, pp. 1–74). Greenwich, CT: JAI Press.

Zellars, K. L., Perrewé, P. L., & Hochwarter, W. A. (2000). Burnout in health care: The role of the five factors of personality. *Journal of Applied Social Psychology, 30*, 1570–1598.

CHAPTER 8

STRESS AND EMPLOYEE EFFECTIVENESS

**Steve M. Jex, Christopher J. L. Cunningham,
Gabriel De La Rosa, and Alison Broadfoot**

Stress is a feature of most, if not all, organizational environments. For most managers, however, it is unclear whether or not stress has a negative impact on employee effectiveness. In this chapter we examine research evidence regarding the relationship between stress and employee effectiveness, with a primary emphasis on translating these findings into practical terms. The primary conclusion drawn in this chapter is that research does not support a strong relationship between stress and employee effectiveness, primarily because researchers have focused on formally mandated tasks. When viewed in a broader sense however, there is evidence that stress detracts from employee effectiveness. The other major conclusion is that not all stressful aspects of the work environment will necessarily detract from employee effectiveness. Generally speaking, stressors that place short-term quantitative demands on employees (e.g., deadlines, workload) will probably be less problematic than stressors, which directly hinder performance (e.g., interruptions from others, poor equipment). The primary practical implication conveyed is that employees experiencing workplace stressors may be quite capable of performing required job-related tasks. However, at the same time, these same employees may be unable to engage in a variety of other

Stress and Quality of Working Life: Current Perspectives in Occupational Health, 101–119
Copyright © 2006 by Information Age Publishing
All rights of reproduction in any form reserved.

behaviors that could contribute to the overall effectiveness of an organization.

INTRODUCTION

Work-related stress is a topic that has captured the interest of researchers and the general public. Much of this interest is due to the impact of stress on employee health; in financial terms, stress costs organizations billions of dollars annually in increased health care costs and lost work time (e.g., Manning, Jackson, & Fusilier, 1996; Matteson & Ivancevich, 1987). An equally important, yet understudied consequence of workplace stress is its potential to reduce employee effectiveness. Unfortunately, researchers and managers in organizations have devoted relatively little attention to understanding the impact of workplace stress on employee effectiveness (Beehr, Jex, Stacy, & Murray, 2000; Jex, 1998).

In this chapter we provide a thorough examination of the relationship between workplace stress and employee effectiveness. The chapter begins with a brief overview of workplace stress. Our purpose here is not to inundate the reader with complex models and theories, but to simply explain how researchers conceptualize the stress process in terms of everyday life in organizations. The second portion of the chapter defines the rather nebulous concept of *employee effectiveness*. As will be evident, we view employee effectiveness as much more than just "doing one's job." The fourth and final portion of the chapter explores the practical implications of research on workplace stress and employee effectiveness.

STRESS IN THE WORKPLACE

Before any discussion of the relationship between stress and effectiveness can begin, several terms need to be clarified. Inconsistent usage of the words *stress* and *strain* has been common across different research literatures (e.g., Beehr, Jex, & Ghosh, 2001; Jex, Beehr, & Roberts, 1992; McEwen, 2000; Sapolsky, 1998; Sutherland & Cooper, 2002). In general, stress refers to an individual's perception of a *stressor*, which is typically defined as conditions and/or events that result in strain (Kahn & Byosiere, 1992). In the short run, perceived stress can affect the attitudes and behaviors of an individual, but it is over a longer duration of time that these effects more frequently take on negative tones. This is the reason for the concept of *strain*, which refers to the consequences of stress over time (Beehr, 1995; Beehr & Newman, 1978).

Sequentially, we view job stress as a process that can be viewed in terms of an expanded response-based model. In such a model, stressors lead directly to a stress response, which then may lead to one of three types of outcomes (strains and/or longer term consequences): *physiological* (e.g., increased risk of cardiovascular disease or hypertension, inability to sleep, psychosomatic symptoms; Jex, 1998; Landsbergis, Schnall, Schwartz, Warren, & Pickering, 1995), *psychological* (e.g., frustration, anxiety, negative work-related attitudes; Beehr, 1995; Jex, 1998; Jex & Beehr, 1991; Jex, Bliese, Buzzell, & Primeau, 2001; Spector, 1997; Thomas & Jex, 2002), and *behavioral* (e.g., increased absenteeism, counterproductive behaviors, drug and alcohol use, withdrawal from work and family, reduced performance; Bachrach, Bamberger, & Sonnenstuhl, 2002; Frone, 1999; Gupta & Beehr, 1979; Jex, 1998; Motowidlo, Packard, & Manning, 1986).

These consequences notwithstanding, stress is more than a negative, symptom-causing experience that simply "happens to people" (Sutherland & Cooper, 2002, p. 34). There is no established reason that all stressors must lead to negative consequences. While the effects of stress arousal may be physiologically similar for most stressors (e.g., Sapolsky, 1998; Selye, 1936 as cited in Sutherland & Cooper, 2002), psychological and behavioral responses may differ greatly depending on the stress situation and this difference may be especially visible at the level of organizational outcomes. Recent research suggests that different types of stressors may lead to different outcomes (e.g., Boswell, Olson-Buchanan, & LePine, 2004; Cavanaugh, Boswell, Roehling, & Boudreau, 2000) and that some stressors may actually result in positive outcomes. In truth, stress is an evolutionary necessity, forcing us to react, respond, and change; these actions might not otherwise be taken unless one is faced with a stressful situation (e.g., McEwen, 2000; Sapolsky, 1998; Sutherland & Cooper, 2002). Within a work setting however, stress becomes problematic when it is mismanaged, which is increasingly becoming the case when employees are unable to effectively handle many of the stressors in their environments (Sutherland & Cooper, p. 35). Within organizations, although stress may promote certain behaviors, this promotion may come with a heavy cost.

EMPLOYEE EFFECTIVENESS

Employee effectiveness is difficult to define and even more difficult to measure. In the most general sense, effectiveness represents the sum total of an employee's contributions to an organization. This definition is certainly consistent with the literature that has attempted to describe and model employee performance (e.g., Campbell, 1990; Campbell, McCloy, Oppler, & Sager, 1993; Campbell, McHenry, & Wise, 1990; Murphy, 1994). We view employee effectiveness, however, as a much broader and more multidimensional concept than performance. In describing effectiveness, we distinguish between *in-role/task* versus *extra-role/contextual* behaviors (e.g., Borman & Motowidlo, 1993),[1] a distinction that is developed more fully in the sections that follow.

Task Performance Behavior

Employee effectiveness is clearly at least partially linked to employees' task performance behaviors (echoed by Borman, 1991). Task performance behaviors are those that "contribute to the organization's technical core" and are "formally recognized" as part of an individual's job (Borman & Motowidlo, 1993, p. 73). A typical manager, for example, is *required* to supervise other employees, rate their performance, and engage in standard paperwork and administrative duties. These behaviors are not permitted to vary a great deal within most work environments (e.g., bank tellers must follow standardized withdrawal procedures).

Contextual Performance Behaviors

While performing one's required tasks may contribute to one's effectiveness, there is much more to being effective that simply doing what's required. The most effective employees are those who go above and beyond required job tasks in order to help others and to further the goals of their organization. Such non-required behaviors can take many forms, many of which are often referred to as *contextual performance behaviors*. For example, a manager exhibiting these behaviors might offer to help another employee learn a new software program, work to improve the public image of the organization to the local community, or demonstrate internal drive and passion for her own work that influences other employees in a positive fashion. The most common contextual performance behaviors examined in the literature have been *organizational citizenship behaviors, prosocial organizational behaviors,* and *personal initiative*.

Organizational citizenship behaviors (OCBs). By definition OCBs contribute to organizational effectiveness and are not a part of an employee's required job tasks (Borman & Motowidlo, 1993; Jex, Adams, Bachrach, & Sorenson, 2003; Organ, 1988; Smith, Organ, & Near, 1983).[2,3] In a detailed quantitative review of the literature, Organ and Ryan (1995) identified two main OCB dimensions: *altruism* and *generalized compliance*. Altruistic behaviors directly aid people within the organization, while generalized compliance behaviors represent more impersonal organizational contributions (i.e., following rules, showing up on time, efficiently using time).

Prosocial organizational behavior (POB).   This form of contextual performance is defined as behavior: (a) performed by a member of an organization, (b) directed toward an individual, group, or organization with whom that individual interacts while carrying out his or her organizational role, or (c) performed with the goal of promoting the welfare of the individual, group, or organization to which it is directed (Brief & Motowidlo, 1986, p. 711).[4] Examples of POB might be assisting coworkers with work or personal matters, providing extra assistance to customers, complying with organizational policies, volunteering for additional work assignments, and representing the organization favorably to outsiders (Brief & Motowidlo, 1986).

Personal initiative.   A third form of contextual performance is personal initiative. A unique feature of this construct is its long-term, persistent proactive focus (Fay & Frese, 2001; Fay & Sonnentag, 2002), which drives people to overcome obstacles and setbacks. In addition, personal initiative includes only those actions that fit within and contribute to an organization's goals. Examples of personal initiative include preparing for future demands or making personal efforts to increase long-term organizational efficiency.

Other Forms Of Effectiveness-Related Behavior

In addition to task and contextual performance behaviors, employees may engage in additional forms of behaviors that contribute to their effectiveness within organizations. Several forms of this type of behavior have been identified, including *creative and innovative behavior,* and (absence of) *counterproductive work behaviors.*

Creative and innovative behavior.   Creativity is commonly defined as "both a novel and appropriate, useful, correct, or valuable response to the task at hand [when] the task at hand is heuristic [i.e., open-ended] rather than algorithmic [i.e., clearly prescribed]" (Amabile, 1983; Amabile, Goldfarb, & Brackfield, 1990). A related concept, innovation, is defined as the successful implementation of creative ideas (Amabile & Conti, 1999). In organizations, creative performance represents instances where employees generate novel and useful ideas (Amabile, 1988). Creativity and innovation are certainly relevant in organizational functions such as research and new product development, but may help to improve more mundane aspects of organizational life such as the design of organizational structures or the utilization of human resources (Damanpour, 1991).

Avoidance of counterproductive work behaviors (CWB). By definition, CWBs are behaviors that run counter to the goals of an organization. Such behaviors may be intentionally directed at harming the organization or other employees (e.g., theft, violence), or they may simply run counter to organizational goals (e.g., wasting time, daydreaming on the job). Because of their detrimental effects on organizational performance and employee health and well-being, CWBs are important to understand. Commonly researched CWBs include larceny, absenteeism, drug abuse, safety violations, and mistreatment of others.

PAST RESEARCH ON STRESS AND EFFECTIVENESS

Most research on the impact of stress on employee effectiveness comes from studies examining the relationship between role stressors and task performance. Summaries of this literature have shown that this relationship is very weak (e.g., Jackson & Schuler, 1985; Tubre & Collins, 2000), but negative nonetheless. There is reason to believe however, that the relationship between stressors and task performance may vary considerably depending on the type(s) of stressor(s) and the type(s) of effectiveness-related behaviors being examined (e.g., Beehr et al., 2000). LePine, Podsakoff, and LePine (2004), for example, found evidence supporting their assertion that the inconsistent relationship between stress and task performance was due to the fact that different types of stress affect performance differently. They found that both challenge and hindrance stressors (defined earlier) were associated with higher levels of psychological strain, but that challenge stressors also *positively* influenced performance (cf., Boswell et al., 2004; LePine, LePine, & Jackson, 2004).

Further complicating the relationship between stress and employee effectiveness is the presence of *mediator* and *moderator* variables. Mediator variables are intermediate links between stress and effectiveness. For example, a stressor may cause an employee to feel depressed, which ultimately leads to decreased effectiveness. The mediator variable in this example is depression. Moderator variables, on the other hand, alter the strength (and sometimes the form) of relationships between other variables. As an example of this, a stressor might decrease the effectiveness of an employee who has been on the job for a short period of time, but have no effect on an employee with several years of experience. In this example, job experience is the moderator variable. Given the importance of intervening variables, our discussion of the relationships between stress and each of the previously defined effectiveness criteria will incorporate mediators and moderators.

Table 8.1.   Previously Researched Individual-Level Mediators and Moderators of the Stress Process

Mediator/Moderator	Observed Effect
(1) *Reactivity* (i.e., strength of sensitivity to stimuli)	Low reactivity is associated better performance under pressure (e.g., Strelau & Maciejczyk, 1977)
(2) *Locus of control* (i.e., perception that control over events is internal or external)	Internal locus is associated with higher job satisfaction in demanding jobs (e.g., Perrewé, 1986)
(3) *Participation in decision making* (i.e., involvement in making personally relevant decisions)	Those engaged in decision making experience higher levels of perceived satisfaction and accomplishment and reduced perceptions of stress (e.g., Miller, Ellis, Zook, & Lyles, 1990)
(4) Perceptions of *social support* and *supervisor support*	May buffer effects of stress,[a] reducing negative emotional (e.g., frustration, depression) and behavioral strain (e.g., decreased effectiveness outcomes (Beehr, 1995; Kahn & Byosiere, 1992; Kirmeyer & Doughtery, 1988)
(5) *Organizational commitment* (i.e., level of attachment to an organization)	High commitment seems to reduce effects of stress on performance (e.g., Jamal, 1985) and may increase beneficial nontask performance behaviors (e.g., Morrison, 1994; Organ & Ryan, 1995)
(6) Level of *depression*	Stress may increase depression, which may then lead to decreased performance of task and nontask behaviors (e.g., Motowidlo, Packard, & Manning, 1986)
(7) Perceived *self-efficacy* (i.e., one's confidence in one's abilities to complete a given task)	High self-efficacy is associated with a tendency to appraise stressors as challenging rather than threatening, leading to fewer negative consequences of stress (e.g., Bandura, 1997). Alternatively, those with high self-efficacy may be more able to handle job stress while experiencing fewer strains (e.g., Grau, Salanova, & Peiró, 2001; Jex & Bliese, 1999; Salanova, Peiró, & Schaufeli, 2002; Schaubroeck & Merritt, 1997)

[a]But this "buffering" effect has not always been identified as it is hard to detect within organizational samples (Cohen & Wills, 1985).

Stress and Task Performance Behaviors

As mentioned previously, task and contextual performance behaviors may be differentially influenced by different types of stressors (i.e., hindrance or challenge) (Cavanaugh et al., 2000; LePine et al., 2004). An employee's task performance is not likely to decrease when she is faced with either hindrance or challenge stressors, since employee behavior of this sort is basically required. Research has in general shown, however, that stressors and task performance are typically weakly, but nevertheless negatively related (as mentioned above). We believe a stronger and more consistent relationship may be observed between stress and contextual performance behaviors.

Stress and Contextual Performance Behaviors

It is conceivable that stress of any kind could decrease the prevalence of contextual performance behaviors, due to the fact that stress tends to foster negative attitudes toward one's job and the organization as a whole (e.g., Cavanaugh et al., 2000; LePine et al., 2004; Spector & O'Connell, 1994; Stanton, Balzer, Smith, Parra & Ironson, 2001; Vigoda, 2002). However, it is also possible that certain forms of stress might actually *increase* the frequency of some contextual performance behaviors. Thus, it is important to consider research on stress and each form of contextual performance separately.

Stress and OCB.   Both hindrance and challenge stress may negatively affect employees' tendency to engage in OCBs, possibly due to a narrowing of employees' attention to task performance issues (e.g., Kahneman, 1973; discussed as a survival reaction by Sapolsky, 1998). Employees' affective organizational commitment also appears to moderate the stress—OCB relationship, such that those with high affective commitment are more likely to engage in altruistic behaviors (i.e., helping others) when faced with organizational constraints (e.g., inadequate training, resources, coworker assistance, intense time pressures, organizational policies, red tape, authority, lack of information access) and less likely to be altruistic when experiencing role conflict (Jex, Adams, et al., 2003). Jex, Adams, et al. suggest this may be the result of committed employees pulling together to overcome organizational constraints, as was the case when employees in their study responded to conflicting role demands by committing themselves more highly to their immediate work group than to the organization as a whole. This may have lead to increasing altruistic behavior within their immediate work group.

Stress and POB and personal initiative.   Both of these forms of behavior are typically demonstrated not in reaction to events, but out of an individual's desire to make a difference. One moderator of these behaviors may be an individual's *proactive personality* (or lack thereof), which has been linked with several organizational outcomes such as job performance (Crant & Bateman, 1993), leader effectiveness (Bateman & Crant, 1993; Crant & Bateman, 2000; Deluga, 1998), work team performance (Kirkman & Rosen, 1999), and career success (Siebert, Crant, & Kraimer, 2000). In regards to stress, proactive personality appears to have nonuniform buffering effects (i.e., highly proactive individuals respond negatively to stress regardless of their level of control on their jobs, while less proactive individuals react more favorably to stressors when their job control was low; Jex, Burnfield, Grauer, Adams, & Morgan, 2003). This makes intuitive sense as highly proactive individuals, who tend toward active problem-solving methods, may be thwarted when their job scope is low—this may cause them additional strain.

Employee characteristics may also moderate the relationship between stress and personal initiative, as is visible through the lens of *control theory* (Edwards, 1992). Control theory suggests that employees evaluate perceptions of their present state against their values, goals, and desires for that state. Discrepancies between the present state and employees' desired state might initiate behaviors or actions to resolve any difference. Thus, control theory suggests individuals react to stress, by attempting to bring their environment closer to some ideal.

Interestingly, the work of Fay and Frese (2001) and Fay and Sonnentag (2002) suggests individuals may play a more proactive role, often anticipating future stressors and taking preemptive actions to prevent negative consequences. While personal initiative may potentially reduce the stress faced by employees, other individual differences may weaken this effect. As Fay and Frese note, *learned helplessness* (e.g., Seligman, 1991) may develop when an individual is repeatedly unable to overcome a barrier or stressor. It is also possible that the *degree of discrepancy* between an individual's current and preferred situation may influence whether he will engage in personal initiative to resolve the discrepancy. Personal initiative toward resolution is most likely to evolve from moderate discrepancies, as opposed to extremely small or large gaps that may lead an individual to forego attempts at resolution.

Stress and Other Effectiveness Behaviors

Stress and creative/innovative behavior.   Research to date suggests that stressors (e.g., time pressure and workload) may influence an employees' ability to creatively function within the workplace (e.g., Farr & Ford, 1990; Ford, 1996; Jehn, 1994; Smith, Michael, & Hocevar, 1990; Van Dyne, Jehn, & Cummings, 2001). In a study of organizational downsizing within a technology company, Amabile and Conti (1999) found that the inherent increases in workload pressures and decreases in organizational encouragement, group support, and supervisory encouragement were all accompanied by a decrease in self-reported creativity.

A more complete understanding of the effects of stress on creativity requires attention to possible intervening variables specific to this relationship, between stress and creative performance. One such moderator that plays a particularly strong role in the relationship between stress and creative performance is an individual's affective state or mood. Murray, Sujan, Hirt, and Sujan (1990) found that positive mood was associated with more cognitively flexibility than neutral mood. Negative mood also seems to impair people's ability to engage in divergent thinking (Vosburg, 1998). In addition, the creative performance of depressed individuals has been shown to be worse than that of elated individuals (Mitchell & Madigan, 1990). Further, since emotionally charged situations elicit impulsive thoughts and behavior (Pretcher, 2001), this could also reduce creative performance since impulsive thoughts and actions will tend to be dominated by routine behavior scripts.

Stress and CWB.   While research has demonstrated that stress may increase CWB, this effect is not always direct; several variables may play moderating or mediating roles. *Employee characteristics* in general may be especially influential since those who perceive the workplace as stressful are more likely to avoid the work environment (Beehr, 1995; Greiner, Krause, Ragland, & Fisher, 1998; Siu, 2001). An employee's *locus of control* (described above), also appears to moderate the incidence of CWB, such that persons with an external locus of control were found to engage in more CWB (Storms & Spector, 1987), while those with an internal locus of control were found to experience lower levels of occupational stress (Spector & O'Connell, 1994).

A second factor influencing the effects of stress on CWB appears to be an individual's level of *negative affectivity* (i.e., tendency to experience negative emotions across situations) (Chen & Spector, 1991; Spector & O'Connell, 1994). Findings suggest that a person with high levels of this trait (i.e., a propensity toward negative emotionality) will be more likely to perceive neutral environmental stimuli as threatening (i.e., as stressors), and thus be more likely to respond by engaging in CWBs. In a similar fashion, employees' *negative emotional reactions* (e.g., frustration, job dissatisfaction) have been shown to mediate the relationship between work stressors and CWB (Fox, Spector, & Miles 2001). For example, high levels of organizational constraints have been shown to increase frustration, which may then manifest itself in the form of CWB (Storms & Spector, 1987).

Evidence also suggests that *employee perceptions of* (a) the *cause of stressors*, (b) *fairness,* and (c) the *likelihood of punishment for engaging in CWBs* also play roles. If employees perceive that organizations *can* prevent stressors, but does not do so, they will be more likely to rectify this perceived injustice by acting out against their organization (Skarlicki & Folger, 1997). As a good example of this, Greenberg (1990) found that theft following a mandatory reduction in pay was found to be moderated by whether an explanation for the pay cut was provided. Theft was most likely to occur when no explanation was given. It has also been found that when employees believe no punishment is likely, higher levels of CWB may result (Fox & Spector, 1999). In a similar fashion, but at a more organizational level, *existence and perception of organizational policies* dictating punishment for CWB, and their *severity,* appears to moderate performance of CWB (e.g., Farrell & Stamm, 1998; Hollinger & Clark, 1983). *Group norms* regarding behavior also appear to mediate and moderate the stress—CWB relationship for alcohol use (e.g., Bachrach et al., 2002), absence behaviors (e.g., Martocchio, 1994; Mathieu & Kohler, 1990), and unsafe behavior on the job (Hofmann & Stetzer, 1998).

CONCLUSIONS AND IMPLICATIONS

Few occupational stress theories have addressed the link between stress and performance (e.g., Hart & Cooper, 2002), and fewer still have examined how the effects of stress on employee effectiveness might be mediated by employee well-being. The concepts discussed in this chapter are potentially most clearly summarized in the interactive model presented in Figure 8.1. It is hoped this model will facilitate a general understanding of the stress—effectiveness relationship.

The most important practical implication of this chapter is that employees who are performing their required job tasks relatively well may still be impacted by stress. Thus, managers must look at more than just whether required job tasks are being performed in assessing whether or not employee effectiveness is compromised workplace stress. Managers should consider, for example, whether employees are: (a) going "above and beyond" their required job tasks, (b) taking initiative to solve work-related problems before they occur, (c) exhibiting creativity and innovation when faced with work-related challenges, and (d) refraining from CWBs. If any of these areas are lacking, this may be a sign that stressors in the workplace are taking their toll on employee effectiveness and some action should be taken.

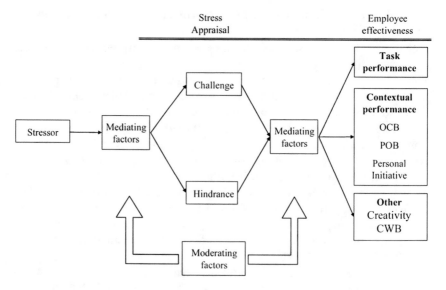

Figure 8.1.   An integrative model of the occupational stress-employee effectiveness relationship.

Another general practical implication of this chapter is that stress does not always have an immediately observable negative impact on employee effectiveness. In this chapter a distinction was made between "hindrance" and "challenge" stressors, and we believe this to be a distinction of practical importance. While organizations should always try to keep hindrance stressors to a minimum so as not to prevent their employees from completing their job tasks, this is not always the case with challenge stressors. Some research suggests organizations should manage challenge stressors and, in some cases, allow employees to experience them (e.g., McCauley, Ruderman, Ohlott, & Morrow, 1994).

For example, allowing employees to work on projects that have tight deadlines may be stressful, but may also help employees to develop useful time management skills that could prevent stressful experiences in the future. As an analogy, consider the activity of physical training with weights. Muscles strengthen because a certain amount of stress is placed on them, forcing them to grow to handle this extra stress. Employees' abilities to function within the work environment may also need to be developed and surely stress of a positive nature (i.e., challenge stress) may serve this goal well. There are many ways to develop an employee though and constantly "stressing them out" with excessive work demands is unlikely to be the most effective in the long run. The most effective employees are likely to be those who are supervised by the most effective managers. Managers need to have some understanding of the complexities of the relationship between stress and employee effectiveness, how it develops, how it can be managed, and what it means for the organization and the employee. As is so often the case, trade-offs must be constantly considered by organization executives when considering the well-being of their workers and the well-being of their organization.

NOTES

1. The use of *in-role* and *extra-role* as descriptors of two separate forms of performance has been debated (e.g., Morrison, 1994; Van Dyne, Graham, & Dienesch, 1994). See MacKenzie, Podsakoff, and Ahearne (1998) for additional information on this distinction. We rely on the task versus contextual distinction as it tends to be more easily understood and less subjective (e.g., Bachrach & Jex, 2000; Morrison, 1994).
2. Organ (1988) identifies five dimensions of OCBs: altruism (helping others), conscientiousness (going above and beyond work duties), civic virtue (responsible participation), sportsmanship (tolerance without complaining), and courtesy (preventing work-related problems with others).
3. While treated here as contextual performance behaviors, individuals with high levels of organizational commitment may enact OCBs as if such behaviors were associated with task performance (see Morrison, 1994).
4. Both functional and dysfunctional POB have been identified; we are focusing on functional POB.

REFERENCES

Amabile, T. M. (1983). The social psychology of creativity. *Journal of Personality and Social Psychology, 45*, 357–376.

Amabile, T. M. (1988). From individual creativity to organizational innovation. In K. Gronhaug & G. Kaufmann (Eds.), *Innovation: A cross-disciplinary perspective* (pp. 139–166). Oslo: Norwegian University Press.

Amabile, T. M., & Conti, R. (1999). Changes in the work environment for creativity during downsizing, *Academy of Management Journal, 42*, 630–640.

Amabile, T. M., Goldfarb, P., & Brackfield, S. C. (1990). Social influences on creativity: Evaluation, coaction, and surveillance. *Creativity Research Journal, 3*, 6–21.

Bachrach, S., Bamberger, P. A., & Sonnenstuhl, W. J. (2002). Driven to drink: Managerial control, work-related risk factors, and employee problem drinking. *Academy of Management Journal, 45*(4), 637–658.

Bachrach, D. G., & Jex, S. M. (2000). Organizational citizenship and mood: An experimental test of perceived job breadth. *Journal of Applied Social Psychology, 30*, 641–663.

Bandura, A. (1997). *Self-efficacy: The exercise of control.* New York: Freeman.

Bateman, T. S., & Crant, J. M. (1993). The proactive component of organizational behavior. *Journal of Organizational Behavior, 14*, 103–118.

Beehr, T. A. (1995). *Psychological stress in the workplace.* London: Routledge.

Beehr, T. A., Jex, S. M., & Ghosh, P. (2001). The management of occupational stress. In C. M. Johnson, w. k. redmon, & t. c. mawhinney (eds.), *handbook of Organizational Performance* (pp. 225–254). New York: The Haworth Press.

Beehr, T. A., Jex, S. M. Stacy, B. A., & Murray, M. A. (2000). Work stressors and coworker support as predictors of individual strain and job performance. *Journal of Organizational Behavior, 21*, 391–405.

Beehr, T. A., & Newman, J. E. (1978). Job stress, employee health, and organizational effectiveness: A facet analysis, model, and literature review. *Personnel Psychology, 31*, 665–699.

Borman, W. C. (1991). Job behavior, performance, and effectiveness. In M. D. Dunnette & L. M. Houghs (Eds.), *Handbook of industrial and organizational Psychology* (Vol. 2, pp. 271–326). Palo Alto: Consulting Psychologists Press.

Borman, W. C., & Motowidlo, S. J. (1993). Expanding the criterion domain to include elements of contextual performance. In N. Schmitt, W. C. Borman, & Associates (Eds.), *Personnel Selection in Organizations* (pp. 71–98). San Francisco: Jossey-Bass.

Boswell, W., Olson-Buchanan, J. B., & LePine, M. A. (2004). Relations between stress and work outcomes: The role of felt challenge, job control, and psychological strain. *Journal of Vocational Behavior, 64*, 165–181.

Brief, A. P., & Motowidlo, S. J. (1986). Prosocial organizational behavior. *Academy of Management Review, 11*, 710–725.

Campbell, J. P. (1990). Modeling the performance prediction problem in industrial and organizational psychology. In M. D. Dunnette & L. M. Hough (Eds.), *Handbook of industrial and organizational psychology, Vol. 1* (2nd ed., pp. 687–732). Palo Alto, CA: Consulting Psychologists Press.

Campbell, J. P., McCloy, R. A., Oppler, S. H., & Sager, C. E. (1993). A theory of performance. In N. Schmitt, W. C. Borman, & Associates (Eds.), *Personnel selection in organizations* (pp. 35–70). Princeton, NJ: Erlbaum.

Campbell, J. P., McHenry, J. J., & Wise, L. L. (1990). Modeling job performance in a population of jobs. *Personnel Psychology, 43*, 313-333.

Cavanaugh, M. A., Boswell, W. R., Roehling, M. V., & Boudreau, J. W. (2000). An empirical examination of self-reported work stress among U.S. managers. *Journal of Applied Psychology, 85*(1), 65–74.

Chen, P. Y., & Spector, P. E. (1991). Negative Affectivity as the underlying cause of correlations between stressors and strains. *Journal of Applied Psychology, 76*, 398–407.

Cohen, S., & Wills, T. (1985). Stress, social support, and the buffering hypothesis. *Psychological Bulletin, 98*, 310–357.

Crant, J. M., & Bateman, T. S. (2000). Charismatic leadership viewed from above: The impact of proactive personality. *Journal of Organizational Behavior, 21*, 63–75.

Damanpour, F. (1991). Organizational innovation: A meta-analysis of effects of determinants and moderators. *Academy of Management Journal, 34*(3), 555–590.

Deluga, R. (1998). American presidential proactivity, charismatic leadership, and rated performance. *Leadership Quarterly, 9*, 265–291.

Edwards, J. R. (1992). A cybernetic theory of stress, coping, and well-being in organizations. *Academy of Management Review, 17*, 238–274.

Farr, J. L., & Ford, C. M. (1990). Individual innovation. In M. A. West & J. L. Farr (Eds.), *Innovation and creativity at work* (pp. 63–80). Oxford, England: Wiley.

Farrell, D., & Stamm, C. L. (1998). Meta-analysis of the correlates of absenteeism. Human Relations, *41*, 211–227.

Fay, D., & Frese, M. (2001). The concept of personal initiative: An overview of validity studies. *Human Performance, 14*, 97–124.

Fay, D., & Sonnentag, S. (2002). Rethinking the effects of stressors: A longitudinal study of personal initiative. *Journal of Occupational Health Psychology, 7*, 221–234.

Ford, C. M. (1996). A theory of individual creative action in multiple social domains. *Academy of Management Review, 21*, 1112–1142.

Fox, S., & Spector, P. E. (1999). A model of work frustration-aggression. *Journal of Organizational Behavior, 20*, 915–921.

Fox, S., Spector, P. E., & Miles, D. (2001). Counterproductive work behavior (CWB) in response to job stressors and organizational justice: Some mediator and moderator test for autonomy and emotions. *Journal of Vocational Behavior, 59*, 291–309.

Frone, M. R. (1999). Work stress and alcohol use. *Alcohol Research & Health, 23*(4), 284–291.

Grau, R., Salanova, M., & Peiro, J. M. (2001). Moderator effects of self-efficacy on occupational stress. *Psychology in Spain, 5*(1), 63–74.

Greenberg, J. (1990). Employee theft as a reaction to underpayment inequity: The hidden cost of pay cuts. *Journal of Applied Psychology, 75*, 561–568.

Greiner, B. A., Krause, N., Ragland, D. R., & Fisher, J. M. (1998). Objective stress factors, accidents, absenteeism in transit operators: A theoretical framework and empirical evidence. *Journal of Occupational Health Psychology, 3*, 130–146.

Gupta, N., & Beehr, T. A. (1979). Job stress and employee behaviors. *Organizational Behavior & Human Performance, 23*(3), 373–387.

Hart, P. M., & Cooper, C. L. (2002). Occupational stress: toward a more integrated framework. In N. Anderson, D. S. Ones, H. K. Sinangil, & C. Viswesvaran (Eds.), *Handbook of industrial, work, and organizational psychology: Organizational psychology* (Vol. 2, pp. 93–114). Thousand Oaks, CA: Sage.

Hofmann, D. A., & Stetzer, A. (1998). The role of safety climate and communication in accident interpretation: Implications fro negative events. *Academy of Management Journal, 41*, 644–657.

Hollinger, R. C., & Clark, J. P. (1983). Deterrence in the workplace: Perceived certainty, perceived severity, and employee theft. *Social Forces, 62*, 398

Jackson, S. E., & Schuler, R. S. (1985). A meta-analysis and conceptual critique of research on role ambiguity and role conflict in work settings. *Organizational Behavior and Human Decision Processes, 36*, 16–78.

Jamal, M. (1985). Relationship of job stress to job performance: A study of managers and blue-collar workers. *Human Relations, 38*, 409–424.

Jehn, K. A. (1994). Enhancing effectiveness: An investigation of advantages and disadvantages of value-based intragroup conflict. *International Journal of Conflict Management, 5*, 223–238.

Jex, S. M. (1998). *Stress and job performance: Theory, research, and implications for managerial practice*. Thousand Oaks, CA: Sage.

Jex, S. M., Adams, G. A., Bachrach, D. G., & Sorenson, S. (2003). The impact of situational constraints, role stressors, and commitment on employee altruism. *Journal of Occupational Health Psychology, 8*(3), 171–180.

Jex, S. M., & Beehr, T. A. (1991). Emerging theoretical and methodological issues in the study of work-related stress. In G. R. Ferris & K. M. Rowland (Eds.), Research in personnel and human resources management (Vol. 9, pp. 311–364). Greenwich, CT: JAI Press.

Jex, S. M., Beehr, T. A., & Roberts, C. K. (1992). The meaning of occupational stress items to survey respondents. *Journal of Applied Psychology, 77*(5), 623–628.

Jex, S. M., & Bliese, P. D. (1999). Efficacy beliefs as a moderator of the impact of work-related stressors: A multilevel study. *Journal of Applied Psychology, 84*(3), 349–361.

Jex, S. M., Bliese, P. D., Buzzell, S., & Primeau, J. (2001). The impact of self-efficacy on stressor-strain relations: Coping style as an explanatory mechanism. *Journal of Applied Psychology, 86*(3), 401–409.

Jex, S. M., Burnfield, J. L., Grauer, E., Adams, G. A., & Morgan, E. (2003, April). *The role of proactive personality in occupational stress*. Poster presented at the annual Society for Industrial and Organizational Psychology Convention, Orlando, FL.

Kahn, R. L., & Byosiere, P. (1992). Stress in organizations. In M. D. Dunnette & L. M. Hough (Eds.), *Handbook of industrial & organizational psychology* (Vol. 3, pp. 571–650). Palo Alto, CA: Consulting Psychologists Press.

Kahneman, D. (1973). *Attention and effort*. Englewood Cliffs, NJ: Prentice-Hall.

Kirkman, B. L., & Rosen, B. (1999). Beyond self-management: Antecedents and conseuences of team empowerment. *Academy of Management Journal, 42*, 58–74.

Kirmeyer, S. L., & Dougherty, T. W. (1988). Workload, tension and coping: Moderating effects of supervisor support. *Personnel Psychology, 41*, 125–139.

Landsbergis, P. A., Schnall, P. L., Schwartz, J. E., Warren, K., & Pickering, T. G. (1995). Job strain, hypertension, and cardiovascular disease: Empirical evidence, methodological issues, and recommendations for future research. In S. L. Sauter, & L. R. Murphy (Eds.), *Organizational risk factors for job stress* (pp. 97–112). Washington, DC: American Psychological Association.

LePine, J. A., LePine, M. A., & Jackson, C. L. (2004). Challenge and hindrance stress: relationships with exhaustion, motivation to learn, and learning performance. *Journal of Applied Psychology, 89*(5), 883-891.

LePine, J. A., Podsakoff, N. P., & LePine, M. A. (2004, April). *A meta-analytic test of the challenge stress-hindrance stress framework: An alternative explanation for inconsistent stress-performance relationships*. Poster presented at the annual conference of the Society for Industrial and Organizational Psychology, Chicago.

MacKenzie, S. B., Podsakoff, P. M., & Ahearne, M. (1998). Some possible antecedents and conseuences of in-role and extra-role salesperson performance. *Journal of Marketing, 62*, 87–98.

Manning, M. R., Jackson, C. N., & Fusilier, M. R. (1996). Occupational stress,
social support, and the costs of health care. *Academy of Management Journal,
39*, 738–750.

Martocchio, J. J. (1994). The effects of absence culture on individual absence.
Human Relations, 47, 243–262.

Mathieu, J. E., & Kohler, S. S. (1990). A cross-level examination of group absence
influences on individual absence. *Journal of Applied Psychology, 75*, 217–220.

Matteson, M. T., & Ivancevich, J. M. (1987). *Controlling work stress*. San Francisco:
Jossey-Bass.

McCauley, C. D., Ruderman, M. N., Ohlott, P. J., & Morrow, J. E. (1994). Assessing
the developmental components of managerial jobs. *Journal of Applied Psychology, 79*(4), 544–560.

McEwen, B. S. (2000). The neurobiology of stress: from serendipity to clinical relevance. *Brain Research, 886*, 172–189.

Miller, K. I., Ellis, B. H., Zook, E. G., & Lyles, J. S. (1990). An integrated model of
communication, stress, and burnout in the workplace. *Communication
Research, 17*, 300–326.

Mitchell, J. E., & Madigan, R. J. (1990). The effects of induced elation and
depression on interpersonal problem solving. *Cognitive Therapy and Research,
8*, 277–285.

Morrison, E. W. (1994). Role definitions and organizational citizenship behavior:
The importance of the employee's perspective. *Academy of Management
Journal, 37*(6), 1543–1567.

Motowidlo, S. J., Packard, J. S., & Manning, M. R. (1986). Occupational stress: Its
causes and conseuences for job performance. *Journal of Applied Psychology,
71*(4), 618–629.

Murphy, K. R. (1994). Toward a broader conceptualization of jobs and job performance: Impact of changes in the military environment on the structure,
assessment, and prediction of job performance. In M. G. Rumsey, C. B.
Walker, & J. H. Harris (Eds.), *Personnel selection and classification* (pp. 157–176).
Hillsdale, NJ: Erlbaum.

Murray, N., Sujan, H., Hirt, E. R., & Sujan, M. (1990). The influence of mood on
categorization: A cognitive flexibility interpretation. *Journal of Personality and
Social Psychology, 59*, 411–425.

Organ, D. W. (1988). *Organizational citizenship behavior: The good soldier syndrome*.
Lexington, MA: Lexington Books.

Organ, D. W., & Ryan, K. (1995). A meta-analytic review of attitudinal and dispositional predictors of organizational citizenship behavior. *Personnel Psychology,
48*(4), 775–802.

Perrewé, P. L. (1986). Locus of control and activity level as moderators in the uan-
titative job demands-satisfaction/psychological anxiety relationship: An
experimental analysis. *Journal of Applied Social Psychology, 16*, 620–632.

Pretcher, R. R. (2001). Unconscious herding behavior as the psychological basis of financial market trends and patterns. *Journal of Psychology and Financial Markets, 2*, 120–125.

Salanova, M., Peiro, J. M., & Schaufeli, W. B. (2002). Self-efficacy specificity and burnout among information technology workers: An extension of the job demand-control model. *European Journal of Work and Organizational Psychology, 11*(1), 1–25.

Sapolsky, R. M. (1998). *Why zebras don't get ulcers: An updated guide to stress, stress-related diseases, and coping*. New York: W. H. Freeman.

Schaubroeck, J., & Merritt, D. E. (1997). Divergent effects of job control on coping with work stressors: they key role of self efficacy. *Academy of Management Journal, 40*(3), 738–754.

Seligman, M. E. P. (1991). *Learned optimism*. New York: Knopf.

Siebert, S. E., Crant, J. M., & Kraimer, M. L. (1999). Proactive personality and career success. *Journal of Applied Psychology, 84*, 416–427.

Siu, O. (2001). Predictors of job satisfaction and absenteeism in two samples of Hong Kong nurses. *Journal of Advanced Nursing, 40*, 218–229.

Skarlicki, D. P., & Folger, R. (1997). Retaliation in the workplace: The roles of distributive, procedural, and interactional justice. *Journal of Applied Psychology, 82*, 434–443.

Smith, C. A., Organ, D. W., & Near J. P. (1983). Organizational citizenship behavior: Its nature and antecedents. *Journal of Applied Psychology, 68*, 653–663.

Smith, K. L. R., Michael, W. B., & Hocevar D. (1990). Performance on creativity measures with examination-taking instructions intended to induce high or low levels of test anxiety. *Creativity Research Journal, 3*, 265–280.

Spector, P. E. (1997). The role of frustration in antisocial behavior at work. In R. A. Jiacalone & J. Greenberg (Eds.), *Anti-social behavior in organizations* (pp. 1–17). Thousand Oaks, CA: Sage.

Spector, P. E., & O'Connell, B. J. (1994). The contribution of personality traits, negative affectivity, locus of control and Type A to the subseuent reports of job stressors and job strains. *Journal of Occupational and Organizational Psychology, 67*, 1–11.

Stanton, J. M., Balzer, W. K., Smith, P. C., Parra, L. F., & Ironson, G. (2001). A general measure of work stress: The stress in general scale. *Educational and Psychological Measurement, 61*(5), 866–888.

Storms, P. L., & Spector, P. E. (1987). Relationships of organizational frustration with reported behavioral reactions: The moderating effects of locus of control. *Journal of Occupational Psychology, 60*, 227–234.

Strelau, J., & Maciejczyk, J. (1977). Reactivity and decision making in stress situations in pilots. In C. D. Spielberger & I. G. Sarason (Eds.), *Stress and anxiety* (pp. 29–42). Washington, DC: Hemisphere.

Sutherland, V. J., & Cooper, C. L. (2002). Models of job stress. In J. T. M. Hersen (Ed.), *Handbook of mental health in the workplace* (pp. 33–59). Thousand Oaks, CA: Sage.

Thomas, J. L., & Jex, S. M. (2002). *Relations between stressors and job performance: An aggregate-level investigation using multiple criterion measures*. Paper presented at the annual conference of the Society for Industrial and Organizational Psychology, Toronto, Canada.

Tubre, T. C., & Collins, J. M. (2000). Jackson and Schuler (1985) Revisited: A meta-analysis of the relationships between role ambiguity, role conflict, and job performance. *Journal of Management, 26*(1), 155–169.

Van Dyne, L., Graham, J. W., & Dienesch, R. M. (1994). Organizational citizenship behavior: Construct redefinition, measurement, and validation. *Academy of Management Journal, 37*(4), 765–802.

Van Dyne, L., Jehn, K. A., & Cummings, A. (2001). Differential effects of strain on two forms of work performance: Individual employee sales and creativity. *Journal of Organizational Behavior, 23*, 57–74.

Vigoda, E. (2002). Stress-related aftermaths to workplace politics: the relationships among politics, job distress, and aggressive behavior in organizations. *Journal of Organizational Behavior, 23*, 571–591.

Vosburg, S. K. (1998). The effects of positive and negative mood on divergent thinking performance. *Creativity Research Journal, 2*, 165–172.

CHAPTER 9

EUSTRESS AND HOPE AT WORK

Accentuating the Positive

Debra L. Nelson and Bret L. Simmons

In this chapter, we describe our journey in developing a research stream that focuses on a more positive approach to the study of work stress. We present the roots of our research in terms of positive psychology and positive organizational behavior, and describe our early studies of eustress. These studies led us to focus on the central role of hope in promoting health and performance at work, and we briefly describe two of our more recent studies in which hope is the central construct. We conclude with recommendations for managers and researchers. Our hope is that readers will become engaged with us in this process of positive discovery.

INTRODUCTION

Movements are afoot in both organizational behavior and in psychology toward studying more positive concepts, including individual and organizational strengths and the "goods" in work life. In accordance with these

Stress and Quality of Working Life: Current Perspectives in Occupational Health, 121–135
Copyright © 2006 by Information Age Publishing
All rights of reproduction in any form reserved.

aims, this chapter focuses on our journey toward a more positive examination of work, health, and performance. We begin with our point of departure, which lies squarely within positive psychology and positive organizational behavior. Next, we describe the early stages of our research, which focused on eustress, the positive stress response. These early investigations of eustress led us down a different path to discover that hope plays a central role in work life, and we next discuss two studies along that path. Finally, we present some recommendations for managers, some ideas that researchers might consider, and a look at the future of research and practice within this positive framework.

POSITIVE ROOTS

The roots of research that accentuates the positive are deep, beginning with the philosophical writings of Aristotle, who described eudaemonia as the realization of one's true potential (Rothman, 1993). Philosophy's focus on the positive began with eudaemonia, as writers began to explore other notions of human thriving and strengths. More recently, Russell (1930/1958) defined the causes of happiness as zest, work, and affection. Ryff and Singer (1998, 2002) extended this philosophical analysis by noting that researchers and health practitioners alike tended to define health as the absence of negative states as opposed to the presence of positive states. They called for a more complete view of health, one that would include both mind-body interactions and wellness.

Seligman and Csikszentmihalyi (2000) called for positive psychology, which they defined as a science of positive subjective experience. They noted that psychology's focus on the negative was a product of history, and that at the time, a focus on healing human suffering was quite appropriate. Even in traumatic times such as war, however, there emerged certain individuals who retained their integrity and purpose. Characteristics such as courage and optimism seemed to protect against the mental and physical symptoms normally associated with traumatic experiences. Seligman and Csikszentmihalyi included in positive psychology's mission the need to focus on both human strengths and positive institutions. Positive psychology, like the positive philosophical tradition, emphasizes human resilience and flourishing.

Extending the ideas of positive health and positive psychology, Luthans (2002a, 2002b) called for a positive organizational behavior (POB) to focus on building human strengths at work rather than altering weaknesses. He contended that POB researchers should investigate states that are positive psychological strengths, can be validly measured, and are malleable in terms of interventions in organizations to improve work performance. The value of focusing on states is that they are more malleable than traits and thus lend themselves more readily to managerial interventions. Luthans proposed that hope, confidence, and resiliency meet these criteria. Other POB characteristics that appear to have promise include the states engagement (Britt, Adler, & Bartone, 2001), interpersonal trust (Mayer, Davis, & Schoorman, 1995), and vigor (Shirom, 2004) and the traits interdependence (Quick, Nelson, & Quick, 1987) and sense of coherence (Antonovsky, 1987).

In summary, the roots of our research follow from a philosophical tradition that emphasizes human flourishing and health research that defines health as the presence of the positive. Positive psychology, with its emphasis on human strengths, is another cornerstone, as is positive organizational behavior, which emphasizes studying human strengths and positive outcomes at work. These roots prompted us to carefully examine the research on work stress.

IN THE BEGINNING

In traditional studies of work stress, the working model is that certain stressors, or demands, elicit responses in individuals that can have adverse impacts on their health. Much of the research, including our own, had been designed under this model. Some authors mentioned positive stress, or eustress, as coined by Selye (1976). Quick, Quick, Nelson, and Hurrell (1997) described eustress as being associated with positive outcomes. They acknowledged the promotion of the positive in their definition of preventive stress management but, like other researchers, focused more heavily on the prevention of the negative (distress).

Perhaps the most extensive treatment of eustress in the literature was that of Edwards and Cooper (1988), who reviewed a variety of sources, including anecdotal evidence, studies of positive life events, and laboratory studies. They noted suggestive, rather than conclusive, evidence for a connection between eustress and health. The health-promoting effects of eustress, they reasoned, might be explained by hormonal and biochemical changes, or by individuals' directing their efforts toward coping with distress. Most importantly, Edwards and Cooper suggested that measuring eustress would require the assessment of positive psychological states and that these must be the presence of the positive, not the absence of negative, states. They viewed positive states and negative states as two separate constructs. This raises the possibility that eustress and distress may be experienced simultaneously.

The literature on cognitive appraisal also gave us some support for the study of eustress and guidance on how to approach it. When an individual encounters a demand or stressor, he or she appraises it with respect to its significance to well-being. Positive appraisals occur if the outcome of the encounter with the stressor is seen as preserving or enhancing well-being. Conversely, negative appraisals include perceptions of harm and/or loss or threat. Lazarus and Folkman (1984) proposed that appraisals of a single stressor as both a threat and a challenge can occur simultaneously. Appraisals can be complex and mixed, depending on the situation and the individual. Thus, for any given stressor, a person may have a degree of both a positive and a negative response.

Our review of the work stress literature led us to conclude that traditional studies had overwhelmingly focused on the negative (distress) rather than the positive (eustress). We found a need for a more complex model of stress that would include both eustress and distress. The evidence cited above represents a brief summary of our review. For a more complete review, including a detailed review of the physiological evidence regarding eustress, please see Simmons (2000). In designing a new, more comprehensive approach to stress that acknowledged the complexities of the stress response, we proposed what we have come to call the "bathtub metaphor."

The Bathtub Metaphor

Perhaps the best way to describe our approach to stress is to use what we refer to as the "bathtub metaphor." When you want to take a comfortable bath, you use the cold and hot water faucets to control both the temperature and the level of the water in the bathtub. The level of water in the bathtub is controlled by two things—the flow of water into the tub from the faucets, and the flow of water out of the tub from the bathtub drain. The temperature of the bath water is controlled by the simultaneous flow of water from both faucets—hot and cold.

The study of stress can be described in a similar fashion. Our past approaches to studying stress are like studying a bathtub with only one water faucet; that is, we've only been studying the cold water (distress). We have discovered quite a lot about the sources of cold water, and we have advised individuals of ways to either decrease the flow of cold water into the bathtub, or to increase the flow of cold water out of the bathtub (control the distress response or cope with distress). Our knowledge of the physiological, psychological, and behavioral consequences of sitting in a tub of cold water (distress) for a long time is fairly well developed.

Using this metaphor, it is easy to see that our knowledge of stress (bathtub) is incomplete. We need to study the source of hot water (eustress) to construct a more complete understanding of an individual's experience of stress. A more complete model must contain both faucets (eustress and distress) to get the level and temperature of the bathtub just right.

A Model for Understanding Eustress

The framework that guides our research is the holistic stress model, which, in line with the bathtub metaphor, is a more comprehensive model of stress. The assumption underlying the holistic model is that both eustress, the positive response, and distress, the negative response, comprise the complete stress response.

In this model, stressors are neutral stimuli. It is the cognitive appraisal of the stressor that determines whether the stress response will be eustress, distress, or more likely, a combination of the two. Thus, it is the interpretation of the stressor, and not the stressor itself, that is most important. Individual differences such as optimism, interdependence, and hardiness can affect the pathway between the stressors and the stress response, largely because of their influences on the appraisal or perception of stressors. We believe that the two parts of the stress

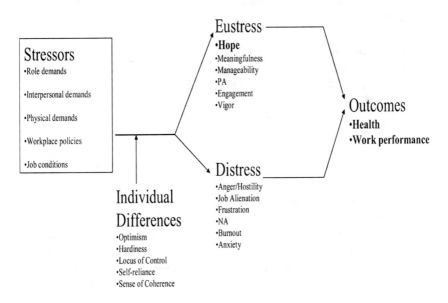

Figure 9.1.   Holistic Model of Stress.

response, eustress and distress, can be modeled using established positive and negative states as indicators of each. For example, hope, meaningfulness, and manageability, among others, are potential indicators of eustress. larly, anger, hostility, and burnout, among others, are potential indicators of distress. Finally, the stress response is linked with important outcomes. Previous stress research has emphasized negative outcomes such as psychological, behavioral, and physical symptoms. In accordance with the positive psychology and positive organizational behavior roots of the model, we proposed that positive outcomes such as health and performance should be our focus (Nelson & Simmons, 2004).

Studies of Nurses

We conducted two studies that focused on aspects of the holistic stress model, one involving hospital nurses and a second study involving home health care nurses. In our study of hospital nurses, we used hope as an indicator of eustress, defined as the positive psychological response to a stressor, as indicated by the presence of positive psychological states (Simmons & Nelson, 2001). As such, hope reflects the extent to which cognitive appraisal of a situation or event was seen to either benefit the nurses or enhance their well-being. We suggested that goal directed behavior of hope represented a state of active engagement in work.

Despite the demands of their work situations, the nurses in our study reported a high degree of the positive psychological state of hope (Simmons & Nelson, 2001). The nurses remained actively engaged in their work, and the positive response to the demands they faced showed a significant relationship to their own well-being. ICU nurses, whose work involves significantly greater exposure to the stressor death and dying, were even more hopeful and engaged in their work than their colleagues in other parts of the hospital.

In a second study, we examined the relationships between attachment styles, interpersonal trust, hope, and health among 175 home healthcare nurses (Simmons, Nelson, & Quick, 2003). Attachment styles are trait variables that determine how individuals form relationships with others. Once again, we found a strong relationship between hope and health. We also found that the attachment style of interdependence (also called self-reliance) had a significant and positive effect on hope, and this effect was partially mediated by trust in the supervisor. Interdependent individuals, those who form healthy relationships with others, were more likely to be hopeful, in part because they formed better relationships with their supervisors.

DETOUR TO HOPE

Our studies of hospital and home health care nurses underscored the importance of hope as an indicator of the positive response to demands at work. Hope has been identified as a positive emotion reflecting a degree of expected benefit resulting from an evaluation of a particular situation (Lazarus, 1993; Smith, Haynes, Lazarus, & Pope, 1993). Hope was defined as a cognitive set that is based on a sense of successful goal directed determination and planning to meet goals (Snyder, Sympson, Ybasco, Borders, Babyak, & Higgins, 1996). Snyder's State Hope Scale is presented in Figure 9.2.

Hope is therefore the belief that one has both the will and the way to accomplish one's goals at work. It is this conceptualization of hope that Luthans (2002a) declared was the most unique positive organizational capacity—a positive construct that could be developed in individuals. In an exploratory study, hopeful leaders had more profitable work units and had better satisfaction and retention rates among their subordinates than leaders with low levels of hope (Peterson & Luthans, 2003). Our studies of eustress in nurses, described above, led us to take a

- If I should find myself in a jam, I could think of many ways to get out of it.
- At the present time, I am energetically pursuing my goals.
- There are lots of ways around any problem that I am facing now.
- Right now, I see myself as being pretty successful.
- I can think of many ways to reach my current goals.
- At this time, I am meeting the goals I have set for myself.

Source: Snyder (1996).

Figure 9.2.   Items from the State Hope Scale.

slight detour, consistent with our journey but focusing on hope as the central construct of interest in two subsequent studies.

University Professor Study

Having established what seemed to be a strong relationship between hope and health, we conducted a third study to examine the antecedents of hope among 319 university professors (Simmons, Joseph, & Nelson, 2004). Our study included individual's job satisfaction with work, promotion, coworkers, pay, supervision, and hope. We also examined whether plateauism, a condition that has traditionally been considered in terms of hierarchical movement whereby future promotions are limited or not forthcoming, would mediate any relationships that might exist between job satisfaction and hope.

Plateauism fully mediated the relationship between satisfaction with promotion and hope but had no effect on the strong, positive relationships between satisfaction with work, the supervisor, and hope. The sample of university professors was characterized by a high level of hope, despite the fact that they were not very satisfied with pay and promotion. The goal directed behavior of hope remained high for the faculty members primarily due to the satisfaction they derived from the work itself, as well satisfaction with their supervision. University faculty members usually have a high degree of autonomy and are relatively free to pursue goals that they value. Although the results should be generalized to other populations of workers with caution, these initial results suggest that the nature of work and the nature of supervision have a strong impact on the development of hope in workers. Even workers who feel that they are plateaued can remain hopeful and thereby healthy and productive at work.

Pastor Study: A First Look at the Relationship Between Hope and Performance

In our most recent investigation, we studied the job of pastor (Little, Simmons, & Nelson, 2004). This is an ideal job for examining issues of hope, burnout, health, and stress because a pastor's work involves emotional labor. Our sample included 117 pastors from a large denomination; of these pastors, 87 were matched with at least one elder from their congregation who rated their performance. The pastors in the study were predominately male and married, age 45–54.

Hypotheses were developed to examine the effects of both positive and negative psychological states on both health and performance. The negative psychological state that we included in our study was burnout; and the positive psychological states were ministry optimism, self-efficacy, engagement, positive affect, and hope. We controlled for the stressors work/family conflict, family/work conflict, and role ambiguity, all of which have significant negative relationships with health. After entering these stressors into the regression equation, we entered, in order, self-efficacy, ministry optimism, engagement, burnout, and then hope. We found that hope had a significant, positive relationship and burnout had a significant, negative relationship with health. For the variable hope, these results confirm what was previously asserted in the study of nurses. Unlike the study of nurses, however, where no negative variables had a significant effect on health, burnout was significant in this sample of pastors. Role ambiguity was the sole stressor negatively related to health, and burnout mediated the relationship while ministry burnout partially mediated it. Thus, our results in the pastor study supported the connection between burnout and health.

We developed two measure of performance for this study. The first was a survey that each pastor was instructed to give to an elder in the church to independently rate his performance. The 14-item elder survey we developed was intended to capture aspects of the pastor's personal behavior deemed necessary for growing a healthy church. Representative items were "this pastor is very patient," "most people in our congregation would say that this pastor treats the people in the congregation with love," and "The people that know this pastor well would say that he has a heart for the people in the community that he serves." We label this measure performance-elder rating.

The second measure of performance we used was growth of the church through newly baptized attendees. We asked both the pastors and their elders to estimate how many new believers had been baptized in the church in the last 12 months. We also asked the pastors "How many people attended services at your church on an average Sunday last month?" We averaged the number of new believers reported by both the pastor and the elder and divided it by the average attendance to form the measure that we call performance-growth percentage.

Using regression procedures described above, we found that elder-rated performance was significantly predicted by any of the variables of interest, including hope and burnout; however, hope was the only significant predictor of performance-growth percentage. We concluded that the relationship between hope and performance was equivocal and therefore merits further investigation.

RECOMMENDATIONS FOR MANAGERS

Our research suggests that managers can intervene to improve employees' hope and that these interventions may serve to improve health and possibly improve performance. Given the definition of hope, managers must help employees enthusiastically pursue their goals and help them devise solutions as obstacles to goal achievement arise. These goals must be meaningful and must be derived from a two-way negotiation between the employee and manager. The employee must own or "buy into" the goal for it to be motivating.

Managers must also provide employees with critical resources for achieving their goals. This gives employees a sense of hope in that they are armed with the necessary ammunition to get things done and to resolve problems as they arise. In the knowledge-based economy, perhaps the most important resource managers must provide is information. Because our research across several studies indicates that role ambiguity (having unclear expectations placed on you) is a critical stressor, this information should include a process of negotiating out the employee's role within the system. Additionally, practicing participating in decision making whenever possible will help keep employees informed not only about possible changes in the priorities of the organization, but also about potential changes in the resources available to employees. For employees who have valued goals at work and the will to accomplish those goals, this will help employees continue to find "the way" to accomplish those goals.

Employees and managers alike must cope with constant change, and hope is essential to successfully managing change. Frequent and inspirational dialogues between managers and employees can increase hope. Managers' expressions of support can go a long way in helping employees believe they have both the will and the way to accomplish meaningful work-related goals.

Related to this dialogue, a trusting relationship with the manager is important. Expressions of support must be viewed as genuine by the employee, and the manager's intentions must be transparent. A trusting relationship with one's supervisor may be an important driver of work-related hope. The relationship with the supervisor is less important for individuals with a personality type that forms healthy relationships with others at work (interdependence) and very important for individuals with a personality type that either relies too heavily on the support of others or pushes others away.

In addition to the relationship with the manager, employees can benefit from a supportive mentor. Having a mentor provides the employee with a role model to emulate in terms of successful performance, and employees who have mentors can increase their own hope for successful performance by adopting the behaviors that made the mentor success-ful.

GUIDELINES FOR RESEARCHERS

We hope that researchers will be energized by the results of our studies to investigate positive constructs like hope and eustress. In that regard, we offer a few suggestions to help them in their endeavors.

Our studies demonstrate convincingly that hope at work is related to health, which is a positive finding in its own right. But we have measured health with a simple self-report scale, so future studies could extend our findings by incorporating different measures of health. The challenge will be to identify behaviors and physiological symptoms that represent the presence of the positive as well as the absence of disease in individuals.

In addition to verifying our results with respect to the relationship between hope and health, the next natural step is to investigate hope's connection to performance at work. We encourage researchers to look not only at job-specific performance, but also at such extra-role performance such as organizational citizenship behavior and innovative behavior. Taking the examination to a new level, we need to explore the relationship between hope, work teams, and indicators of organizational performance that matter to managers. Only then can we make the strong case for managers to spend time, money, and effort on interventions focused on improving the hope of their employees.

With respect to the equivocal relationship between hope and performance that we found in our preliminary study of pastors, we think this suggests that researchers should consider potential moderators in the hope-performance relationship. It is possible that supervisors and employees hope for significantly different things at work, which might explain the nonsignificant relationship we found between hope and elder-rated performance. If that is the case, then variables that assess aspects of goal congruence should be included in any future studies of the relationship between hope and other-rated performance.

Once we make the case for the link between hope and outcomes that matter to managers, we need to know more about the antecedents of hope at work. Specifically, what are the managerial behaviors that are most strongly related to hope among employees? What are the job characteristics that promote work-related hope? Are there organizational climate and culture factors related to employees' hope? Identifying the antecedents will help researchers work with managers to design interventions for increasing hope at work.

Along the way, it will be critical to empirically distinguish hope from other positive organizational behavior constructs. Self-efficacy, optimism, and positive affect are constructs that may conceptually overlap with hope. Carefully defining and measuring POB constructs, along with assessing discriminant validity, must be a part of our future research agenda.

Finally, we plan to refine our concept of eustress and to reexamine our holistic model of stress. We have preferred to view stressors and demands as neutral, reserving the assignment of positive and negative to the stress response. We did this because we believed that the value of the holistic stress model hinged on the validity of eustress, the positive stress response. Unless and until we establish this as a construct separate and distinct from distress, the model has little value. Once researchers validate eustress, and identify several other positive states in addition to hope that have efficacy as indicators, then, and only then, we may want to shift our focus to identifying "eustressors," or demands that have stronger, positive relationships with indicators of eustress.

Another challenge will be verifying the moderating effects of traits in the model. We have suggested that this moderating effect takes place before the cognitive appraisal of demands manifests itself in indicators of eustress and distress. In other words, aspects of an individual's personality affect how they take demands at work and therefore how they experience eustress and distress. It is also possible that traits may have a moderating effect between the stress response and organizational outcomes. Aspects of an individual's personality affect how the experience of eustress and distress manifests itself in indicators of health and performance. Either way, there are methodological challenges to testing this complete model: from demands, through two mediators (eustress and distress), to multiple outcomes of health and performance, with moderation of traits at one point.

A HOPEFUL FUTURE

We have barely scratched the surface in terms of defining and measuring eustress. To revisit our bathtub metaphor, we need to study the sources of hot water (eustress) and examine ways for individuals to either increase the flow of hot water into the bathtub (increase eustress), or to increase the flow of hot water out of the bathtub (turn eustress into high performance). When distress flows out of the tub (one of the ways that we seek to relieve the "level" of the cold water), that is often dysfunctional for our lives and job performance. But as eustress flows out of the tub, that can be functional for our individual lives and work performance and perhaps have a spillover affect in both areas. So it is not enough that to have a "positive response" to work demands (e.g., they are meaningful, satisfying, engaging), but we must find ways to turn that positive response into outcomes that individuals and their organizations value. Eventually, even a warm tub turns cold, so we would rather not just sit in it until it turns cold, but rather enjoy it, empty it, and then return to refill it again and again.

In mapping our research journey, we must admit that we have made progress but that we have not reached our destination. One of the lessons we have learned along the way is that a positive view of work life is worthy of study. This is not to say that we should ignore the negative; instead, we believe that it is time to lift up the study of positive strengths and attributes such as hope, resilience, vigor, eustress, and engagement. In addition, we need to focus on positive outcomes such as health and performance. A review of our journey gives us a sense of hope for both managers and researchers. If managers can harness the power of positive attributes and create a work environment that allows individuals to flourish, work will be a more positive and productive endeavor. By focusing on positive traits, states, and context, researchers can more effectively partner with managers to design interventions that maximize worker health and performance and, ultimately, maximize organizational performance. Healthy workers and healthy organizations constitute a hopeful vision for the future. We invite both managers and researchers to join us on our journey.

REFERENCES

Antonovsky, A. (1987). *Unraveling the mystery of health: How people manage stress and stay well*. San Francisco: Jossey-Bass.

Britt, T. W., Adler, A. B., & Bartone, P. T. (2001). Deriving benefits from stressful events: The role of engagement in meaningful work and hardiness. *Journal of Occupational Health Psychology, 6*, 53–63.

Edwards, J. R., & Cooper, C. L. (1988). The impacts of positive psychological states on physical health: A review and theoretical framework. *Social Science Medicine, 27*, 1147–1459.

Lazarus, R. S. (1993). From psychological stress to the emotions: A history of changing outlooks. In L. W. Porter & M. R. Rosenzweig (Eds.), *Annual review of psychology* (Vol. 44, pp. 1-21). Palo Alto, CA: Annual Reviews.

Lazarus, R. S., & Folkman, S. (1984). *Stress, appraisal, and coping*. New York: Springer.

Little, L. M., Simmons, B. L., & Nelson, D. L. (2004). *Does burnout affect performance? An unanswered question*. Working paper, Oklahoma State University.

Luthans, F. (2002a). The need for and meaning of positive organizational behavior. *Journal of Organizational Behavior, 23,* 695–706.

Luthans, F. (2002b). Positive organizational behavior: Developing and managing psychological strengths. *Academy of Management Executive,* 16, 57–72.

Mayer, R. C., Davis, J. H., & Schoorman, F. D. (1995). An integrative model of organizational trust. *Academy of Management Review, 3,* 709–734.

Nelson, D.L., & Simmons, B. (2004). Eustress: An elusive construct, an engaging pursuit. In P. L. Perrewe & D .C. Ganster (Eds.), *Research in occupational stress and well being: Emotional and physiological processes and positive intervention strategies* (Vol. 3, pp. 265–322). Oxford, England: Elsevier.

Peterson, S. J., & Luthans, F. (2003). The positive impact and development of hopeful leaders. *Leadership and Organizational Development, 24,* 26–31.

Quick, J. C., Nelson, D. L., & Quick, J. D. (l987). Successful executives: How independent? *Academy of Management Executive, 1,* 139–145.

Quick, J. C., Quick, J. D., Nelson, D. L., & Hurrell, J. J. (1997). *Preventive stress management in organizations.* Washington, DC: American Psychological Association.

Rothman, J. C. (1993). *Aristotitle's eudaemonia, terminal illness, and the question of life support.* New York: P. Lang.

Russell, B. (l958). *The conquest of happiness.* New York: Liveright. (Original work published 1930)

Ryff, C. D., & Singer, B. (1998). The contours of positive human health. *Psychological Inquiry, 9,* 1–28.

Ryff, C. D., & Singer, B. (2002). From social structures to biology: Integrative science in pursuit of human health and well-being. In C. R. Snyder & S. J. Lopez (Eds.), *Handbook of positive psychology* (pp. 541–555). New York: Oxford University Press.

Seligman, M. E. P., & Csikszentmihalyi, M. (2000). Positive psychology. *American Psychologist, 55,* 5–14.

Selye, H. (1976). *Stress in health and disease.* Boston: Butterworths.

Shirom, A. (2004). Feeling vigorous at work? The construct of vigor and the study of positive affect in organizations. In P. L. Perrewe & D. C. Ganster (Eds.), *Research in occupational stress and well being: Emotional and physiological processes and positive intervention strategies* (Vol. 3, pp. 135–164). Oxford, England: Elsevier.

Simmons, B. L. (2000). *Eustress at work: Accentuating the positive.* Unpublished doctoral dissertation, Oklahoma State University.

Simmons, B. L., Joseph, J. J., & Nelson, D. L. (2004, August). *What keeps plateaued workers hopeful?* Paper presented at the annual meeting of the American Psychological Association, Hawaii, Honolulu.

Simmons, B. L., & Nelson, D. L. (2001). Eustress at work: The relationship between hope and health in hospital nurses. *Health Care Management Review, 26,* 7–18.

Simmons, B. L., Nelson, D. L., & Quick, J. C. (2003). Health for the hopeful: A study of attachment behavior in home health care nurses. *International Journal of Stress Management, 10,* 361–371.

Smith, C. A., Haynes, K. N., Lazarus, R. S., & Pope, L. K. (1993). In search of the "hot" cognitions: Attributions, appraisals, and their relation to emotion. *Journal of Personality and Social Psychology, 65,* 916–929.

Snyder, C. R., Sympson, S. C., Ybasco, F. C., Borders, T. F., Babyak, M. A., & Higgins, R. L. (1996). Development and validation of the state hope scale. *Journal of Personality and Social Psychology, 70,* 321–335.

CHAPTER 10

HEALTHY LEADERS, HEALTHY ORGANIZATIONS

Primary Prevention and the Positive Effects of Emotional Competence

James Campbell Quick, Marilyn Macik-Frey, David A. Mack, Nathan Keller, David A. Gray, and Cary L. Cooper

Stress, toxic emotions, and safety hazards in organizations are three of the chronic problems leaders and followers face at work. The public health notions of prevention, used effectively with chronic health disorders, can be translated to address these chronic organizational problems. By exhibiting positive executive health, we suggest that authentic transformational leaders can play a key role in the primary prevention of distress at work while the engendering of emotionally healthy work environments for themselves and others.

Stress in organizations is one of a number of chronic problems that can be managed using the public health notions of prevention. Although stress at certain levels, effectively managed can lead to productive and healthy workplaces, the goal of prevention is to keep the levels of stress from esca-

Stress and Quality of Working Life: Current Perspectives in Occupational Health, 137–153
Copyright © 2006 by Information Age Publishing
All rights of reproduction in any form reserved.

lating to a point where negative health and well-being outcomes occur. Providing primary, secondary, and tertiary prevention can reduce or eliminate the negative personal and organizational outcomes of distress in the work-place (Quick, Quick, Nelson, & Hurrell, 1997). Many factors lead to stress in the workplace. Our chapter focuses on two important and inter-related aspects, leadership and emotion and the positive impact on the health of the organization. We expand, however, our view of a healthy organization to include the dimension of safety. Just as leaders can play a critical role in preventing stress, they can also positively influence safety. Thus the healthy leader impacts the *total* realm of health and well-being within the organization

Poor leadership can be a source of stress in the workplace through the direct impact on subordinates and through the indirect influence over the work environment (Kelloway, Sivanathan, Francis, and Barling, 2004). Conversely, healthy leadership can provide the healthy work setting and social support foundations that drive the successful organization (Quick, Mack, Gavin, Cooper, & Quick, 2004). Borrowing from the positive organization behavior (Luthans, 2002) paradigm, we approach occupational stress from the positive perspective. That is, we believe more progress can be achieved by addressing what works to create health rather than following the traditional psychological model of analyzing dysfunction. In that light, this chapter looks at how leaders can foster a healthy work environment with particular emphasis on the authentic transformational leader's critical influence on positive emotion.

Emotion in the workplace can serve as a toxin or as a foundation for trust, motivation and shared vision. The effective management of emotion in the workplace can be a critical determinant of the ultimate outcome and leaders are in a unique position to influence that path. To lead with authentic transformational leadership requires the supple ability to manage emotion or emotional competence. We propose that the authentic transformational leader who is strong in emotional competence plays a key role in the primary prevention of distress and can engender an emotionally healthy and psychologically and physically safe work environment. Thus, healthy leaders foster organizational health and well being for themselves and others through the influence of emotional competence.

TOXIC EMOTIONS AND PREVENTIVE STRESS MANAGEMENT

Preventive stress management is an approach to enhancing health while averting distress in the workplace. The core notions of this theory for organizations come from the public health notions of prevention (Quick, Quick, Nelson, & Hurrell, 1997). When translated into an organizational context, these notions target three points for preventive intervention in the organizational stress process. The organizational stress process itself begins with (1) a demand or stressor that triggers (2) the stress response in individuals and groups at work, thus setting the stage for potential (3) distress, which takes the forms of behavioral, medical, or psychological problems as well as their collective direct and indirect organizational costs, such as absenteeism and turnover. The three points of preventive intervention in this process are: (1) primary prevention, which aims to address the source of the stress so as to eliminate, reduce, or manage it; (2) secondary prevention, which aims to modify one's stress response; and (3) tertiary prevention, which aims to heal the wounded and alleviate suffering.

Toxic emotions are one powerful and potentially harmful source of stress for both leaders and followers (Frost, 2002; Frost & Robinson, 1999). Toxic emotions often trigger defensive responses from others in the workplace, may cause bad feelings, broken communication, and disrupted relationships. However, toxic emotions are part and parcel of the human condition, including those occurring within organizations. Frost (2002) suggests that compassionate leaders are able to handle toxic emotions such as pain and conflict in a way that metabolizes the toxicity within the organization. While these compassionate leaders reduce the adverse effects of toxic emotions throughout the workplace, they do expose themselves to health risks in the process. Therefore, organizations need to have mechanisms and professionals who can help heal the handlers of toxic emotions at work (Quick & Macik-Frey, 2004).

Any form of therapeutic intervention in organizations constitutes tertiary prevention. However, looked at through a different lens, while good therapy with one key executive or leader may be tertiary prevention for that leader, it becomes primary prevention for the tens, hundreds, or even thousands of men and women who work for that leader. Therefore, executive health is important: healthy leaders in organizations are among the best primary preventive interventions that organizations can offer for occupational stress and individual strain (Quick, Cooper, Gavin, & Quick, 2002; Quick, Gavin, Cooper, & Quick, 2004). We define healthy leaders as ones who are authentic transformational leaders and ones who are emotionally competent such that they manage their own emotions in healthy ways and are sensitive to the emotions and feelings of those with whom they work.

OCCUPATIONAL STRESS, SAFETY, AND RISK REDUCTION

In addition to stress prevention, safety and risk reduction are often overlooked, but critical components of a healthy organization. Therefore, healthy leaders and healthy organizations should use stress audits, risk management, and risk reduction to create a safe and healthy workplace (Clarke & Cooper, 2004). Safety and health at work go hand in hand and reducing risks in organizations can compliment primary prevention and the positive organizational behavior approach of Luthans (2002). Thus, leaders' attempts to reduce safety risks enhance the sense of security and reduce the experience of occupational stress at work. Further, when this is accomplished with emotional competence, it promotes trust and commitment in followers who then embrace health and safety initiatives.

Safety Risks at Work

Most stress interventions are designed to improve employee health and, therefore, positively influence organizational health and reduce costs as well. However, many interventions are often fairly narrowly defined and conceptualized as health initiatives (Clarke & Cooper, 2004). The assessment of safety risks allows for the design of intervention programs that enhance both a safe and a healthy work environment. For example, health-promotion schemes can be employed to improve both health and safety outcomes. The positive benefits of health programs (e.g., improved diet, increased exercise, weight loss, smoking cessation, and the acquisition of stress-reduction techniques) have been demonstrated to improve employees' health (Cooper, Dewe, & O'Driscoll, 2001; Quick, Quick, Nelson, & Hurrell, 1997). While having favorable results in organizations, there is little recognition that such programs can be integrated into interventions aimed at safety risks. For example, lost time injuries may be reduced through health promotion. Health promotion by leaders may influence safety outcomes in one of two ways. One is by showing concern for employee health and well-being, which improves the safety climate. The other is through improved worker health that increases resistance to stress and, therefore, reduces accident liability.

Safety interventions that are specifically targeted at improving the safety climate are more effective when they are carried out in the context of a positive organizational climate and supported by a transformational leader. For example, interventions aimed at improving safety behavior that are communicated by an empathetic and committed leader are likely to be viewed more positively than rigid, inflexible safety environments that emphasize behavioral compliance. Just, fair and trusting safety environments that reward positive behavior are healthier than punitive environments aimed at identifying and sanctioning unacceptable behavior.

The synergy between authentic transformational leadership based on emotional competence and a safety-oriented work environment can be positive and consistent with a systematic risk management process. We suggest that a risk management model be applied to both the health and safety risks of occupational stressors to compliment the primary prevention approach of authentic transformational leadership. Thus, stress interventions can reduce risks and have positive benefits for organizations in terms of employee health (e.g., sickness absence) and safety (e.g., lost time injuries and accidents).

Risk Reduction

The final stage of a risk management model requires monitoring the effects of risk control measures, and evaluating their effectiveness (Clarke & Cooper, 2004). Leaders can be instrumental in promoting this stage through the use of stress audits. These audits can identify the effects of the risk control measures in terms of levels of exposure and the effects of stressors on employee health. Indicators of organizational health (e.g., absenteeism, productivity, lost-time injuries, and accidents) should be monitored. Interventions aimed at safety risks should evaluate the extent to which risk control measures have affected safety-related behavior.

Employee participation is as important in reducing safety risks at work and transformational leaders using positive approaches can facilitate this aspect as well. Interviews and focus groups with employees can help to identify the impact of measures on employees, assess their reactions and evaluate the extent to which the measures are having the desired effect. Any intervention program needs to be ongoing, with the monitoring and review of the program providing feedback to this process. Information from ongoing reviews can be used to adapt the program to reflect changes in the organization. The continuing nature of the program allows employees to take advantage of support as they need it. Stress counseling can be useful, as many individuals may need this service at some point in their careers. Training can increase stress awareness, thus allowing individuals to recognize the symptoms of being "under stress" and gives them to the knowledge of how to deal with stressors and recognize the point at which they would benefit from help and support.

EXECUTIVES AND HEALTHY WORK ENVIRONMENTS

As the leaders of their organizations, executives have many responsibilities. Efficient use of capital, maximization of return on investment/equity, strict adherence to accounting standards, and consistent profitability are just a few of the major ones. Each of these concerns the financial health of the organization and helps to ensure the continued survival of the organization. An equal, but often underrated responsibility in our opinion is the health of the employees in the organization. We do not suggest that the company should assume the responsibility for the individual health of each employee but rather that the leadership should seek to create a healthy work environment that encourages positive work relationships and attitudes toward work (Forward, Beach, Gray, & Quick, 1991).

The alternative is the creation of a toxic work environment. A toxic work environment is one in which the employees feel undervalued, are not trusted, and are not encouraged to trust each other. In a toxic work environment, employees are considered a resource to be expensed rather than an asset which should be developed and protected. A toxic work environment will quite literally poison the workplace, inhibit productivity, create hostile employee interactions and ultimately affect the company's bottom line (Frost, 2002).

Creating an environment that is supportive and healthy for employees, does not mean creating an environment that is stress free (Quick, Mack, Gavin, Cooper, & Quick, 2004). Stress is a necessary element in creating motivation for employees. A workplace that is free of stress is not necessarily highly productive. Creating the needed amount of stress without abusing employees is the crucial element here. Obviously, executives should avoid bullying behavior, harsh demands, and outbursts of anger directed at employees. These types of actions create feelings of distress, which is the negative or harmful aspect of stress (Bell, Quick, & Cycyota, 2002). These abusive behaviors and malevolent approach to the treatment of people at work causes significant emotional pain and dysfunction (Frost & Robinson, 1999). This in turn leads to such negative outcomes as employee absenteeism, health issues (and subsequent health care cost increases), lowered productivity and, in the extreme, even may lead to instances of workplace violence (Mack, Shannon, Quick, & Quick, 1998).

Executives can, and should, create positive stress in their workplaces. Although this is not an exact science, there are a number of steps that executives can take to ensure that they maximize the positive (motivational) aspects of creating stress while minimizing the harmful aspects. Quick, Mack, et al. (2004) proposes three broad areas that must be effectively managed. The first is the proper and effective use of political skills. Perrewé, Ferris, Frink, and Anthony (2000) describe political skill as an interpersonal style that manifests itself in social astuteness and the ability to engage in behaviors that enhance employee confidence and trust and a belief that leaders are acting sincerely. This is a type of interpersonal control that, if used properly, will enable executives to cope more positively with chronic workplace stressors such as uncertainty and interpersonal conflicts and allow them to create a workplace that values trust and positive interpersonal relationships.

The second area for which executives must pay attention is creating cooperative work environments that value individual and group contribution without the *adverse* affects of conflict. This does not mean a workplace that is free of conflict. Fostering healthy competition between employees and/or work groups is an effective motivational technique and should be utilized where appropriate. The concern is that competitions not create situations where the overall goals of the organization are compromised, as a result of the perceived adverse goals of the individuals or groups within the organization. This is the negative aspect of conflict that is both unhealthy and unproductive (Cosier & Dalton, 1990). The successful leader encourages healthy conflict but is ever vigilant to the possibility that negative behaviors can result if not monitored.

The third and final area that must be addressed is the most critical. Executives must create work environments that foster a culture of open communication. This is the counter-agent for the toxic environment that was addressed above and the key to unlocking social support for preventive stress management (Macik-Frey, Quick, & Quick, 2005). A culture of open communication exists when employees feel that they can freely express their ideas and feelings, without fear of retribution. This allows the leadership of the organization to understand the concerns of the employees and take positive action to avert problems before they become destructive. It is also important for the leader to communicate freely and openly with the employees. They can do this through reflective listening and the use of nondefensive communication (Athos & Gabarro, 1978; Wells, 1980). Reflective listening is a learned skill that allows the listener to focus attention on the speaker's message and allows the listener to provide feedback regarding his/her level of understanding. Jablin (1979) proposes that the most effective leaders are those who can listen empathetically, are respectful of egos, and sensitive to the feelings of their followers. These leaders do not have to have "open door policies" because their employees know from experience that their input is valued and welcome.

While we do not have room here to discuss all of the steps (nor the accompanying pitfalls) that a leader should take to ensure the creation of positive stress in a healthy workplace, Quick, Mack, et al. (2004) have outlined nine principle-based dimensions that form a framework for executive action that can be used to craft a *positive* stressful environment in the workplace. These dimensions are outlined in Table 10.1.

AUTHENTIC TRANSFORMATIONAL LEADERSHIP

Our principle argument for the leader's ability to positively influence the health and safety of the organization rests in the leader possessing an authentic transformational leadership style. Authentic transformational leadership theories, which overlap with theories of charismatic leadership, represent the latest paradigm shift in the leadership research. Bass (1999) defines authentic transformational leadership as a leader's capability to move the follower beyond immediate self-interests and generate awareness and acceptance of the purposes and mission of the group. Bass (1999) postulates authentic transformational leadership raises the follower's level of maturity and inspires innovative ideals as well as fosters concerns for achievement, self-actualization, and the well being of others, the organization, and society. Bass and Avolio (1993) characterize authentic transformational leaders as positive self-aware individuals that employ one or more of the "four I's" (idealized influence, or charisma; inspirational motivation, individual consideration, and intellectual stimulation); these concepts will be discussed further in the following section.

Training to increase authentic transformational leadership behaviors begins with assessing one's perception of an ideal leader, and evaluating his/her potential to make perceptions of quality leadership a reality (Bass, 1999). Luthans and Avolio (2003) posit the core of authentic transformational leadership is the concept of self-awareness, which includes knowledge of one's emotions, values and beliefs, along with an accurate assessment of one's strengths and weaknesses. An assessment individual intelligence, technical skills, and expertise are not sufficient in determining their abilities to become authentic transformational leaders. Rather, an introspective evaluation of an individual's character, morals, values, and beliefs, essentially their emotional intelligence (EI), is more accurate in predicting transformational leadership behavior. Authentic transformational leaders must know what is important to them, be totally immersed in their core beliefs and values, and transparently convey their values and beliefs in everyday behaviors and interactions (May, Hodges, Chan, & Avolio, 2003)

Idealized Influence

Idealized influence or charisma is the leader's ability to provide vision and a sense of mission, instill pride, gain respect, trust, and increase optimism. Such a leader excites and inspires subordinates. Establishing idealized influence requires the leader to possess positive self-regulation, described by Luthans and Avolio (2003) as the ability to exert self-control by setting internal standards, evaluating discrepancies between such standards and potential or actual outcomes, and identifying possible means of rectifying such discrepancies. Authentic transformational leaders use positive self-regulation to promote ethical policies, procedures, and processes within their organizations and create clearly stated, continually enforced

Table 10.1. Principles for Positive Executive Health

	Principle	Executive Actions	
1	Craft challenging goals	Negotiate with employees to establish goals that a stretch challenges. Treat failure to meet challenging goals as an opportunity for analysis and growth. Align personal and organizational goals to achieve unity of action.	Lathan & Locke, 1990 Drucker, 1954
2	Create trusting relationships	Act in ways that display an observable link between positive intention and action. Be willing to be vulnerable, approached, and questioned for understanding. Trustworthiness sets a stage for trust and invites trusting responses.	Farson & Keyes, 2002 Cannon & Edmonson, 2001
3	Encourage learning culture	Examine failures as opportunities for learning and development. Be slow to punish, but do so swiftly and clearly when appropriate. Positively reinforce the generation of new ideas, then test ideas against reality.	Forward, Beach, Gray & Quick, 1991 Senge, 1990
4	Communicate openly	Invite feedback and responses to ideas and initiatives in the workplace. Engage in nondefensive communication rather than defensive communication. Develop empathetic listening skills to compliment effective speaking skills.	Scott & Mitchell, 1976 Penley, et al., 1991
5	Encourage exploratory behavior	Allow employees to take actions and see results without sanctions. Support self-correction actions when problems are encountered at work. Practice extinction, or the nonconsequencing of behavior, whenever possible.	Weick, 1988 Olson, 1990
6	Celebrate small wins and success	Positively reinforce achievements and successes, especially the small ones. Practice positive organizational behavior to reinforce successes. Focus on positive, short term effects as successive approximations to goals.	Luthans, 2002 Komaki, Coombs & Schepman, 1996
7	Capitalize on diversity at work	Build alliances with diverse constituencies and individuals in the workforce. Seek out diverse opinions and perspectives, looking for the devil's advocate. Value qualifications and expertise, emphasizing employee strengths and skills.	Joplin & Daus, 1997 Cox & Blake, 1991
8	Accept constructive conflict	Frame conflicts around problems and ideas, not around persons. Value conflicts as opportunities to explore new ideas or ways to doing business. Confront unresolved conflicts by talking through difficult conversations.	De Dreu & Van de Vliert, 1997 Wall & Callister, 1995
9	Select for goodness of fit	Test for individual differences to identify strengths and interests; train for skills. Seek alignment of individual skills, abilities, and interests with work requirements. Reinforce upward, positive dynamic interactions between person and environment.	Hough & Furham, 2003 Edwards, 1996

Source: Quick, Mack, Gavin, Cooper, and Quick (2004, p. 369).

code of ethical conduct which helps establish acceptable standards (Avolio & Bass, 1991).

Inspirational Motivation

The inspirational motivation of transformational leadership provides followers with challenges and meaning for engaging in shared goals and undertakings (Bass & Steidlmeier, 1999). Authentic transformational leaders communicate positive psychological capabilities, including the positive organizational behavior states of confidence, hope, optimism, and resilience. This helps authentic leaders to clearly frame moral dilemmas, transparently respond to them and thus become ethical role models. Essentially a transformational leader develops a vision for the organization, which serves as a source of self-esteem, and common purpose for organizational members (Donohue & Wong, 1994). The vision should convey an inspiring, appealing picture of what the organization can be in the future without discounting the past. The vision is more than a goal or objective, it is a value or collection of values that the followers can rally around (Donohue & Wong, 1994). Additionally, the leader expresses confidence in the follower's abilities in attaining the vision, demonstrates sincere individualized concern for their efforts, and exhibits the willingness to take personal risks and self sacrifice to accomplish organizational goals.

Intellectual Stimulation

Intellectual stimulation is concerned with the degree to which followers are provided with interesting and challenging tasks and encouraged to solve problems in their own way. The leader stimulates followers to rethink old ways of doing things and to reassess their old values and beliefs. Transformational leadership incorporates an open architecture dynamic into processes of situation evaluation, vision formulation, and patterns of implementation, resulting in followers questioning assumptions and generating creative solutions to problems (Bass & Steidlmeier, 1999).

Individualized Consideration

The authentic transformational leader treats each follower as an individual and provides coaching, mentoring and growth opportunities (Bass, 1985). This is not simply "supportive behavior" or "taking care of the welfare of the followers" collectively. A transformational leader shows self-sacrifice in achieving the vision such as personal risk taking and incurring high costs to attain the vision the leader espouses. They are committed to growth and development, wherein they seek to continually promote and even restore these positive states in themselves and others (Luthans & Avolio, 2003). Authentic transformational leaders strive to fully understand themselves and better prepare for future challenges; they try to help others do the same by modeling and supporting the professional and moral development of their associates (Gardner & Schermerhorn, 2004). Through transparent decisions and processes, authentic transformational leaders help employees better understand themselves and the organization, which goes a long way in promoting a positive and productive organizational climate (May, Chan, Hodges, & Avolio, 2003). This self-sacrificing attitude increases the trust the followers have in the leader, and demonstrates the leader's strategy that shows more concern for the followers and the organization than for the leader's self-interest (Donohue & Wong, 1994).

EMOTIONAL COMPETENCE AT WORK

We argue that an essential way that authentic transformational leaders are able to impact the health of organizations is through their impact on emotion. The increasing emphasis on emotion in the workplace has been likened to an affective revolution (Barsade, Brief, & Spataro, 2003). Both in the academic and business world, emotion in the workplace is perceived as critical to understanding organizational behavior. Ashford & Humphrey (1995) believe organizational change occurs through the evoking, framing and mobilizing of emotion. They suggest the work environment is intrinsically emotional and value laden and that you can not separate cognition or rational behavior from emotion. Work stress and employees' response to stressors is equally influenced by emotion. Thus, to fully understand and prevent negative outcomes of occupational stress, and to promote a safe environment, emotion, and emotional management must be addressed.

One well studied aspect of the affective revolution is the concept of emotional intelligence (EI) or emotional competence (EC). Emotional intelligence is "the ability to perceive emotions, to access and generate emotions so as to assist thought, to understand emotions and emotional knowledge, and to reflectively regulate emotions so as to promote emotional and intellectual growth" (Mayer & Salovey, 1997, p. 5). This definition is increasingly being adopted as the standard, although there continues to be some concern regarding consistent definitions across studies. Ashkanasy and Daus (2002) outline four key points that seem to be generally accepted about EI; (1) EI is related to, but distinct from other intelligences; (2) EI is an individual difference construct; (3) EI develops over the lifespan and can be enhanced through training and (4) EI involves a person's ability to identify, perceive, understand, and manage emotion (in self and others). Montemayor & Spree (2004) also hypothesized, based on analysis of multiple definitions of EI (Goleman, 1998; Mathews, Zeidner, & Roberts, 2002; Mayer & Salovey, 1997), that distinguish between self and other focus and between awareness and management operations to arrive at four dimensions (self-awareness, other awareness, self-management, other management). Their results found general support for these distinctions.

Goleman (1998) distinguishes between emotional competence and emotional intelligence as the skills, abilities, and capabilities underlying the intelligence. Mayer and Salovey's (1997) model is also based on "abilities" as the descriptors of the EI construct and they argue this focus is more theoretically linked to the psychological study of other intelligences. In line with this reasoning, we prefer the term emotional competence to focus on the skills and abilities of emotional awareness and management which are those observable aspects of emotional intelligence, but acknowledge that the terms are used interchangeably within the literature.

Emotional competence has been shown to positively affect the response to stressors. Salovey, Stroud, Woolery, and Epel (2002) found that emotional competence factors of clarity of mood (awareness) and skill at repair (self-management) were negatively correlated with depression and social anxiety. These abilities were positively related to empathy and interpersonal satisfaction. They found that higher perceived emotional competence was related to adaptive psychological coping, attenuated cortisol release, decreased cardiovascular response, and greater habituation to repeated stressors (lessening their psychological and physical response). The ability to understand and manage emotions, key aspects of emotional competence, should positively affect the health and well-being of the individual in stressful situations. Likewise, the emotionally competent person's ability to manage or influence other's emotions suggests a potential to influence the stress response of others as well.

Emotional competence has been linked to transformational leadership (Ashkanasy & Tse, 2000; Barling, Slater, & Kelloway, 2000; Gardner & Sivanathan & Fekken, 2002; Stough, 2002). Barbuto and Burbach (2004) found a strong positive relationship between emotional competence and transformational leadership. We have previously identified authentic transformational leadership as a powerful and effective means of leading. Research suggests that aspects of EI are critical components of transformational leadership (Bass, 1985, 2002) based on the emotional relationship between leader and follower. We propose that authentic transformational leaders are also high in emotional competence.

A leader's attitude and behavior can have a profound effect on an organization's climate and culture. The authentic transformational leader, possessing strong emotional competence has the skills and abilities to promote healthy and safe emotional work environments above that of other leadership styles. The ability to understand and manage emotional undertones in self and others and to promote appropriate emotions puts the transformational leader in a unique position to influence the health of the entire organization. Emotionally competent leaders are better able to identify and communicate a mission, deal with emotionally challenging situations, provide empathetic support, and encouragement, inspire, and arouse their followers with positive emotion, and deal affectively with followers reactions to negative events or trauma. The influence and modeling that result from an emotionally competent leader leads to a more emotionally competent organizational environment. Work stress, safety, and emotion are inherently linked and the authentic transformational leader's emotional competence places his/her in a unique position to influence healthy outcomes in the workplace.

Leaders' attitudes, beliefs, and behaviors can and do shape the entire organization. Leaders who can effectively manage their own emotions and respond positively to those of others at work help create healthy work life. Because of their important influence from the top of the organization, authentic transformational leaders who are emotionally competent are positive agents for preventive stress management, safety, and risk management in organizations.

CONCLUSION

Stress in organizations is one of a number of chronic problems that can be managed using the public health notions of prevention. Toxic emotions in the workplace are a second category of chronic workplace problem. Safety in the work environment is a third health issue for leaders and executives. We suggest that authentic transformational leaders exhibit positive executive health and can play a key role in the primary prevention of distress and the engendering of emotionally healthy work environments. Thus, healthy leaders foster organizational health and well being for themselves and others at work.

ACKNOWLEDGMENT

Portions of this chapter were previously presented as "Authentic transformational leaders: Developing character and personal integrity through emotional competence" by N. Keller, J.C. Quick, M. Macik-Frey, and D.A. Gray at the 2004 Gallup Leadership Summit in Omaha, NE. The authors wish to thank John and Judy Goolsby for the generous direction of an anonymous gift in concert with Dean Daniel D. Himarios of UTA's College of Business Administration to create the Goolsby Leadership Academy. This gift has enabled to Academy and College to look more closely at authentic leadership, emotional health in the workplace, and personal integrity for all. We thank Stacy M. Deutsch and Anjali Mishra for their help in the preparation of the references and manuscript.

REFERENCES

Ashford, B. E., & Humphrey, R. H. (1995). Emotion in the workplace: A reappraisal. *Human Relations, 48,* 97–125.

Ashkanasy, N. M., & Daus, C. S. (2002). Emotion in the workplace: The new challenge for managers. *Academy of Management Executive, 16,* 76–86.

Ashkanasy, N. M., & Tse, B. (2000). Transformational leadership as management of emotion: A conceptual review. In N. M. Ashkanasy, C. E. Hartel, & W. J. Zerbe (Eds.), *Emotions in working life: Theory, research and practice* (pp. 221–235). Westport, CT: Quorum.

Athos, A. G., & Gabarro, J. J. (1978). *Interpersonal behavior.* Englewood Cliffs, NJ: Prentice Hall.

Avolio, B. J., & Bass, B. M. (1991). *Full-range training of leadership. Manual.* Binghamton, NY: Bass/Avolio & Associates.

Barbuto, J. E. Jr., & Burback, M. E. (2004, June). *The emotional intelligence of transformational leaders: A field study.* Paper presented at the 2004 Gallup Leadership Summit, Omaho, NE.

Barling, J., Slater, F., & Kelloway, E. K. (2000). Transformational leadership and emotional intelligence: An exploratory study. *Leadership & Organization Development Journal, 21,* 157–161.

Barsade, S. E., Brief, A. P., & Spataro, S. E. (2003). The affective revolution in organizational behavior: the emergence of a new paradigm. In J. Greenberg (Ed.), *Organizational behavior: The state of the science* (pp. 3–52). Mahway, NJ. Erlbaum.

Bass, B. M. (1985). *Leadership and performance beyond expectations.* New York: Free Press.

Bass, B. M. (1999). Two decades of research and development in transformational leadership. *European Journal of Work & Organizational Psychology, 8,* 24–33.

Bass, B. M. (2002). Cognitive, social and emotional intelligence of transformational leaders. In Riggio, R. E., Mujrphy, S. E., & Pirozzolo, F. J. (Eds.), *Multiple intelligences and leadership* (pp. 105–118). Mahwah, NJ: Erlbaum.

Bass, B. M., & Avolio, B. J. (1993). Transformational leadership: A response to critiques. In M. M. Chemmers & R. Ayman (Eds.), *Leadership theory and research: Perspectives and directions* (pp. 49–88). San Diego, CA: Academic Press.

Bass, B. M., & Steidlmeier, P, (1999). Ethics, character, and authentic transformational leadership behavior. *Leadership Quarterly, 10,* 187–218.

Bell, M. P. Quick, J. C., & Cycota, C. (2002). Assessment and prevention of sexual harassment: An applied guide to creating healthy organizations. *International Journal of Selection and Assessment, 10,* 160–167.

Cannon, M., & Edmonson, A. (2001). Confronting failure: Antecedents and consequences of shared beliefs about failure in organizational work groups. *Journal of Organizational Behavior, 22,* 161-177.

Clarke, S., & Cooper, C. L. (2004). *Managing the risk of workplace stress.* London: Routledge.

Cooper, C. L., Dewe, P., & O'Driscoll, M. (2001). *Organizational stress: A review and critique of theory, research and applications.* Thousand Oaks, CA: Sage.

Cosier, R. A., & Dalton, D. R. (1990). Positive aspects of conflict: A field experiment. *International Journal of Conflict Management, 1,* 81–92.

Cox, T., & Blake, S. (1991). Managing cultural diversity: Implications for organizational competitiveness. *Academy of Management Executive, 5*(3), 45-56.

De Dreu, C. K., & Van de Vlier, E. (1997). *Using conflict in organizations.* London: Sage.

Donohue, K., & Wong, L. (1994). Understanding and applying transformational leadership. *Military Review, 8,* 24–32.

Drucker, P. F. (1954). *The practice of management.* New York: Harper & Bros.

Edwards, J. R. (1996). An examination of competing versions of the person-environment fit approach to stress. *Academy of Management Journal, 39,* 292-339.

Farson, R., & Keyes, R. (2002). The failure-tolerant leader. *Harvard Business Review, 80*(8), 3-8.

Forward, G., Beach, D., Gray, D., & Quick, J. C. (1991). Mentofacturing: A vision for American industrial excellence. *Academy of Management Executive, 5*(3), 32–44.

Frost, P. (2002). *Toxic emotions at work: How compassionate managers handle pain and conflict.* Boston: Harvard Business School.

Frost, P., & Robinson, S. (1999). The toxic handler: Organizational hero—and casualty. *Harvard Business Review, 77,* 97–106.

Gardner, W., & Schermerhorn, J. R., (2004). Performance gains through positive organizational behavior and authentic leadership. *Organizational Dynamics, 33,* 270–281.

Gardner, L., & Stough, C. (2002). Examining the relationship between leadership and emotional intelligence in senior level managers. *Leadership and Organization Development Journal, 23,* 68–78.

Goleman, D. (1998). *Working with emotional intelligence.* New York: Bantam Books.

Hough, L. M., & Furham, A. (2003). Use of personality variables in work settings. In W. C. Borman, D. R. Ilgen, & R. J. Klimoski (Eds.), *Handbook of Psychology, 12,* 131-169.

Joplin, J., & Daus, C. S. (1997). Challanges of leading a diverse workforce. *Academy of Management Executive, 11,* 32-47.

Jablin, F. M. (1979). Superior-subordinate communication: The state of the art. *Psychological Bulletin, 86,* 1201–1222.

Kelloway, E. K., Sivanathan, N., Francis, L., & Barling, J. (2004). Poor leadership. In J. Barling, E. K. Kelloway, & M. R. Frone (Eds.), *Handbook of work stress* (pp. 89–112). Thousand Oaks, CA: Sage.

Komaki, J., Coombs, T., & Schepman, S. (1996). Motivational implications of reinforcement theory. In R. M. Steers, L. W. Porter, & G. A. Begley (Eds.), *Motivation and leadership at work* (pp. 34-52). New York: McGraw-Hill.

Latham, G. P., & Locke, E. A. (1990). *A theory of goal setting and task performance.* Englewood Cliffs, NJ: Prentice-Hall.

Luthans, F. (2002). Positive organizational behavior: Developing and managing psychological strengths. *Academy of Management Executive, 16*(1), 57–72.

Luthans, F., & Avolio, B. (2003). Authentic leadership: A positive developmental approach. In K. S. Cameron, J. E. Dutton, & R. E. Quinn (Eds.), *Positive organizational scholarship* (pp. 241–258). San Francisco: Berrett-Koehler.

Macik-Frey, M., Quick, J. C., & Quick, J. D. (2005). Interpersonal communication: The key to social support for preventive stress management. In C. L. Cooper (Ed.), *Handbook of stress, medicine, and health, second edition* (pp. 265–292). Boca Raton, FL: CRC Press.

Mack, D. A., Shannon, C., Quick, J. D., & Quick, J. C. (1998). Stress and the preventive management of workplace violence. In R. W. Griffin, A. O'Leary-Kelly, & J. Collins (Eds.), *Dysfunctional behavior in organizations: Violent behavior in organizations* (Vol 1, pp. 19–141). Greenwich, CT: JAI Press.

Mathews, G., Zeidner, M., & Roberts, R. D. (2002). *Emotional intelligence: Science and myth.* Cambridge, MA: MIT Press.

May, D., Chan, A., Hodges, T., & Avolio, B., (2003). Developing the moral component of authentic leadership. *Organizational Dynamics, 32,* 247–260.

Mayer, J. D., & Salovey, P. (1997). What is emotional intelligence. In P. Salovey & D. J. Sluyter (Eds.), *Emotional development and emotional intelligence: Educational implication* (pp. 3–31). New York: Basic Books.

Montemayor, E. F., & Spree, J. (2004, August). *The dimensions of emotional intelligence: Construct validation using manger and self ratings.* Best conference paper (OB) presented at the annual meeting of the Academy of Management, New Orleans, LA.

Olson, E. E. (1990). The transcendent function in organizational change. *Journal of Applied Behavioral Science, 26*(1), 69-81.

Penley, L. E., Alexander, E. R., Jernigan, I. E., & Henwood, C. (1991). Communications abilities of managers: The relationship to performance. *Journal of Management, 17*(1), 57-77.

Perrewé, P. L., Ferris, G. R., Frink, D. D., & Anthony, W. P. (2000). Political skill: An antidote for workplace stressors. *Academy of Management Executive, 14,* 115–123.

Quick, J. C., Gavin, J. H., Cooper, C. L., & Quick, J. D. (2004). Working together: Balancing head and heart. In N. G. Johnson, R. H. Rozensky, C. D. Goodheart, & R. Hammond (Eds.), *Psychology builds a healthy world* (pp. 219–232). Washington, DC: American Psychological Association.

Quick, J. C., & Macik-Frey, M. (2004). Behind the mask: Coaching through deep interpersonal communication. *Consulting Psychology Journal: Practice and Research, 56,* 67–74.

Quick, J. C., Mack, D., Gavin, J. H., Cooper, C. L., & Quick, J. D. (2004). Executives: Engines for positive stress. In P. L. Perrewé and D. C. Ganster (Eds.), *Research in Occupational Stress and Well-Being* (pp. 359–405). New York: Elsiver Press.

Quick, J. C., Quick, J. D., Nelson, D. L., & Hurrell, J. J., Jr. (1997). *Preventive stress management in organizations.* Washington, DC: American Psychological Association. (Original work in 1984 by Quick & Quick)

Quick, J. D., Cooper, C. L., Gavin, J. H., & Quick, J. C. (2002). Executive health: Building self-reliance for challenging times. In C. L. Cooper & I. T. Robertson (Eds.), *International review of industrial and organizational psychology* (Vol. 17, pp. 187–216). Chichester, England: Wiley.

Salovey, P., Stroud, L. R., Woolery, A., & Epel, E. S. (2002). Perceived emotional intelligence, stress reactivity, and symptom reports: Further explorations using the Trait Meta-Mood Scale. *Psychology and Health, 17,* 611–627.

Scott, W. G., & Mitchell, L. R. (1979). *Organization theory: A structural and behavioral analysis* (3rd ed.). Homewood, IL: Richard D. Irwin.

Senge, P. (1990). The leaders' new work: Building learning organizations. *Sloan Management Review, 32*(1), 7-23.

Sivanathan, N., & Fekken, G. C. (2002) Emotional intelligence and transformational leadership. *Leadership & Organization Development Journal, 23,* 198–204.

Wall, J. A., & Callister, R. R. (1995). Conflict and its management. *Journal of Management, 21,* 515-558.

Weick, K. E. (1988). Enacted sense making in crisis situations. *Journal of Management Studies, 25*(4), 305-317.

Wells, T. (1980). *Keeping your cool under fire: Communicating nondefensively.* New York: McGraw-Hill.

CHAPTER 11

THE CONSEQUENCES OF ORGANIZATIONAL POLITICS PERCEPTIONS AS A WORKPLACE STRESSOR

**Gerald R. Ferris, Robyn L. Brouer,
Mary Dana Laird, and Wayne A. Hochwarter**

Perceptions of organizational politics have been conceptualized as a source of stress in the work environment with the potential to promote dysfunctional consequences and strain reactions. Research has demonstrated that a variety of individual difference variables, such as personal commitment and affective disposition, either intensify or neutralize these effects. An additional variable that holds considerable promise for altering politics perceptions- strain associations is political skill. Political skill is characterized by social perceptiveness and the ability to adjust one's behavior to different situational needs in ways that enhance personal or organizational goals. As such, high political skill is argued to be a coping mechanism used to ameliorate the politics perceptions-strain reaction relationship. This chapter begins with a brief overview of the politics perceptions literature followed by a discussion of politics perceptions as a workplace stressor. Next, we outline recent political skill literature and continue by outlining political skill's potential to serve as a coping mecha-

Stress and Quality of Working Life: Current Perspectives in Occupational Health, 155–165
Copyright © 2006 by Information Age Publishing
All rights of reproduction in any form reserved.

nism. We conclude with directions for future research and implications for practice.

THE CONSEQUENCES OF ORGANIZATIONAL POLITICS PERCEPTIONS AS A WORKPLACE STRESSOR

Organizational politics has influenced organizational behavior for centuries. However, it has been only recently that organizational scientists have investigated perceptions of organizational politics, and considered the potential roles this construct plays in explaining employee reactions in the workplace. One role proposed for politics is that of a workplace stressor, which can promote a host of physiological, psychological, and work-related strain reactions. We suggest such a characterization is only partially accurate. Instead, we contend that the dynamics of politics perceptions are more complex than can be depicted by a simple direct effect, and vary as a function of individual differences. It is our contention that political skill, a factor that represents interpersonal astuteness, plays an important role in this relationship.

The purpose of the present chapter is to propose a model that suggests that the effects of politics perceptions as a stressor on strain reactions varies as a function of political skill. Specifically, political skill is argued to neutralize, or serve as an antidote for, the dysfunctional effects of politics perceptions as a stressor. This chapter unfolds as follows. First, we briefly discuss the ever-expanding politics perceptions literature. Second, the conceptual underpinnings of politics perceptions as a workplace stressor are outlined. Third, we review recent contributions to the political skill literature. We conclude by presenting future research opportunities and implications for practice.

Perceptions of Organizational Politics

While managers have acknowledged the prevalence of politicking for decades, scientific inquiry is a relatively new endeavor. Much of the research in this domain can be attributed to a model offered by Ferris, Russ, and Fandt (1989), which integrated antecedent, moderating, and reaction constructs. Since the debut of this model over 15 years ago, research has been grouped into two distinct categories: (1) studies of actual political behaviors and their consequences, and (2) studies of individuals' perceptions of organizational politics and the antecedents and consequences of these perceptions (see Ferris, Adams, Kolodinsky, Hochwarter, & Ammeter, 2002, for a review of empirical research).

Throughout the years, numerous definitions of organizational politics have been proposed. However, a recurring theme of self-serving behavior that is not sanctioned by organizations has unified these definitions (e.g., Burns, 1961; Farrell & Peterson, 1982; Ferris et al., 1989; Gandz & Murray, 1980; Mayes & Allen, 1977; Schein, 1977). This is illustrated by Mintzberg's (1983, p. 172) definition of organizational politics as "individual or group behavior that is informal, ostensibly parochial, typically divisive, and above all in a technical sense, *illegitimate*—sanctioned neither by formal authority, accepted ideology, nor certified expertise (although it may exploit any one of those)." Critical to Mintzberg's definition is the acknowledgement that organizational politics may promote antagonistic reactions among individuals and groups with different agendas, who are often vying for resources considered scarce (Ferris, Frink, Gilmore, & Kacmar, 1994).

Although the study of political behaviors and organizational politics is still growing, some researchers have focused their efforts on investigating perceptions of organizational politics. According to Gandz and Murray (1980), politics should be envisioned as a subjective evaluation, not an objective reality. Because individuals respond to their perceptions of reality (Lewin, 1936), perceptions of organizational politics represent an important area of study, even if they are misperceptions of objective conditions (Porter, 1976).

Ferris, Harrell-Cook, and Dulebohn (2000) stated that perceptions of organizational politics "involve an individual's attribution to behaviors of self-serving intent, and is defined as an individual's subjective evaluation about the extent to which the work environment is characterized by co-workers and supervisors who demonstrate such self-serving behavior" (p. 90). The key aspects of this definition are that perceptions of politics include an attribution of intent regarding other organizational members' behavior, that these behaviors are interpreted as self-serving actions, and that the perceptions involve individuals' subjective assessments about political behavior in the workplace (Ferris et al., 2002). Despite the fact that studies have shown direct relationships with politics perceptions and favorable outcomes (Hochwarter, 2003), the majority of the empirical research documents destructive individual and organizational consequences (Ferris et al., 2002).

Politics Perceptions as a Workplace Stressor

Exhaustive reviews of stress research can be found in the literature, and with them, a myriad of construct definitions (Hurrell, Nelson, & Simmons, 1998). Seyle (1975) viewed stress as an organism's psychological, physiological, or behavioral reactions to anxiety-provoking events. Another perspective envisions stress as the subjective feeling that work demands exceed the individual's belief in his or her coping capacity (Cropanzano, Howes, Grandey, & Toth, 1997; Edwards, 1992; Folkman & Lazarus, 1991). For the purposes of this paper, Beehr's (1990) conceptualization of stress as a workplace characteristic that causes employee discomfort is utilized. In this context, politics perceptions is conceptualized a workplace *stressor*. The discomfort experienced by the individual is referred to as the *strain* response.

Numerous negative stress-induced strain reactions have been reported in the literature including incidences of coronary heart disease, mental breakdown, and perceptions of and external reports of poor health (Cooper & Cartwright, 1994). In addition to the negative strain reactions produced by stressors on the individual, there are also links to adverse organizational consequences. These links include accidents, absenteeism, and lost productivity (Cooper & Cartwright, 1994; Hurrell et al., 1998). Further, work-related stressors have been found to increase voluntary turnover suggesting, "withdrawal from the organization is an impulsive and emotionally generated behavioral response to high experienced stress or psychological strain" (Parasuraman & Alutto, 1984, p. 18). Finally, it has been shown consistently that job satisfaction and organizational commitment are greatly impacted by job stressors (Cordes & Dougherty, 1993).

Empirical studies confirm the stress-provoking qualities of perceived politics (Ferris, Frink, Galang, Zhou, Kacmar, & Howard, 1996; Kacmar & Baron, 1999). Surprisingly, the idea that organizational politics might be a work-related stressor is relatively new to organizational scientists. Matteson and Ivancevich (1987) were the first to identify politics as one of many potential stressors associated with the work environment. Since this initial work, several studies have theoretically discussed, or empirically demonstrated, the stress-related implications of workplace politics (e.g., Ferris et al., 1996; Gilmore, Ferris, Dulebohn, & Harrell-Cook, 1996; Jex & Beehr, 1991; Matteson & Ivancevich, 1987). From a conceptual standpoint, these results are not surprising. For example, three main features that integrate stress and organizational politics perceptions: (1) both are perceptual in nature, (2) both have uncertain characteristics and, (3) both can be seen as either threats or opportunities (Ferris et al., 1996).

Similar to the preceding conceptualization of perceptions of organizational politics, stress is often viewed as an individually experienced phenomenon instead of a characteristic of the environment (McGrath, 1976; Schuler, 1980; Schuler & Jackson, 1986). As previously stated, individuals respond to their perceptions of reality, not to objective reality (Lewin,

1936). As such, individual perceptions are integral to both stress and perceptions of organizational politics (Ferris et al., 1996).

A second characteristic that integrates job stress and politics perceptions is uncertainty. According to Ferris et al. (1989), uncertainty leads to increases in both political behavior and perceptions of organizational politics. Similarly, stress researchers have emphasized the role of uncertainty of processes and outcomes in their definitions of stress (e.g., Beehr, 1998; Schuler, 1980). For example, Schuler and Jackson (1986) argued that stress represents the level of uncertainty that individuals encounter, and that a careful examination of uncertainty should provide a greater understanding of stress.

The final feature that unifies politics perceptions and stress is the possibility of categorizing each as either an opportunity or a threat. For example, stress has been characterized in terms of both constraints (e.g., threats) and opportunities (McGrath, 1976), whereas Schuler (1980) viewed anxiety as dynamic conditions in which people deal with opportunities, constraints, or demands. According to Ferris et al. (1996, p. 236), "it seems quite reasonable to conceive of politics as providing situations of potential gain (i.e., opportunity) as well as situations of potential loss (i.e., threats)." As evidence of positive manifestations, Hochwarter (2003) reported that political behavior was associated with favorable attitudinal outcomes when coupled with increases in politics perceptions.

Finally, evidence of politics perceptions—stress associations has been substantiated in the literature. For example, Valle and Perrewé (2000) found a direct positive relationship between perceptions of politics and job anxiety, and Ferris et al. (1996) reported a perceptions of politics-job anxiety association. Cropanzano et al. (1997) corroborated significant direct associations between perceptions of politics and several forms of stress, including job tension, somatic tension, general fatigue, and burnout. Finally, Vigoda (2002) found job distress to be an immediate response to organizational politics perceptions in three distinct organizations.

Political Skill and Organizational Politics

Although politics perceptions have been found to relate to strain reactions, this direct association may not materialize for all individuals. Research on the political influence process, organizational politics, and perceptions of politics has expanded recently (e.g., Vigoda, 2002; Ferris et al., 2002). However, until recently, little attention has been paid to the way in which people engage in the influence process (Jones, 1990). It is plausible that individual differences may affect the execution and outcome of the influence behavior. One individual difference variable we contend will predict the effectiveness of influence tactics is political skill (Ferris, Berkson, Kaplan, Gilmore, Buckley, Hochwarter, & Witt, 1999; Ferris, Davidson, & Perrewé, 2005; Ferris, Treadway, Kolodinsky, Hochwarter, Kacmar, Douglas, & Frink, 2005; Perrewé, Zellars, Ferris, Rossi, Kacmar, & Ralston, 2004).

Mintzberg (1983) first introduced the term political skill as an individual characteristic required to be successful in virtually all organizational environments. Despite this introduction, the notion of political skill did not receive further attention for over 15 years. In order to address this deficit in the literature, Ferris et al. (1999) provided a clear definition of political skill. Stemming from this work, political skill "refers to the ability to effectively understand others at work, and to use such knowledge to influence others to act in ways that enhance one's personal and/or organizational objectives" (Ferris, Treadway et al., p. 127). Political skill, which is comprised of both dispositional and learnable components, represents a proficiency that is critical in contemporary work environments (Ferris, Davidson, & Perrewé, 2005). Whereas the study of influence tactics and political behaviors is important, this represents the "what" of influence. On the other hand, political skill is aimed at addressing the "how" of influence, about which we know much less (Ferris, Treadway et al., 2005).

For example, when investigating the influence behavior of self-promotion, the "what" involves describing oneself in a complimentary manner, which is comprised of two related aspects: (1) providing precise narratives of one's attitudes and behaviors, and (2) behaving in ways that show that one indeed possesses these characteristics (Kumar & Beyerlein, 1991). However, the "how" of influence is not nearly as discernible. If one does not demonstrate influence tactics appropriately, the target will likely respond with antagonism, agitation, or avoidance. On the other hand, if self-promotion is utilized fittingly, positive reactions are to be expected (Ferris, Davidson, & Perrewé, 2005). Through this brief example, it is clear that political skill plays a prominent role in the demonstration and interpretation of influence behaviors because it can affect the ways tactics of influence are perceived and interpreted, often changing a positive interpretation to a negative one.

Political Skill as Antidote for Dysfunctional Effects of Politics Perceptions

Politically skilled individuals possess a fundamental understanding of the individuals in their environment, which manifests itself in feelings of self-confidence and control. As such, it is expected that these individuals have at their disposal a larger reservoir of resources that can be used to minimize the debilitating effect of stressors such as such as politics perceptions (Ferris et al., 1999; Perrewé, Ferris, Frink, & Anthony, 2000; Perrewé et al., 2004). Furthermore, Ferris et al. (1996) found that the extent to which individuals perceived that they had discretion in decision making weakened the positive relationship between perceptions of politics and job anxiety. In support, political skill is believed to represent a form of interpersonal control that permits individuals to perceive and interpret workplace stressors in ways that are less aversive because they know that their political skill will help them to cope more effectively by influencing others (Ferris, Davidson, & Perrewé, 2005).

Implications for Future Research

Although this paper has presented formative ideas regarding the influence of political skill on politics perceptions-strain reaction relationships, empirical research is required to support its proposed effect. A second recommendation for future research is to examine multiple strain reactions, which include both physiological and psychological variables. For example, much of the research in this domain has been restricted to work-relevant consequences, when, in fact, it is plausible that stressors cause strain across domains. For example, can the positive effects of political skill on stress-strain relationships minimize the crossover strain that individuals experience at home? Because the boundaries of work and non-work domains have become much more blurred in recent years, anxiety caused at work likely permeates to other environments.

Finally, future research is warranted concerning the effects of political skill on individuals' responses to political organizations. When involved in political work environments, employee generally react in one of three ways: (1) they leave the organization, (2) they stay in the organization, but refuse to participate in organizational politics or, (3) they stay in the organization, but actively participate in organizational politics. If the ideas proposed in this chapter are supported, individuals high in political skill will choose to stay in political environments, but individuals low in political skill will opt to leave the organization or stay in the organization and avoid politicking. Future research should investigate the relationship between political skill and the three reactions to perceptions of politics noted above.

Implications for Practice

The implication that political skill can serve to minimize strain can be extrapolated to other benefits deemed valuable by decision makers. Because an important component of political skill is empathy (Ferris et al., 1999), the ability to develop an appreciation for the way others view organizational dynamics can serve multiple roles. For example, developing a work force that is comprised of individuals who are more interpersonally astute can be beneficial in terms of conflict resolution and team decision-making. In this regard, individuals are able to see the big picture, which allows employees to focus their energies on activities that are aligned with the goals of the organization, and not on bickering, protecting turf, and one-upsmanship.

In terms of the direct contribution to the organization, research has shown interpersonal acuity to represent a significant predictor of both group (Ahearn, Ferris, Hochwarter, Douglas, & Ammeter, 2004) and individual (Ferris, Witt, & Hochwarter, 2001) performance. As noted, political skill is characterized as the possession of abilities that are both dispositional and learnable. As such, assessments of prehire political skill may be a useful tool when coupled with other validation selection procedures. Furthermore, management develop programs may find utility in incorporating political skill training. A program of this nature would inherent require exposure to a comprehensive, yet overlapping, set of skills such as network building, empathy, and active listening.

Finally, acknowledging that politics pervades all work environments may allow decision makers to direct attention to workplace dynamics that are amenable to control. In terms of pervasiveness, politics intensify in settings laden with ambiguity. Specifically, when rules are absent or unclear, or performance expectations are ambiguous, employees are left to their own devices to construct reality, which often take the form of behaviors viewed by many as disreputable. It is clear that organizations worldwide are experiencing unprecedented levels of uncertainty caused by a variety of factors including political unrest, governmental manipulation on trade dynamics, and terrorism. A consequence of operating in unpredictable environments is the increased use of work-force modifications such as outsourcing and layoffs. When job continuance is in question, individuals are likely to rely on tactics not considered in more stable settings, like policking. Because eliminating the cause of tension (i.e., uncertainty) may be outside the parameters of managerial control, focusing on the manner in which individuals cope at work may represent a more viable focus of attention. We contend that political skill can not only assist individuals to cope with politics, but also to adapt to the wide array of uncertainties that they are likely to experience in the coming years.

REFERENCES

Ahearn, K. K., Ferris, G. R., Hochwarter, W. A., Douglas, C., & Ammeter, A. P. (2004). Leader political skill and team performance. *Journal of Management, 30*, 309–327.

Beehr, T. A. (1990). Stress in the workplace: An overview. In J. W. Jones, B. D. Steffy, & D. W. Bary (Eds.), *Applying psychology in business* (pp. 7–31). Lexington, MA: Lexington Books.

Beehr, T. A. (1998). Research on occupational stress: An unfinished enterprise. *Personnel Psychology, 51*, 835–844.

Burns, T. (1961). Micropolitics: Mechanisms of institutional change. *Administrative Science Quarterly, 6*, 257–281.

Cooper, C. L., & Cartwright, S. (1994). Healthy mind; healthy organization—a proactive approach to occupational stress. *Human Relations, 47*, 455–472.

Cordes, C. L., & Dougherty, T. W. (1993). A review and an integration of research on job burnout. *Academy of Management Review, 18*, 621–656.

Cropanzano, R., Howes, J. C., Grandley, A. A., & Toth, P. (1997). The relationship of organizational politics and support to work behaviors, attitudes, and stress. *Journal of Organizational Behavior, 18*, 159–180.

Edwards, J. R. (1992). A cybernetic theory of stress, coping, and well-being in organizations. *Academy of Management Review, 17*, 238–274.

Farrell, D., & Petersen, J. C. (1982). Patterns of political behavior in organizations. *Academy of Management Review, 7*, 403–412.

Ferris, G. R., Adams, G., Kolodinsky, R. W., Hochwarter, W. A., & Ammeter, A. P. (2002). Perceptions of organizational politics: Theory and research directions. In F. J. Yammarino & F. Dansereau (Eds.), *Research in multi-level issues: The many faces of multi-level issues* (Vol. 1, pp. 179–254). Oxford, England: Elsevier.

Ferris, G. R., Berkson, H. M., Kaplan, D. M., Gilmore, D. C., Buckley, M. R., Hochwarter, W. A., & Witt, L. (1999, August). *Development and initial validation of the political skill inventory*. Paper presented at the 59th Academy of Management Meetings, Chicago, IL.

Ferris, G. R., Davidson, S. L., & Perrewé, P. L. (2005). *Political skill at work: Impact on work effectiveness*. Mountain View, CA: Davies-Black.

Ferris, G. R., Frink, D. D., Galang, M. C., Zhou, J., Kacmar, K. M., & Howard, J. L. (1996). Perceptions of organizational politics: Predictors, stress-related implications, and outcomes. *Human Relations, 49*, 233–266.

Ferris, G. R., Frink, D. D., Gilmore, D. C., & Kacmar, K. M. (1994). Understanding as an antidote for the dysfunctional consequences of organizational politics as a stressor. *Journal of Applied Social Psychology, 24*, 1204–1220.

Ferris, G. R., Harrell-Cook, G., & Dulebohn, J. H. (2000). Organizational politics: The nature of the relationship between politics perceptions and political behavior. In S. B. Bacharach & E. J. Lawler (Eds.), *Research in the sociology of organizations* (pp. 89–130). Stamford, CT: JAI Press.

Ferris, G. R., Russ, G. S., & Fandt, P. M. (1989). Politics in organizations. In R. A. Giacalone & P. Rosenfeld (Eds.), *Impression management in the organization* (pp. 143–170). Hillsdale, NJ: Erlbaum.

Ferris, G. R., Treadway, D. C., Kolodinsky, R. W., Hochwarter, W. A., Kacmar, C. J., Douglas, C., & Frink, D. D. (2005). Development and validation of the political skill inventory. *Journal of Management, 31*, 126–152.

Ferris, G. R., Witt, L. A., & Hochwarter, W. A. (2001). The interaction of social skill and general mental ability on work outcomes. *Journal of Applied Psychology, 86*, 1075–1082.

Folkman, S., & Lazarus, R. S. (1991). Coping and emotion. In A. Monat, & R. S. Lazarus (Eds.), *Stress and coping: An anthology* (pp. 207–227). New York: Columbia University Press.

Gandz, J., & Murray, V. (1980). The experience of workplace politics. *Academy of Management Journal, 23*, 237–251.

Gilmore, D. C., Ferris, G. R., Dulehorn, J. H., & Harrell-Cook, G. (1996). Organizational politics and employee attendance. *Group and Organization Management, 21*, 481–494.

Hochwarter, W. A. (2003). The interactive effects of pro-political behavior and politics perceptions on job satisfaction and affective commitment. *Journal of Applied Social Psychology, 33*, 1360–1378.

Hurrell, J., Nelson, D., & Simmons, B. (1998). Measuring job stressor and strains: Where have we been, where we are, and where do we need to go? *Journal of Occupational Health Psychology, 3*, 368–389.

Jex, S. M., & Beehr, T. A. (1991). Emerging theoretical and methodological issues in the study of work-related stress. In G. R. Ferris & K. M. Rowland (Eds.), *Research in personnel and human resource management* (Vol. 9, pp. 311–365). Greenwich, CT: JAI Press.

Jones, E. E. (1990). *Interpersonal perception*. New York: W. H. Freeman.

Kacmar, K. M., & Baron, R. A. (1999). Organizational politics: The state of the field, links to related processes, and an agenda for future research. In G. R. Ferris (Ed.), *Research in personnel and human resources management* (Vol. 17, pp. 1–39). Stamford, CT: JAI Press.

Kumar, K., & Beyerlein, B. (1991). Construction and validation of an instrument for measuring ingratiatory behaviors in organizational settings. *Journal of Applied Psychology, 76*, 619–627.

Lewin, K. (1936). *Principles of topological psychology*. New York: McGraw-Hill.

Matteson, M. T., & Ivancevish, J. M. (1987). *Controlling work stress*. San Francisco: Jossey-Bass.

Mayes, B., & Allen, R. (1977). Toward a definition of organizational politics. *Academy of Management Review, 4*, 672–677.

McGrath, J. E. (1976). Stress and behavior in organizations. In M.D. Dunnette (Ed.), *Handbook of industrial and organizational psychology* (pp. 390–419). Chicago: Rand McNally.

Mintzberg, H. (1983). *Power in and around organizations*. Englewood Cliffs, NJ: Prentice-Hall.

Parasuraman, S., & Alutto, J. A. (1984). Sources and outcomes of stress in organizational settings: Toward the development of a structural model. *Academy of Management Journal, 27,* 330–351.

Perrewé, P. L., Ferris, G. R., Frink, D. D., & Anthony, W. P. (2000). Political skill: An antidote for workplace stressors. *Academy of Management Executive, 14,* 115-123.

Perrewé, P. L., Zellars, K. L., Ferris, G. R., Rossi, A. M., Kacmar, C. J., & Ralston, D. A. (2004). Neutralizing job stressors: Political skill as an antidote to the dysfunctional consequences of role conflict stressors. *Academy of Management Journal, 47,* 141–152.

Porter, L. W. (1976, September). *Organizations as political animals.* Presidential address, Division of Industrial-Organizational Psychology, 84th annual convention of the American Psychological Association, Washington, DC.

Schein, V. E. (1977). Individual power and political behavior in organizations: An inadequately explored reality. *Academy of Management Review, 2,* 64–72.

Schuler, R. (1980). Definitions and conceptualizations of stress in organizations. *Organizational Behavior and Human Performance, 25,* 184–215.

Schuler, R. S., & Jackson, S. E. (1986). Managing stress through PHRM practices: An uncertainty interpretation. In K. M. Rowland & G. R. Ferris (Eds.), *Research in personnel and human resources management* (Vol. 4, pp. 183–224). Greenwich, CT: JAI Press.

Seyle, H. (1975). *Stress without distress.* New York: Signet.

Valle, M. P., & Perrewé, P. L. (2000). Do politics perceptions relate to political behaviors? *Human Relations, 53,* 359-386.

Vigoda, E. (2002). Stress-related aftermaths to workplace politics: The relationship among politics, job distress, and aggressive behavior in organizations. *Journal of Organizational Behavior, 23,* 571–591.

CHAPTER 12

THE EUROPEAN COMMISSION'S GUIDANCE ON WORK-RELATED STRESS AND RELATED INITIATIVES

From Words to Action

Lennart Levi

Working life and its conditions are powerful determinants of occupational health, well-being, and productivity. The European Framework Directive, the guidance on work-related stress, a series of activities related to the concept "Corporate Social Responsibility (CSR)" and the recent Framework agreement on work-related stress, covering some 190 million employees in 25 European Union member states, jointly provide a solid basis for integrated occupational health promotion and disease prevention. The great challenge now is two-fold: (1) to implement and evaluate available evidence, and (2) to serve as a model in this field for other continents to consider, adjust, and assimilate. Given the triple global burden of high occupational morbidity, low productivity, and wide-spread poverty, there is now an urgent need for such promotive and preventive actions across societal sec-

Stress and Quality of Working Life: Current Perspectives in Occupational Health, 167–182
Copyright © 2006 by Information Age Publishing
All rights of reproduction in any form reserved.

tors and levels for beneficial outcomes for all concerned—workers, management, and society.

In the constitution of the World Health Organization (WHO), *health* is
defined as "a state of complete physical, mental and social well-being and
not merely the absence of disease or infirmity." There is no doubt whatso-
ever that working life and its conditions are powerful determinants of
health, for better or for worse. The relationship works both ways. Work
affects health. But health more often than not also affects a person's productivity and earning capacity as well as his or her social and family relationships. Needless to say, this holds true for all aspects of health, both
physical and *mental*.

In 2000, the European Commission published its *Guidance on Work-
Related Stress: Spice of Life or Kiss of Death*,[1] in English, French, German,
Italian, and Spanish. This development had its roots in a major European
Conference held in Brussels on 9–10 November, 1993, on "Stress at work
—A call for action," organized jointly by the European Foundation, the
European Commission and the Belgian Labor Ministry, and supported by
the Belgian Presidency of the Council of Ministers. The conference highlighted the increasing impact of stress on the quality of working life,
employees' health and company performance. Special attention was paid
to stress monitoring and prevention at company national and European
level. Instruments and policies for better stress prevention were presented and discussed. Finally, a round table on "Future perspectives on
stress at work in the European Community" brought together representatives from national governments, the European Commission, UNICE,
CEEP, ETUC, and the Foundation.

Based on what came out of these deliberations, the commission set up
an ad hoc group to the Advisory Committee on Safety and Health on
"stress at work." The ad hoc group proposed, and the Advisory Committee endorsed, that the commission should draw up "guidance" in this
field. The author is proud to have had a hand in the above developments.

The Present Situation

The many causes and consequences of work-related stress are widespread in the 15 European Union Member States at the turn of the century. Over half the EU's 160 million workers report working at very high
speeds (56%), and to tight deadlines (60%). More than a third have no
influence on task order. Forty percent report having monotonous tasks.
Such work-related "stressors" are likely to have contributed to the present

spectrum of ill health: 15% of the workforce complain of headaches, 23% of neck and shoulder pains, 23% of fatigue, 28% of "stress," and 33% of backache (European Foundation, 2001), plus a host of other illnesses, including life-threatening ones.

Sustained work-related stress is an important determinant of *depressive disorders*. Such disorders are the fourth biggest cause of the global disease burden. They are expected to rank second by 2020, behind ischaemic heart disease, but ahead of all other diseases (World Health Organization, 2001a, 2001b). In the 15 EU member states, the cost of these and related mental health problems is estimated to average 3–4% of GNP (ILO, 2000), amounting to approximately *675 billion euros a year* (2003).

It is also likely that sustained work-related stress is an important determinant of *metabolic syndrome* (Björntorp, 2001; Folkow, 2001). This disorder features a combination of: accumulation of abdominal fat; a decrease in cellular sensitivity to insulin; dyslipidemia (increased levels of LDL cholesterol and triglycerides, and lowered levels of HDL cholesterol); and raised blood pressure, in turn probably contributing to *ischaemic heart disease* and *diabetes type 2* morbidity.

In these ways, virtually every aspect of work-related health and disease can be affected. Such influences can also be mediated through emotional, and/or cognitive *misinterpretation* of work conditions as threatening, even when they are not, and/or trivial symptoms and signs occurring in one's own body as manifestations of serious illness (cf. p. xiii of this volume). All this can lead to a wide variety of disorders, diseases, loss of well-being— and loss of productivity. Examples discussed in some detail in the CEC guidance include ischaemic heart disease, stroke, cancer, musculoskeletal, and gastrointestinal diseases, anxiety, and depressive disorders, accidents, and suicides.

THE EUROPEAN COMMISSION'S GUIDANCE

What is Stress?

According to the CEC guidance,[1] *stress* consists of a pattern of "stone-age" reactions preparing the human organism for fight or flight, that is, for physical activity, in response to *stressors*, that is, demands and influences that tax the organism's adaptational capacity. Stress comprises the common denominators in an organism's adaptational reaction pattern to a variety of such influences and demands (Selye, 1936, 1971). Stress was adequate when stone-age man was facing a wolf pack, but not so when today's worker is struggling to adjust to rotating shifts, highly monotonous and fragmented tasks, or threatening or over-demanding customers. If sustained, it is often maladaptive and even disease-provoking.

As mentioned above, health and well-being can be influenced by work, both positively (spice of life) and negatively (kiss of death). Work can provide goal and meaning in life. It can give structure and content to our day, week, year, and life. It may offer us identity, self-respect, social support, and material rewards. This is likely to happen when work demands are optimal (and not maximal or minimal), when workers are allowed to exercise a reasonable degree of autonomy, when the "climate" of the work organization is friendly and supportive, and when the worker is adequately rewarded for his or her effort. When this is so, work can be one of the most important health-promoting (salutogenic) factors in life.

If, however, work conditions are characterized by the *opposite* attributes, they are—at least in the long run—likely to cause, accelerate the course or trigger the symptoms of ill health. *Pathogenic mechanisms* include *emotional* reactions (anxiety, depression, hypochondria, and alienation), *cognitive* reactions (loss of concentration, recall, inability to learn new things, be creative, make decisions), *behavioral* reactions (abuse of drugs, alcohol, and tobacco, destructive and self-destructive behavior, refusal to seek or accept treatment, prevention, and rehabilitation), and *physiological* reactions (neuroendocrine and immunological dysfunction, such as persistent sympathotonia and/or a dysfunctional hypothalamic-pituitary-adrenal axis).[2]

Can Work-Related Stress be Prevented?

Work-related stress can be approached on four levels—the individual worker, the work organization, the nation, and the European Union. Whatever the target(s), conditions are usually man-made and open to interventions by all relevant stakeholders.

According to the guidance, there is a need, at all levels, first to identify work-related stressors, stress reactions, and stress-related ill health. There are several reasons for doing this: stress is a problem for workers, their work organization and society alike; work stress problems are on the increase; it is a legal obligation under the EU Framework Directive on health and safety; and many of the stressors and consequences are avoidable and can be adjusted by all three parties on the labor market if they act together in their own and mutual interests.

According to the EU Framework Directive, employers have a "duty to ensure the safety and health of workers in every aspect related to the work." The directive's principles of prevention include "avoiding risks," "combating the risks at source," and "adapting the work to the individual." In addition, the directive indicates the employers' duty to develop "a coherent overall prevention policy." The European Commission's Guidance aims at providing a basis for such endeavors.

Based on surveillance at individual workplaces and monitoring at national and regional levels, work-related stress should be prevented or counteracted by job-redesign (e.g., by empowering the employees, and avoiding both over and under load), by improving social support, and by providing reasonable reward for the effort invested by workers, as integral parts of the overall management system. And, of course, by adjusting occupational physical, chemical, and psychosocial settings to the workers' abilities, needs, and reasonable expectations—all in line with the requirements of the EU Framework Directive and Article 152 of the Treaty of Amsterdam, according to which "a high level of human health protection shall be ensured in the definition and implementation of all Community policies and activities."

Supporting actions include not only research, but also adjustments of curricula in business schools, schools of technology, medicine and behavioral and social sciences, and in the training and retraining of labor inspectors, occupational health officers, managers and supervisors, in line with such goals.

Tools to Prevent Stress

To identify the existence, causes, and consequences of work-related stress, we need to *monitor* our job content, working conditions, terms of employment, social relations at work, health, well-being, and productivity. The CEC guidance provides many references to checklists and questionnaires to enable stakeholders to do this. Once the parties on the labor market know "where the shoe pinches," action can be taken to "adjust the shoe" to fit the "foot," that is, to improve stress-inducing conditions in workplaces.

The guidance argues that much of this can be accomplished through organizational changes, for example, by:

- Allowing adequate time for the worker to perform his or her work satisfactorily.
- Providing the worker with a clear job description.
- Rewarding the worker for good job performance.
- Providing ways for the worker to voice complaints and have them considered seriously and swiftly.
- Harmonizing the worker's responsibility and authority.

- Clarifying the work organization's goals and values and adapting them to the worker's own goals and values, whenever possible.
- Promoting the worker's control, and pride, over the end product of his or her work.
- Promoting tolerance, security, and justice at the workplace.
- Eliminating harmful physical exposures.
- Identifying failures, successes, and their causes and consequences in previous and future health action at the workplace; learning how to avoid the failures and how to promote the successes, for a step-by-step improvement of occupational environment and health (Systematic work environment management, see below).

On a company or national level, all parties on the labor market may wish to *consider* organizational improvements to prevent work-related stress and ill health, with regard to :

- *Work schedule.*   Design work schedules to avoid conflict with demands and responsibilities unrelated to the job. Schedules for rotating shifts should be stable and predictable, with rotation in a forward (morning-afternoon-night) direction.
- *Participation/control.*   Allow workers to take part in decisions or actions affecting their jobs.
- *Workload.*   Ensure assignments are compatible with the worker's own capabilities and resources, and allow for recovery from especially demanding physical or mental tasks.
- *Content.*   Design tasks to provide meaning, stimulation, a sense of completeness, and an opportunity to use skills.
- *Roles.*   Define work roles and responsibilities clearly.
- *Social environment.*   Provide opportunities for social interaction, including emotional and social support and help between fellow workers (Social Capital, cf. Marmot, 2004; Putnam, 2000).
- *Future.*   Avoid ambiguity in matters of job security and career development; promote life-long learning and employability.

Systematic Work Environment Management

According to the guidance, actions to reduce noxious work-related stress need not be complicated, time consuming, or prohibitively expensive. One of the most common-sense, down-to-earth and low-cost approaches is known as *systematic work environment management*. It is a self-regulatory process, carried out in close collaboration between stakeholders. It can be coordinated by, for example, an in-house occupational health service or a labor inspector, or by an occupational or public health nurse, a social worker, a physiotherapist, or a personnel administrator.

The first step is to *identify* the incidence, prevalence, severity, and trends of work-related stressor exposures and their causes and health consequences, for example, by making use of some of the survey instruments listed in the CEC guidance or the ILO SOLVE program. Then, the characteristics of such exposures as reflected in the content, organization and conditions of work are analyzed in relation to the outcomes found. Are they likely to be *necessary*, or *sufficient*, or *contributory* to work-stress and stress-related ill health? Can they be changed? Are such changes acceptable to relevant stakeholders? In a third step, the stakeholders may design an integrated *package of interventions*, and implement it in order to prevent work-related stress and to promote both well-being and productivity, preferably by combining top-down and bottom-up approaches.

The short- and long-term *outcomes* of such interventions then need to be *evaluated*, in terms of (a) stressor exposures, (b) stress reactions, (c) incidence and prevalence of ill health, (d) indicators of well-being, and (e) productivity with regard to the quality and quantity of goods or services. Also to be considered are (f) the costs and benefits in economic terms. If the interventions have no effects, or negative ones in one or more respects, the stakeholders may wish to rethink what should be done, how, when, by whom, and for whom. If, on the other hand, outcomes are generally positive, they may wish to continue or expand their efforts along similar lines. It simply means systematic *learning from experience*. If they do so over a longer perspective, the workplace becomes an example of *organizational learning*.

Experiences with such interventions are generally positive, not only for the employees and in terms of stress, health, and well-being, but also for the function and success of work organizations, and for the community. If conducted as proposed, they are likely to create a win-win-win situation for all concerned.

Other Recent Initiatives

This overall approach of the guidance on stress was further endorsed in the Swedish EU presidency conclusions (2001), which said that

employment not only involves focusing on more jobs, but also on better jobs. Increased efforts should be made to promote a good working environment for all, including equal opportunities for the disabled, gender equal-ity, good and flexible work organisation permitting better reconciliation of working and personal life, lifelong learning, health and safety at work, employee involvement and diversity in working life.

The subsequent Belgian EU presidency initiated another European conference, in Brussels on 25–27 October, 2001 on "coping with stress and depression-related problems in Europe." Based on its conclusions, The European Council of Health Ministers in its subsequent "Conclusions" (2001) invited the EU member states to "give special attention to the increasing problem of work-related stress and depression."

In its report *Mental Health in Europe*, the World Health Organization (2001) similarly emphasizes that "mental health problems and stress-related disorders are the biggest overall cause of early death in Europe. Finding ways to reduce this burden is a priority." And, soon after, the Executive Board of the World Health Organization (2002) resolved that

> mental health problems are of major importance to all societies and to all age groups and are significant contributors to the burden of disease and the loss of quality of life; they are common to all countries, cause human suffering and disability, increase risk of social exclusion, increase mortality, and have huge economic and social costs.

This was further discussed in a WHO preconference in Tallinn, Estonia, on 4–5 October, 2004, proposing issues for consideration by the WHO ministerial conference on mental health (Helsinki, 12-15 January, 2005). The conference established a Mental Health Declaration for Europe and a Mental Health Action Plan for Europe, both for the Who European Region, http://www.euro.who.int/mentalhealth2005. Following up on this, the European Commission has launched its Green Paper on promotion and prevention with regard to mental health in Europe (European Commission, 2005), with options for a subsequent White Paper later on.

Four Complementary European Approaches to Work Stress Related ill Health

An obvious interlocking question is—*how* the above objectives will be achieved. The answer to this question is considered in four relatively recent European documents :

- the European Commission's (CEC) *Guidance on Work-Related Stress* (Levi & Levi, 2000), considered extensively above;

- the European Standard (EN ISO 10075-1 and 2) on *Ergonomic Principles Related to Mental Work Load* (European Committee for Standardization, 2000);
- the European Commission's Green Paper on *Promoting a European Framework for Corporate Social Responsibility* (European Commission, 2001a), and
- *The Framework Agreement on Work-Related Stress*, signed on 8 October, 2004 by the European Social Partners, namely ETUC, UNICE, UEAPME and CEEP.

Let us also consider the last three and compare their implications for the protection and promotion of occupational health and well-being.

European Standard on Mental Work Load

The international series of the standard ISO 10075, Part 1[3] and 2[4] related to mental work load have been adopted and published as *European Standards* by CEN on July and March 2000. The CEN members are thereby giving this standard the status of a national standard without any alteration.

This standard defines *mental stress* as "the total of all assessable influences impinging on a human being from external sources and affecting it mentally." *Mental strain* is correspondingly defined as "the immediate effect of mental stress within the individual (*not* the long-term effect) depending on his/her individual habitual and actual preconditions, including individual coping styles." The standard lists some "facilitating" and "impairing" (short-term) effects of mental strain. The former include "warming-up effects" and "activation," whereas the latter comprise "mental fatigue," and "fatigue-like states" such as "monotony," "reduced vigilance" and "mental satiation."

According to the standard, the consequences of mental strain also include other consequences, for example, boredom and feelings of being overloaded, which are, however, not dealt with in the standard, "due to large individual variation, or to as yet inconclusive results of research." The same is said to apply to "possibly unfavourable long-term effects of repeated exposure to mental strain being either too high or too low."

In its "general design principles," the standard emphasizes the need to fit the work system to the user, and in doing this, to utilize his or her experiences and competencies, for example, by using methods of participation. These principles should be applied in order to influence (a) the intensity of the workload, and (b) the duration of the exposure to the workload. Personal factors, like abilities, performance capacities, and motivation will influence the resulting workload. Accordingly, the work system design starts with a function analysis of the system, followed by function allocation among operators and machines, and task analysis, and results in task design and allocation to the operator.

The standard points out that mental workload is not a one-dimensional concept but has different qualitative aspects leading to different qualitative effects. The standard provides guidelines concerning fatigue, monotony, reduced vigilance, and satiation. It presents their determinants in considerable detail and exemplifies them.

Corporate Social Responsibility in Europe

The European Round Table of Industrialists (ERT) (2001), commenting on the European Commission's (2001a) Green Paper on *Corporate Social Responsibility*, concludes that *healthy, profitable, forward-thinking companies have a key contribution to make to the Lisbon goal of Europe becoming the "most competitive and dynamic knowledge-based economy in the world" by 2010.* Such companies have recognized that, in order to operate successfully, they must satisfy the three elements of sustainable development: financial, environmental, and social. According to ERT, this is the essence of what might most accurately be referred to as responsible corporate conduct, rather than "Corporate Social Responsibility," the term used by the European Commission. Failure to satisfy the three elements would lead, over time, to terminal weakness, in terms of credibility and trust among stakeholders and internal organizational resources. Recognition of and respect for corporate social responsibility are therefore key to any business interested in building a healthy future for its employees, shareholders and stakeholders in general (ERT, 2001).

According to the European Commission (2001b), the CSR concept implies that a company conducts its business in a socially acceptable way and is accountable for its effects on all relevant stakeholders. Thus, CSR raises the question of the total impact of an activity on the lives of individuals both within, and external to, the company:

- Within: recruitment and employee retention, wages and benefits, investment in training, working environment, health and safety, labor rights, and so forth.
- Externally: human rights, fair trading, impact on human health and quality of life, acceptable balance of benefits and disbenefits for those most affected, sustainable development, and so forth.

According to the European Commission's Green Paper (2001a), the strategy's basic message is that long term economic growth, social cohesion and environmental protection must go hand in hand. This has numerous implications for companies' relations with their employees. It involves a commitment to aspects such as health and safety, a better balance between work, family and leisure, lifelong learning, greater workforce diversity, gender-blind pay and career prospects, profit-sharing and share ownership schemes. These practices can have a direct impact on profits through increased productivity, lower staff turnover, greater amenability to change, more innovation, and better, more reliable output. Indeed, a major thread throughout the paper is that companies often have an interest in going beyond minimum legal requirements in their relations with their stakeholders. Peer respect and a good name as employer and firm are highly marketable assets.

A number of other initiatives support the promotion of CSR at the global level, such as the U.N. Global Compact, the ILO's Tripartite Declaration on Multinational Enterprises and Social Policy, and the OECD (2001) Guidelines for Multinational Enterprises. While these initiatives are not legally binding codes of conduct for companies, they benefit (in the case of the OECD guidelines) from the commitment of signatory governments to promote effective observance of the guidelines by business. In its invitation to discuss these issues, the Belgian EU presidency (2001) provided a matrix clarifying the three types of responsibilities included and the four categories of actors involved. Based on such considerations, companies could publish annual *"triple bottom line"* reports, addressing financial, environmental, and social (including health) issues.

In preparing such a bottom line, they might wish to consider the *Social Index* (0–100 points)—a self-assessment tool developed by the Danish Ministry of Social Affairs (2000) for measuring the degree to which a com-

Table 12.1.

	Managers	Workers	Consumers	Investors
Quality	Skills and training	Workers' expectations	Economic services of general interest	Index, disclosure, SIF
Convergence	Codes of conduct	Human resources Management reports	Social labels	Reporting and rating criteria
Partnership	Small and medium size enterprises	Social dialogue	Social and ethical clauses in public procurement	Pension funds

pany lives up to its social responsibilities. Various options for such voluntary approaches are discussed in more detail in the recent Report by the
European Multistakeholder Forum on Corporate Social Responsibility
(2004). Additional approaches to measurement components of CSR and
monitoring and ranking of enterprise performance have been developed
in a cooperation between the Dow Jones Indexes, STOXX Ltd and SAM
Indexes GmbH.

A COMPARISON BETWEEN THE APPROACHES

The Stress-Stressor-Strain Concepts

The European standard defines "mental stress" as a stimulus—generally in line with the corresponding definition in physics, as "a force that
tends to strain or deform a body." The guidance has chosen the current
psycho-socio-biological stress concept originally introduced by Selye
(1936), comprising the common denominators in an organism's adaptational reaction pattern to a variety of influences and demands.

According to the European Standard, stress (= the stimulus) induces
"mental strain" (= the reaction). The nonspecific aspects of the latter is
what the guidance refers to as "stress." The European standard's "stress"
concept equals the guidance's concept of "stressor." It is, of course,
important to point out this fundamental difference between the two sets
of definitions, to avoid confusion.

Negative, Positive, or Neutral Connotations

The European standard emphasizes that its stress concept is regarded
as neither intrinsically negative or positive. Depending on the context it
can be both or neither. Similarly, the guidance indicates that stress can be
positive ("the spice of life") or negative ("a kiss of death"), depending on
the context and between-individual variation.

Unfavorable Long-Term Effects?

The European standard excludes consideration of possible negative
long-term effects because of "the yet inconclusive results of research."
The guidance, prepared several years later, takes the opposite view and
presents a wide variety of negative (health) effects of long-term stressor
exposures, documenting its claims. The latter evaluation is also in line

with the World Health Organization's formulation that "mental health problems and stress-related disorders are the biggest overall cause of early death in Europe."

As can be easily seen, these approaches are based on different but related paradigms. The European Commission's Guidance has its roots in workers' protection, stress medicine and psychology, and in an ecological or systems approach. The European standard is based on ergonomics, an applied science of equipment and work process design also intended to improve overall system performance by reducing operator fatigue and discomfort, as well as ensuring their health, safety, and well-being. And CSR has as its basic core a consideration for ethics and human rights.

The guidance was prepared with the awareness that "one size does not fit all." It is a "pick-and-mix," a smorgasbord, from which all stakeholders are invited to choose the combination of interventions considered to be optimal in their specific setting, for subsequent evaluation. It chimes with the European Framework Directive and is aimed at preventing work-related ill health and promoting well-being and productivity.

The standard is more specific about what to include, what to promote and how. It refers to all kinds of human work activity with the express aim of "fitting the work system to the user." Without overtly saying as much, it gives the impression that productivity (rather than health or well-being) are to be considered the primary outcome. On many points, the guidance and the standard overlap, both in terms of objectives and the means by which these objectives should be achieved.

The CSR initiative constitutes a much broader approach, encompassing both employee health and well-being and productivity, as well as economic and ecological sustainable development. Although attempts have been made to instrumentalize the CSR concept by providing quantitative and qualitative measures of targets, interventions and outcomes, there is a considerable risk of some stakeholders paying lip service to CSR without taking more than token action.

Tripartite EU Framework Agreement

Even so, all initiatives constitute important bases for tripartite collaboration for the promotion of high productivity, high occupational and public health and high quality of life. This collaboration has now been formally agreed on by the European Social Partners at the EU25 level. According to ETUC et al. (2004), their recently signed framework agreement marks a big step forward from the framework directive mentioned above:

- it acknowledges *stress as a common concern* (my italics) of European employers, workers, and their representatives;
- it includes work-related stress and its causal factors by name among the risks that should be prevented;
- it lays down a general framework for preventing, eliminating, and managing stress factors (stressors) with specific reference to work organization, content, and the working environment;
- these factors are detailed through a series of relevant examples (that do not constitute a list which could have given rise to errors and omissions);
- the employers' responsibility is clearly spelled out, while participation and cooperation by workers and their representatives in the practical implementation of measures to reduce stress (i.e., tackling stressors are an essential part of the draft agreement);
- the agreement is oriented towards action to tackle stress;
- stress that does not stem from the workplace or working conditions is taken into account if it creates stress inside the workplace ("imported stress").

To conclude, there is an urgent need for preventive measures across societal sectors and levels, aimed at promoting "the healthy job" concept, and humanizing organizational restructuring. The challenge to science of all this is to find out *what* to do, for *whom*, and *how*, and to help bridge the science-policy, policy-implementation and implementation-evaluation gaps. The corresponding challenge to all other stakeholders on the labor market is to implement existing evidence in coordinated and sustainable program for subsequent evaluation.

AUTHOR'S NOTE

An earlier version was published by the European Trade Union Confederation (ETUC) in its Newsletter (TUTB Newsletter No. 19–20, September 2002, pp. 12–17).

NOTES

1. Levi, L and Levi, I: *Guidance on Work-Related Stress: Spice of Life, or Kiss of Death?*, Luxembourg: Office for Official Publications of the European Communities, 2000. URL: www.europa.eu.int/comm/employment_social/health_safety/docs_en.htm#pub7

2. Hypothalamus: a part of the brain that regulates bodily temperature and other autonomic activities; pituitary: a small endocrine gland, whose secretions control other endocrine glands; adrenal glands: two small endocrine glands, secreting cortisol, adrenaline, noradrenaline, and other hormones.
3. EN ISO 10075–1: Ergonomic principles related to mental work-load—Part 1: General terms and definitions.
4. EN ISO 10075–2: Ergonomic principles related to mental work-load—Part 2: Design principles.

REFERENCES

Belgian EU Presidency. (2001, November). *Corporate social responsibility on the European social policy agenda*. Brussels, Belgium: Belgium Government.

Björntorp, P. (2001) Heart and soul: Stress and the metabolic syndrome. *Scand Cardiovasc J, 35*, 172–177.

Danish Ministry of Social Affairs. (2000). *The social index—measuring a company's social responsibility*. Copenhagen, Denmark: Author.

ETUC, UNICE, UEAPME, & CEEP. (2004). *Framework agreement on work-related stress*. Brussels, Belgium: Authors.

European Commission. (2001a). *Promoting a European framework for corporate social responsibility, Green Paper*. Luxembourg: Office for Official Publications of the European Communities.

European Commission. (2001b). *Corporate social responsibility—general information*. Brussels, Belgium: Author

European Commission. (2005). *Improving the mental health of the populaton. Towards a strategy on mental health for the European Union*. Brussels, Belgium: Author. (Green Paper COM(2005)484)

European Committee for Standardization. (2000). *Ergonomic principles related to mental work-load—part 1: General terms and definitions* (EN ISO 10075-1) *and part 2: Design principles*. Brussels, Belgium: CEN.

European Council of Health Ministers. (2001, November). *Combating stress and depression related problems: Council conclusions*. Brussels, Belgium: Author.

European Foundation, Paoli, P., & Merllié, D. (2001). *Third European survey on working conditions*. Dublin, Ireland: Author.

European Multistakeholder Forum on CSR. (2004). *Final results and recommendations*. Brussels, Belgium: Author.

European Round Table of Industrialists. (2001, November). *ERT position on corporate social responsibility*. Brussels, Belgium: Author

Folkow, B. (2001). Mental stress and its importance for cardiovascular disorders: Physiological aspects, "from-mice-to-man." *Scand Cardiovasc J, 35*, 165–172.

ILO (2000). *Mental health in the workplace*. Geneva, Switzerland: International Labour Office.

Levi, L., & Levi, I. (2000). *Guidance on work-related stress. Spice of life, or kiss of death?* Luxembourg: Office for Official Publications of the European Communities.

Marmot, M. (2004). *Status syndrome*. London: Bloomsbury.

OECD (2001). *Corporate social responsibility: Partners for progress*. Paris: Author.

Putnam, R. D. (2000). *Bowling alone*. New York: Simon and Schuster.

Selye, H. (1936). A syndrome produced by diverse nocuous agents. *Nature, 32,* 138.

Selye, H. (1971). The evolution of the stress concept—stress and cardiovascular disease. In L. Levi (Ed.), *Society, stress and disease: The psychosocial environment and psychosomatic diseases* (Vol. 1, pp. 299–311). London: Oxford University Press.

Swedish EU Presidency: Modernizing the European social model. Improving quality of work. (2001, March 23-24). Stockholm European Council. Stockholm: Swedish Government.

World Health Organization Executive Board. (2002, January 17). *Strengthening mental health*. Resolution EB109.R8, 17.

World Health Organization. (2001a). *World health report*. Geneva, Switzerland: Author.

World Health Organization. (2001b). *Mental health in Europe*. Copenhagen, Denmark: Author.

CHAPTER 13

APPROACHES TO PREVENTION OF JOB STRESS IN THE UNITED STATES

Steven L. Sauter and Lawrence R. Murphy

National surveys in the United States (U.S.) find relatively high levels of job stress in the workforce, with a third or more of all workers reporting that their jobs are "often" or "always" stressful. Concerns have been raised that new organizational practices, such as the adoption of lean production work systems and flexible employment policies, may pose yet further risk for stress in the workplace. Interventions to reduce job stress in U.S. organizations have focused primarily on individual-oriented programs such as stress management. While these efforts have demonstrated utility for lowering psychological and physiological signs of stress, interventions that address work organization (organizational practices and job design) are generally preferred because they are believed to more directly address the sources of stress at work. However, for reasons that are unclear at present, research has not consistently shown that these "stressor reduction" interventions actually lower worker levels of stress. Another class of interventions that has become common in U.S. workplaces addresses work-life balance, but data on the effectiveness of this type of intervention in lowering worker stress are also mixed. Suggestions to improve the effectiveness and conduct of interventions that focus on work reorganization in U.S. organizations are

Stress and Quality of Working Life: Current Perspectives in Occupational Health, 183–197
Copyright © 2006 by Information Age Publishing
All rights of reproduction in any form reserved.

offered, including development of guidelines on the design, implementation, and evaluation of interventions, and better integration of work organization interventions into organizational programs to reduce job stress.

STRESS IN U.S. WORKFORCE

This article examines what organizations in the United States are doing to reduce worker stress and identifies obstacles to more widespread and effective job stress interventions. To set the stage for this discussion, we begin by illustrating the scope of job stress in the United States and highlighting changing patterns of work organization that may increase risks of stress, illness, and injury in the workforce.

Claims about exorbitant levels and costs of job stress in the United States are common in the popular media. Within the last decade, however, reliable evidence has begun to emerge on both the prevalence of job stress in the U.S. workforce and the costs to society. For example, nationally representative data obtained from the General Social Survey in 1989, 1998, and 2002 showed that about one-third of workers in the United States reported their jobs to be "often" or "always" stressful during this period (General Social Survey 1972–2002 Cumulative Codebooks, 2002). Other sources support these findings. For example, a 1991 survey by Northwestern National Life found that 40% of workers reported their jobs to be "very" or "extremely" stressful (Northwestern National Life, 1991). Also, a 1997 national survey by the Families and Work Institute reported that 26% of workers were "often" or "very often" burned out or stressed by their jobs and 36% felt "often" or "very often" used up at the end of the day (Bond, Galinsky, & Swanberg, 1998).

These high reporting rates are of concern when considering the economic and health burden of stress in the American workforce. According to the Bureau of Labor Statistics, the median disability period for cases of job stress in the United States exceeds the disability period for most injuries and illnesses. In 1997, for example, the median absence for job stress (23 days) was 4 times greater than the median for all other injuries and illnesses (Webster & Bergman, 1999). Adding to these data is sobering information on excessive health care utilization among workers reporting high levels of stress. In a 1998 study of 46,000 employees, health care costs were nearly 50% greater for workers reporting high levels of stress in comparison to "risk free" workers. The increment rose to nearly 150% (an increase of more than $1,700 per individual annually) for workers reporting high levels of both stress and depression (Goetzel, Anderson, Whitmer, Ozminkowski, Dunn, & Wasserman, 1998).

Emerging Risks—The Changing Organization of Work

Similar to other mature economies, the United States has witnessed sweeping changes in the organization of work in the last 2 decades. Beginning in the mid-1980s, organizations in the United States invested heavily in innovative production processes to foster improvements in quality and efficiency and to increase their ability to respond rapidly to changing market demands. Variations of these new production practices are often described under the rubrics of high performance and high involvement work systems, flexible workplace practices, total quality management (TQM), and lean production. In contrast to mass production technology and traditional command and control management systems, these types of work systems capitalize on the problem-solving ability of workers by shifting decision-making authority downward to workers or worker teams. Other common features among these systems include process simplification, multiskilling, and job combination, just-in-time production, and continuous improvement. Evidence suggests that these types of work practices are spreading rapidly throughout the U.S. economy and across industrial sectors. Recent surveys, for example, suggest that 30% to 50% of organizations with 50 or more workers engage in teamwork, 25% practice job rotation, and 25% to 50% employ TQM practices (Gittleman, Horrigan, & Joyce, 1998; Kaminski, 2001; Osterman, 1994).

These changes in production management have occurred against a backdrop of organizational restructuring and downsizing, and the growth of flexible employment practices involving temporary or contractor-supplied labor. Downsizing rates in the United States reached record levels by the early 1990s when a third or more of major organizations engaged in broad workforce reductions on a yearly basis (American Management Association, 1997), and the recession at the turn of the century produced a new wave of workforce reductions. In the period January 1999 – December 2001, 9.9 million jobs were lost compared to 7.6 million lost jobs in the previous 3-year period (Bureau of Labor Statistics, 2002a). Additionally, steady growth has occurred in the temporary workforce in the U.S. in recent years. Temporary employment multiplied 6-fold to nearly 3 million workers during the period 1982–1998. This trend stands in contrast to total employment growth of only 40% during this same period (CRS, 1999; Government Accounting Office, 2000). By the late 1990s, agency-supplied temporary workers and workers in other alternative employment arrangements (independent contractors, contractor-supplied labor, and on-call workers) constituted nearly 10% of the U.S. workforce (DiNatale, 2001).

Steady increases in working hours and telecommuting are other notable developments in worklife in the United States. Data suggest that the average work year for prime-age working couples in the United States has increased by nearly 700 hours in the last 2 decades of the twentieth century (Bluestone & Rose, 1998; Department of Labor, 1999), and the spread of 24/7 business operations in the United States has resulted in substantial growth in 12-hour work shifts. According to recent data from the International Labor Organization (1999), average annual working hours in the United States exceed the average for Japan and for most European countries. Additionally, evidence points to strong increases in telecommuting in the United States during the decade of the 1990s (Department of Transportation, 1993; International Telework Association and Council, 2000). According to a 2002 report by the Bureau of Labor Statistics, nearly 20% of the nonagricultural workforce currently performs some work at home as part of its primary jobs (Bureau of Labor Statistics, 2002b).

In sum, the organization of work in the United States has undergone radical changes in recent years. This departure is perhaps best illustrated by a 1999 analysis of employment conditions in California, which found that just one in three workers held only one dayshift, on-site job that was permanent, full-time, year-round, and paid by the employer (Institute for Health Policy Studies, 1999, as cited in Karoly & Panis, 2004).

Implications for Worker Stress

Recent trends in the restructuring of work and employment have raised concerns worldwide that these developments present new and unexplored risks of stress, illness, and injury (Aronsson, 2001; Landsbergis, 1999; Quinlan, Mayhew, & Bohle, 2001; Sauter et al., 2002). For example, lengthening work hours and the spread of lean production have created worries of work intensification and overload. Downsizing and temporary employment practices might jeopardize the ability of workers and organizations to accumulate and retain safety knowledge, discourage the reporting of hazards and injuries or utilization of health care due to fear of job loss, or create chronic employment insecurity. Increased telecommuting and flexiplace work arrangements raise concerns about safety oversight and introduction of occupational hazards into the home workplace. But in reality, the diversity, complexity, and speed of these innovations in the organization of work have far outpaced research progress toward understanding and preventing the risks they may pose. Indeed, in the United States and in most countries, there are insufficient means and methods to even track accurately or quantify these changes.

Historical Perspective on Stress Interventions at Work

Concerns raised by rapid organizational change in today's workplace underscore the need for research to better understand and prevent potential risks posed by these changes. Prevention knowledge and research is least developed. In this section, we review efforts in U.S. organizations that are designed to reduce job stress and we identify emergent trends in stress interventions. We use the term stress intervention in its broadest sense and include efforts to eliminate or reduce the sources of stress at work as well as efforts to help workers cope with stress.

By way of background, it was not until the mid-1970s that job stress emerged as a topic of concern in U.S. workplaces. Prior to this, the attention of U.S. organizations was directed more toward providing health promotion programs to foster worker health via early detection of disease (e.g., hypertension screening) and promotion of healthy lifestyle habits (e.g., exercise). Health promotion programs use educational and motivational techniques to encourage behavioral and lifestyle changes to improve worker health and well-being. Health promotion programs supplemented existing employee assistance programs (EAPs) that offered substance abuse and mental health counseling to workers. EAPs, in turn, had their roots in occupational alcohol programs that were begun in the 1940s by Alcoholics Anonymous (Wrich, 1984) and offered an alternative to dismissing employees whose job performance had severely deteriorated due to alcohol abuse. The earliest predecessors of EAPs were mental health counseling programs that appeared in U.S. workplaces in 1915 (Burlingame, 1947) and were motivated by a suspected link between emotional problems of workers and organizational outcomes such as low morale and turnover.

Approaches to Job Stress Prevention

In principle, numerous approaches to the prevention of job stress are possible. As illustrated in Table 13.1, Murphy and Sauter (2004a, 2004b) employed a two-dimensional classification scheme to depict possible approaches to the prevention of job stress. According to this taxonomy, job stress prevention strategies can be described in terms of the level of intervention (legislative/policy, employer/organizational, job/task, individual) and, within each level, according to stage of prevention (primary, secondary, and tertiary). In practice, however, job stress intervention efforts have been limited to just a few of these many possibilities.

Legislative efforts to prompt interventions to reduce worker stress in U.S. organizations are relatively uncommon, although laws forbidding

**Table 13.1.   Levels and Stages of
Interventions for Prevention of Job Stress**

	Primary	Secondary	Tertiary
		Worker Compensation	
Legislative / policy	Legislation to limit hours of work		Social Security disability program
Employer/ organization	Work-family programs	Return to work programs	Company provided long-term disability
Job/task	Job/task redesign Job enrichment Job rotation	Provision of light duty jobs	
Individual/ job interface	Health promotion programs	Stress management programs	
		Employee assistance programs disease management programs	

discrimination and sexual harassment, the Family and Medical Leave Act (FLMA, http://www.dol.gov/esa/whd/fmla) and pending legislation on hours of work (The Patient and Physician Safety and Protection Act, http://www.theorator.com/bills107/hr3236.html) are exceptions. Instead, interventions have been primarily driven by company-initiated efforts, and secondarily via the provision of federal, state, and private grants to universities and other research institutions working in partnership with companies. Although these efforts encompass interventions at the company, job/task, and individual level, evidence suggests that secondary intervention at the individual level (stress management) is the most prevalent form of job stress intervention in today's workplace. Also, experience shows that these company-initiated efforts are rarely evaluated in a scientific sense and seldom appear in the peer-reviewed literature. Indeed, a simple review of the scientific literature would produce a truncated view of stress interventions in U.S. organizations.

Review of the Job Stress Intervention Literature

Reviews of the scientific literature over the past 20 years have turned up a steadily increasing number of stress intervention studies (Bunce, 1997; Murphy, 1984, 1996; Newman & Beehr, 1979; Van der Klink, Blonk, Schene, & van Dijk, 2001) and some general conclusions can be drawn from these reviews. As indicated, most worksite stress intervention studies involve efforts to help employees manage stress, with only an occasional study directed towards reducing sources of stress at work (i.e., stressor reduction). Stress management training includes a wide assortment of techniques including meditation, biofeedback, muscle relaxation, and cognitive-behavioral skills training, all designed to reduce the symptoms of stress and, as such, they represent secondary prevention. Stressor reduction efforts, in contrast, focus on altering company practices or policies and the design of jobs (e.g., increasing worker participation in decision making or reducing heavy workload demands) as the primary means of reducing employee stress, and reflect a primary prevention approach.

Second, stress management training is more often than not associated with benefits to workers in the form of lower physiological arousal level, reduced feelings of distress, and fewer somatic complaints, but significant improvements in job satisfaction are less evident (Bunce, 1997; Murphy, 1996; Van der Klink et al., 2001). This makes sense since the primary target of stress management interventions is the individual, not the organization itself, and one might expect direct effects on the former but indirect effects, if any, on the latter.

Third, stressor reduction interventions, which attempt to eliminate or reduce the sources of stress at work, are not routinely effective in lowering worker levels of stress. This is surprising in light of the fact that these are "preferred" interventions from a theoretical point of view and are routinely advocated by most job stress researchers. Nevertheless, the weight of the evidence in support of stressor reduction interventions is unimpressive. Indeed, a careful review of this literature leads to the conclusion that stressor reduction interventions produce small or insignificant effects on levels of distress (Briner & Reynolds, 1999; Parkes & Sparkes, 1998; Murphy, 1996; Van der Klink et al., 2001).

Why these stressor reduction interventions have not been more successful is unclear. Since a fundamental tenet of stress is that change of any type is stressful, it is possible that interventions focusing on job redesign might increase worker stress in the short-term. Workers may need training and assistance to help them adapt and adjust to new work routines and interpersonal relationships, beyond the need to cope with change per se. This would argue for longer evaluation periods to accurately assess benefits. It is also possible that stressor reduction interventions decrease stress for some workers (the ones who see the change as positive) but increase stress for other workers (those who see the change as negative). This suggests the need for evaluation protocols that include subgroup analyses or which attempt to identify workers who were positively and negatively affected by the interventions. More widespread adoption of stressor reduction interventions is unlikely without a better understanding of why interventions to reduce workplace stressors have not proven more successful.

A number of reasons have been offered to explain why stress management interventions are more prevalent than stressor reduction interventions (e.g., Ganster & Murphy, 2001). For instance, there remains a
common belief in U.S. organizations that stress is a personal, not work-
related, problem, and this view leads many organizations to focus on
helping workers cope with stress instead of efforts to reduce job stressors.
Likewise, individual-oriented stress management interventions directly
address the idiosyncratic nature of stress ("one person's meat is another
person's poison") more so than job-oriented stress interventions. How
does one design an organizational intervention if stress is largely a matter
of individual worker perceptions? Thus, stress management represents a
less risky and less costly choice for practitioners.

Not all of the news is bad with respect to stressor reduction interventions. Murphy (1999) reviewed studies of stressor reduction interventions
in healthcare settings and identified a handful of studies that described
positive effects. Although not all of these studies were scientifically rigor-
ous, the results were sufficiently positive to warrant attention from
researchers and practitioners. For instance, participatory job redesign in
a 50-bed surgical unit (Abts, Hofer, & Leafgreen, 1994) led to improvements in both employee and patient satisfaction. Likewise, a thorough
redesign of the patient care delivery system to resolve role conflicts led to
reduced stress, better cooperation among nurses from different shifts,
and higher job satisfaction. Another study showed that comprehensive
restructuring of work at a large U.S. medical center led to increased feedback, task significance, meaningfulness of work, internal motivation, and
job satisfaction (Parsons & Murdaugh, 1994). In these and other such
studies, Murphy (1999) identified three elements that seemed necessary
for stressor reduction interventions to be successful; namely, worker
involvement in the process, management commitment to long-term stressor reduction, and a supportive organizational culture. These elements
are quite similar to the ingredients for successful stress interventions
listed by other authors (e.g., Kompier, Geurts, Gründemann, Vink, &
Smulders, 1998).

Other Worksite Programs

What is missing from traditional reviews of the stress intervention literature is acknowledgement of the wide assortment of programs commonly
offered to U.S. employees that might serve to reduce worker stress, either
directly or indirectly. Two groups of such programs can be identified.
One group consists of time management seminars, conflict resolution
training, and similar such programs that became popular in the 1980s in

large and medium-sized U.S. organizations. These programs were offered to employees for the avowed purpose of improving performance and productivity at work, although organizations expected post-training dividends across a wide variety of other outcomes, including lower worker stress.

A second and more recent group of programs can be labeled "work-life balance" or "family-friendly" and surfaced in U.S. companies in the past 20 years. Flexible work schedules are perhaps the best example and were initiated to reduce routine work-life conflicts such as taking a sick child to the doctor. Provision of childcare for employees, compressed work schedules, part-time work, flexi-place, elder care, and concierge services are more recent examples of efforts by organizations to help employees achieve a better work-life balance. These programs have grown in frequency in U.S. workplaces in response to changes in the U.S. labor force and in the organization of work noted earlier in this chapter. It is noteworthy that the U.S. federal government took the lead in developing and introducing many work-family initiatives to federal employees and these initiatives became models for the private sector (Saltzstein, Ting, & Saltzstein, 2001).

The Families and Work Institute conducted a survey in 1998 to determine how U.S. companies are responding to the work-life needs of workers. A representative sample of 1,057 for-profit companies with 100 or more employees was surveyed. Sixty-eight percent of companies allowed employees to periodically change their starting and quitting times, but only 24% allowed employees to do this on a regular basis. Eighty-eight percent allowed time off for school/child care functions and 81% allowed female employees to return to work gradually after childbirth. Job-sharing was allowed by 38% of companies, 55% allowed employees to work at home occasionally and 33% allowed workers to work at home regularly. A more recent survey of 945 major U.S. companies by Hewitt Associates (2002) found that 74% offered flexible scheduling, 48% offered part-time work, 40% job sharing, 30% work at home, and 21% compressed work weeks. Fully 94% offered help to employees with childcare, and 38% assisted employees financially with elder care needs.

Effects of Work-life Programs on Employee Stress

Do these "work-life" programs actually reduce employee stress? As noted earlier, company-sponsored work-life programs are not usually subjected to scientific evaluation. Further, most evaluations are not formal but rather involve the collection of anecdotal information from workers who participate in work-life programs and are directed toward discerning if employee needs were met by the program and how well the program was utilized.

Although evidence has accumulated over the past 10 years suggesting that "work-life" programs might improve worker satisfaction and employee attitudes toward their employer (e.g., Ezra & Deckman, 1996; Families and Work Institute, 1998), the results of evaluation studies have not been consistent. For instance, Saltzstein et al. (2001) conducted a detailed analysis of work-life survey data collected from over 32,000 federal employees in 1991. Their analyses indicated that the use of flexible work schedules showed a small but negative effect on satisfaction with work-family balance and job satisfaction; this finding remained the same when analyses were conducted with various demographic subgroups. Compressed work schedules showed no effect on satisfaction with work-like balance or job satisfaction. On the other hand, part-time employment was strongly related to work-life balance but not with job satisfaction. Use of childcare had no link to work-life balance but was associated with improved job satisfaction.

Perhaps most instructive, "working at home on the clock" had a negative influence on work-life balance but a positive influence on job satisfaction. This finding differed dramatically by demographic subgroup: for older, unmarried men, there was a very strong link between working at home and satisfaction with work-life balance. For men and women with dual incomes (with or without children), working at home on the clock had a negative influence on satisfaction with work-family balance and a small positive effect on job satisfaction. The results highlight the complexity of the effects of work-life benefit programs on employee satisfaction with the job and satisfaction with work-life balance (Saltzstein, et al., 2001).

Summary of the Current State of the Art

In summary, there is both good news and bad news with respect to the current state of stress interventions in U.S. organizations. The good news is that organizations have become increasingly responsive to work-family conflicts and have implemented programs and redesigned employee benefits to address this conflict. In addition, many U.S. organizations continue to provide training in stress management, such as relaxation and cognitive-behavioral skills, courses on time management, conflict resolution, and other performance enhancement skills.

The bad news is that U.S. organizations remain reluctant to implement interventions designed to change job characteristics and work routines that cause stress for workers. The likelihood that such interventions will increase depends on four developments. First, organizations need a good deal more information from the research community to support the rationale for and design of stress interventions. Data collected in national surveys of job stress is needed to identify high-risk work practices and would provide organizations with a more solid foundation for designing stress interventions. It is noteworthy that a nationally representative survey of U.S. households was conducted in 2002 that collected information on job conditions and worker well-being. The National Institute for Occupational Safety and Health (NIOSH) funded a "quality of worklife" module on the national survey that consisted of 76 questions addressing job characteristics (workload, autonomy, skill utilization, participation, repetitive work, recognition), organizational culture (safety climate, discrimination, harassment, respect, trust), work/family conflict, supervision, fringe benefits, and worker health (physical health, mental health, injuries). Half of the items in the NIOSH module were taken directly from the older U.S. Quality of Employment Surveys (Quinn, et al., 1971; Quinn & Shepard, 1974; Quinn & Staines, 1978) so that changes in the quality of work life over the past 20 years can be evaluated.

Second, U.S. organizations need to be offered a great deal more evidence that stress interventions will in fact produce reductions in worker distress and improvements in worker well-being. Studies are needed that clearly demonstrate the health and safety benefits of altering aspects of the work environment, such as increasing worker control, lowering workload, or improving role clarity.

Third, authoritative guidelines on how to design, implement, and evaluate stress interventions are desperately needed. These guidelines should be based on a composite of research evidence, not one or two studies, and be applicable to most if not all work organizations. Guidelines for ergonomic interventions provide an example of what is needed (Cohen, Gjessing, Fine, Bernard, & McGlothlin, 1997). In this regard, NIOSH has offered general guidelines for reducing work stressors (NIOSH, 1999; Sauter, Murphy, & Hurrell, 1990) but more specifics need to be provided if they are to be useful to organizations. A recent report prepared by the Manchester School of Management for the Health and Safety Executive (Giga, Faragher, & Cooper, 2001) provides more up-to-date guidelines on how to design and evaluate work stress interventions.

Finally, stress interventions need to adopt a broader conceptual perspective—one that neither treats work stress as a stand-alone issue nor implements stress interventions in isolation from other organization initiatives, but does link stress intervention to organizational-level outcomes (e.g., productivity, absenteeism, injuries, illness, job satisfaction). NIOSH has suggested that stress be viewed within a healthy work organization perspective that fosters both worker well-being and organizational effectiveness (Cooper & Murphy, 2000; Sauter, Lim, & Murphy, 1996). Similarly, Colarelli (1998) has made a strong case for rethinking how interventions are introduced into organizations, giving attention to contextual and historical factors and acknowledging the pressures and counter forces operating in opposition to interventions. For instance, Colarelli (1998) advocates implementing "clusters of interventions" instead of single interventions, as the former are more likely to overcome the existing pressures and counter forces that operate to oppose change.

ACKNOWLEDGMENTS

The authors wish to thank Kellie Pierson and Jessica Keel for their technical support in preparation of this manuscript.

REFERENCES

Abts, D., Hofer, M., & Leafgreen, P. K. (1994). Redefining care delivery: A modular system. *Nursing Management, 25*, 40–46.

American Management Association (1997). *1997 American management association survey: Corporate job creation, job elimination, and downsizing*. New York: Author.

Aronsson, G. (2001). Editorial: A new employment contract. *Scandinavian Journal of Work Environmental Health, 27*, 361–372.

Bluestone, B., & Rose, S. (1998). *Public policy brief no. 39: The unmeasured labor force —the growth in work hours*. Blithewook, Annandale-on-Hudson, NY: The Jerome Levy Economics Institute of Bard College, Bard Publications Office.

Bond, J. T., Galinsky, E., & Swanberg, J. E. (1998). *The 1997 national study of the changing workforce*. New York: Families and Work Institute.

Briner, R. B., & Reynolds, S. (1999). The costs, benefits, and limitations of organizational level stress interventions. *Journal of Organizational Behavior, 20*, 647–64.

Bunce, D. (1997). What factors are associated with the outcome of individual-focused worksite stress management interventions? *Journal of Occupational and Organizational Psychology, 70*, 1–17.

Bureau of Labor Statistics (2002a). *Worker displacement, 1999–2001*. Washington, DC: U.S. Department of Labor, Bureau of Labor Statistics, News USDL No. 02-483.

Bureau of Labor Statistics (2002b). *Work at home in 2001*. Retrieved on December 15, 2004 from ftp://ftp.bls.gov/pub/news.release/History/homey.03012002 .news

Burlingame, C. C. (1947). Psychiatry in industry. *American Journal of Psychiatry, 103*, 549–553.

Cohen, A. L., Gjessing, C. C., Fine, L. J., Bernard, B. P., & McGlothin, J. D. (1997). *Elements of ergonomics programs: A primer based on workplace evaluations of musculoskeletal disorders*. Cincinnati, OH: U.S. Department of Health and Human Services, Public Health Service, Centers for Disease Control and Prevention, National Institute for Occupational Safety and Health, DHHS (NIOSH) Publication No. 97–117.

Colarelli, S. M. (1998). Psychological interventions in organizations: An evolutionary perspective. *American Psychologist, 53,* 1044–1056.

Cooper, C. L., & Murphy, L. R. (2000). Developing healthy corporate cultures by reducing stressors at work. In L. R. Murphy & C. L. Cooper (Eds.). *Healthy and productive work: An international perspective.* London: Taylor-Francis.

CRS (1999). *CRS report for Congress: Temporary workers as member of the contingent labor force.* Washington, DC: The Library of Congress, Congressional Research Service, Order Code No. RL30072.

Department of Labor (1999). *Report on the American workforce.* Washington, DC: Author.

Department of Transportation (1993). *Transportation implications of telecommuting.* Washington, DC: U.S. Department of Transportation, Bureau of Transportation Statistics.

DiNatale, M. (2001). Characteristics of and preference for alternative work arrangements, 1999. *Monthly Labor Review, 124,* 28–49.

Ezra, M., & Deckman, M. (1996). Balancing work and family responsibilities: Flextime and child care in the Federal Government. *Public Administration Review, 56,* 174–179.

Families and Work Institute (1998). *The 1998 business worklife study: A sourcebook.* New York: Families and Work Institute.

Ganster, D., & Murphy, L. R. (2001). Workplace interventions to prevent stress-related illness: Lessons from research and practice. In C. L. Cooper & Edwin Locke (Eds.), *Industrial and Organizational Psychology.* Oxford, England: Blackwell.

General Social Survey 1972-2002 Cumulative Codebook (2002). Retrieved on December 15, 2004, from http://webapp.icpsr.umich.edu/GSS/

Giga, S. I., Faragher, B., & Cooper, C. L. (2001). Identification of good practice in stress reduction/management: A state of the art review. United Kingdom: Crown (Contract Research Report 4301/R54.802).

Gittleman, M., Horrigan, M., & Joyce, M. (1998). "Flexible" workplace practices: Evidence from a nationally representative survey. *Industrial Labor Relations Review, 52,* 99–113.

Goetzel, R. Z., Anderson, D. R., Whitmer, R. W., Ozminkowski, R. J., Dunn, R. L., & Wasserman, J. (1998). The relationship between modifiable health risks and health care expenditure: An analysis of the multi-employer HERO health risk and cost database. *Journal of Occupational and Environmental Medicine, 40,* 843–854.

Government Accounting Office (2000). *Contingent workers: Incomes and benefits lag behind those of rest of workforce.* Washington, DC: U.S. General Accounting Office, Report No. GAO/HEHS–00–76.

Hewitt Associates (2002). *Work/life benefits provided by major U.S. employers in 2001-2002.* Retrieved from http://goliath.ecnext.com/comsites5/bin/pdinventory

.pl?pdlanding=1&referid=2750&item_id=0199-1654625&words=Hewitt_
Study_Shows#abstract

International Labor Organization (1999). *Key indicators of the labor market 1999.* Geneva, Switzerland: International Labor Office.

International Telework Association and Council (2000). *ITAC Press Release—New US teleworkers grow by nearly 3 million.* Retrieved on December 15, 2004 from http://www.workingfromanywhere.org/news/2000newsrelease.htm

Kaminski, M. (2001). Unintended consequences: Organizational practices and their impact on workplace safety and productivity. *Journal of Occupational Health Psychology, 6,* 127–138.

Karoly, L. A., & Panis, W. A. (2004). *The 21st century at work – forces shaping the future workforce and workplace in the United States.* Santa Monica, CA: RAND.

Kompier, M. A. J., Geurts, S. A. E, Gründemann, R. W. M., Vink, P., & Smulders, P. G. W. (1998). Cases in stress prevention: The success of a participative and stepwise approach. *Stress Medicine, 14,* 155–168.

Landsbergis, P. A., Cahill, J., & Schnall, P. (1999). The impact of lean production and worker health. *Journal of Occupational Health Psychology, 4,* 108–130.

Murphy, L. R. (1984). Occupational stress management: A review and appraisal. *Journal of Occupational Psychology, 57,* 1–15.

Murphy, L. R. (1996). Stress management in work settings: A critical review of the research literature. *American Journal of Health Promotion, 11,* 112–135.

Murphy, L. R. (1999). Organizational interventions to reduce stress in health care professionals. In R. Payne & J. Firth-Cozens (Eds.), *Stress in health professionals* (2nd ed., pp. 149-162). Chichester, England: Wiley.

Murphy, L. R., & Sauter, S. L. (2004a). Work organization interventions: Status of research and practice. In *Scientific summary paper—The way we work and its impact on our health* (pp. 112–115). Retrieved November 21, 2005, from http:/ /www.workhealth.org/2004%20California%20Forum/ White%20Paper%20FINAL%204-16-04.pdf

Murphy, L. R., & Sauter, S. L. (2004b, April). *Work organization interventions: Status of research and practice.* Paper presented at The Way We Work and its Impact on Our Health conference, Los Angeles, CA.

National Institute for Occupational Safety and Health (1999). *Stress at work.* Retrieve on December 15, 2004, from http://www.cdc.gov/niosh/pdfs/ stress.pdf

Newman, J. D., & Beehr, T. (1979). Personal and organizational strategies for handling job stress: A review of research and opinion. *Personnel Psychology, 32,* 1–43.

Northwestern National Life Insurance Company (1991). *Employee burnout: America's newest epidemic.* Minneapolis, MN: Author.

Osterman, P. (1994). How common is workplace transformation and who adopts it? *Industrial Labor Relations Review, 47,* 173–188.

Parkes, K., & Sparkes, T. J. (1998). *Organizational interventions to reduce work stress. Are they effective?* United Kingdom: *Health and Safety Executive,* RR193/98 ISBN 0-7176-1625-8.

Parsons, M. L., & Murdaugh, C. L. (1994). *Patient-centered care: A model for restructuring.* Gaithersburg, MD: Aspen.

Quinlan M., Mayhew C., & Bohle P. (2001). The global expansion of precarious employment, work disorganization and consequences for occupational health: A review of recent research. *International Journal of Health Services, 31,* 335–414.

Quinn, R., Seashore, S., Kahn, R., Mangione, T., Campbell, D, Staines, G., & McCullough, M. (1971). *Survey of working conditions: Final report on univariate and bivariate tables.* Washington, DC: U.S. Government Printing Office, Document No. 2916-0001.

Quinn, R. P., & Shepard, L. J. (1974). *The 1972–73 quality of employment survey.* Ann Arbor, MI: Institute for Social Research.

Quinn, R. P., & Staines, G. L. (1977). *The 1977 quality of employment survey.* Ann Arbor, MI: Institute for Social Research.

Saltzstein, A. L. Ting, Y., & Saltzstein, G. H. (2001). Work-family balance and job satisfaction: The impact of family-friendly policies on attitudes of federal government employees. *Public Administration Review, 61,* 452–467.

Sauter, S. L., Brightwell, W. S., Colligan, M. J., Hurrell, Jr., J. J., Katz, T. M., LeGrande, D. E., et al. (2002). *The changing organization of work and the safety and health of working people.* DHHS (NIOSH) Publication No. 2002-116. Cincinnati, OH: National Institute for Occupational Safety and Health. Retrieved from http://www.cdc.gov/niosh/02 116pd.html

Sauter, S. L., Lim, S. Y., & Murphy, L. R. (1996). Organizational health: A new paradigm for occupational stress research at NIOSH. *Japanese Journal of Occupational Mental Health, 4,* 248–254.

Sauter, S. L., Murphy, L. R., & Hurrell, Jr., J. J. (1990). A national strategy for the prevention of work-related psychological disorders. *American Psychologist, 45,* 1146–1158.

Van der Klink, J. J. L., Blonk, R. W. B., Schene, A. H., & van Dijk, F. J. H. (2001). The benefits of interventions for work-related stress. *American Journal of Public Health, 91,* 270–276.

Webster, T., & Bergman, B. (1999). Occupational stress: Counts and rates. *Compensation and Working Conditions Online, 4(3),* 1–4. Retrieved on December 15, 2004, from http://www.bls.gov/opub/ted/1999/oct/wk3/art03.htm

Wrich, J. (1984). *The employee assistance program.* Minneaplis, MN: Hazelden Educational Foundation.

ABOUT THE AUTHORS

Alison A. Broadfoot is a doctoral student at Bowling Green State University. Her current research interests include occupational health psychology, work motivation, and selection. Alison received her bachelor degree from Rice University.

Robyn L. Brouer is a PhD student in management at Florida State University. She has research interests in the areas of the multidimensional aspects of person-environment fit, social influence, and effectiveness processes in organizations, leader-member exchange, and work stress.

Cary L. Cooper is professor of organizational psychology and health, Lancaster University Management School and pro vice chancellor (external relations) at Lancaster University. He is the author of over 100 books (on occupational stress, women at work and industrial and organizational psychology), has written over 400 scholarly articles for academic journals, and is a frequent contributor to national newspapers, TV, and radio. Professor Cooper is the immediate past president of the British Academy of Management. He is a fellow of the Academy of Management (having also won the 1998 Distinguished Service Award) and in 2001 he was awarded a CBE in the Queen's Birthday Honours List for his contribution to organizational health.

Christopher J. L. Cunningham is a second year doctoral student in industrial/organizational psychology at Bowling Green State University. His research has focused on occupational health psychology issues involving the work-family interface, employee fitness, occupational stress and performance, and organizational attraction. In 2003 he graduated with highest honors from Lehigh University, having earned a bachelor of arts in psychology, a minor in Spanish, and concentrations in business, music, and English. While at Lehigh he was recognized with several major academic awards including the Williams Prize for Business and Economics Writing, the College Scholar Excellence Award, and selection as a student associate of the Martindale Center for the Study of Private Enterprise.

Gerald R. Ferris is the Francis Eppes professor of management and professor of psychology at Florida State University. He received a PhD in business administration from the University of Illinois at Urbana-Champaign. Ferris has research interests in the areas of social influence and effectiveness processes in organizations, and the role of reputation in organizations, and he is the author of articles published in such journals as the *Journal of Applied Psychology, Organizational Behavior and Human Decision Processes, Personnel Psychology, Academy of Management Journal*, and *Academy of Management Review.*

David A. Gray is associate dean of the College of Business and professor of management. He was awarded the PhD in business administration from the School of Management at the University of Massachusetts in 1974. His research interests have focused on aspects of human resource management and the labor relations process. More specifically, he has researched strategic and operational rationales of human resource outsourcing; the linkage of the HR value chain to the employee-employer psychological contract and the performance impact of various HR practices; and union management conflict and cooperation before and after labor-management relations by objectives, or RBO. The results of these and other research efforts have been published in the *Academy of Management Review, Academy of Management Executive, California Management Review, OMEGA : The International Journal of Management Science, Journal of Labor Research, Journal of Collective Negotiations in the Public Sector,* and *Journal of Business Research.*

Jonathon R. B. Halbesleben (PhD, University of Oklahoma) is a research assistant professor of health services management in the School of Medicine at the University of Missouri-Columbia. His research has been concerned with burnout, the work/family interface, and health care management. His research on stress and burnout has appeared in *Journal of Applied Psychology, Journal of Management,* and *Work and Stress.* He serves on the editorial board of the *Journal of Organizational Behavior.*

Wayne A. Hochwarter, PhD is associate professor of management at Florida State University. He received a PhD in business administration from Florida State University, and has been on the faculties at Mississippi State University and the University of Alabama. His research interests include social influence processes in organizations, interpersonal effectiveness, accountability, and health consequences of stress at work. He has published articles in *Administrative Science Quarterly,* the *Journal of Applied Psychology,* the *Journal of Management,* and the *Journal of Vocational Behavior* on these topics.

Steve M. Jex, PhD, is currently associate professor of industrial/organizational psychology at Bowling Green State University and guest scientist at Walter Reed Army Institute of Research. He has also held faculty positions at Central Michigan University and the University of Wisconsin Oshkosh. Dr. Jex received his PhD in industrial/organizational psychology from the University of South Florida and has spent most of his post-doctoral career conducting research on occupational stress. His research has appeared in a number of scholarly journals including *Journal of Applied Psychology, Journal of Organizational Behavior, Journal of Occupational Health Psychology, Journal of Applied Social Psychology,* and *Work & Stress.* His also serves on two editorial boards, and is currently associate editor of *Journal of Occupational and Organizational Psychology.* In addition to his research and editorial activities, Dr. Jex is the author of two books, *Stress and Job Performance: Theory, Research, and Implications for Managerial Practice and Organizational Psychology: A Scientist-Practitioner Approach.*

Major Nathan Keller, U.S. Army is Goolsby doctoral fellow, The University of Texas at Arlington. He is completing his doctoral degree in social work with an emphasis in stress and leadership. He earned a BA from Gettysburg College, and a masters of social work from the University of Georgia. He holds a board certification in clinical social work (BCD) by the American Board of Examiners and an advanced clinical social work license (LCSW). Nathan Keller teaches both undergraduate and graduate courses at UT Arlington specializing in clinical social work. He has been practicing social work as an active duty United States Army social work officer since 1994, and has spent the last 6 years providing clinical interventions, developing stress prevention programs, and researching and evaluating stress management programs designed to assist service members and their families cope with the unique stressors of the military lifestyle.

Mary Dana Laird is a PhD student in management at Florida State University. She has research interests in organizational politics and impression management process in organizations, as well as in the nature of political skill and how it can help explain behavior in organizations.

Lennart Levi, MD, PhD is emeritus professor of psychosocial medicine, Karolinska Institutet, Stockholm, Sweden. Born in 1930. MB 1953, MD 1959, PhD 1972, associate professor of experimental psychosomatic medicine 1972, full professor of psychosocial medicine 1978–95, Emeritus professor 1995; all at the Karolinska Institute (Medical University of Stockholm), Sweden. Dr. Levi is founder and director, division of stress research at the Karolinska Institute 1959–1995 (designated WHO Collaborating Research and Training Center, 1973); founder and director, National Swedish Institute for Psychosocial Medicine 1980–1995. Secretary general of the WHO and University of Uppsala sponsored a series of international, interdisciplinary symposia 1970–78 on "Society, Stress and Disease" (also editing their proceedings, published by the Oxford University Press in five volumes, 1971–87). He was a member of the WHO Expert Panel on Mental Health 1973–97. Temporary advisor/consultant to WHO, ILO, UNICEF since 1972 and the European Commission since 1993. Before and after his retirement in 1995, he has been active in WHO's, ILO's and EU's programs in this field. His over 300 scientific papers and books in many languages include the European Commission's *Guidance on Work-Related Stress,* on which the recently signed European Framework Agreement on Work-Related Stress is based in part. He is chair, World Psychiatric Association Section of Occupational Psychiatry since 1983 and president, International Stress Management Association since 2001. Finally, Dr. Levi was awarded the Royal Swedish Medal of Merit for "pioneering achievements in the area of stress research" 2002.

Gabriel M. De La Rosa is currently a doctoral student at Bowling Green State University. His current research interest include occupational health psychology, recruitment, performance, and cross cultural issues in I/O psychology. Gabriel is a graduate of San Jose State University in San Jose, CA.

Marilyn Macik-Frey is the E. F. Faust/Goolsby Doctoral Fellow, Goolsby Leadership Academy, at the University of Texas at Arlington. She is completing her doctoral degree in organization behavior with an emphasis in communication and leadership. She earned a BS for select students from Stephen F. Austin State University, an MS in communicative disorders from the University of Arkansas for Medical Sciences and MBA from Texas A & M University in Corpus Christi. She holds the certificate of clinical competence from the American Speech-Language and Hearing Association. She established a private rehabilitation agency prior to working as a consultant for Therapy Management Innovations, Inc. She served as a national trainer for Prism Rehabilitation. Her academic and applied experiences serve as a foundation for her continued work in the area of interpersonal communication and leadership.

David A. Mack is assistant dean for program development and the associate director of the Goolsby Leadership Academy at The University of Texas at Arlington's College of Business Administration. He received his PhD from UT Arlington in May 2000. Dr. Mack earned an MBA in entrepreneurship from DePaul University in 1993. Dr. Mack has had extensive management experience in the insurance and financial services industry. He is currently a coowner, with his wife, of a financial services marketing/management business in the Dallas-Fort Worth Metroplex. He has published a number of articles and book chapters on job stress, workplace violence, leadership, and small business. Dr. Mack teaches undergraduate and graduate courses at UT Arlington and has taught graduate business courses at both DePaul University and Texas Wesleyan University. His teaching specializes in management consulting, applied research, and organization behavior and he is active in the College's Executive MBA program in China.

Christina Maslach is professor of psychology and the vice provost for undergraduate education at the University of California, Berkeley. She received her AB, magna cum laude, in social relations from Harvard-Radcliffe College, and her PhD in psychology from Stanford University. She has conducted research in social and health psychology, and is best known as a pioneering researcher on job burnout and the author of the widely used Maslach Burnout Inventory (MBI). In addition to numerous articles, her books on this topic include *Burnout: The Cost of Caring*; the coedited volume, *Professional Burnout: Recent Developments in Theory and Research*; and two prior books with Michael Leiter: *The Truth About Burnout* and *Preventing Burnout and Building Engagement*. Maslach's research accomplishments led the American Association for the Advancement of Science to honor her "For groundbreaking work on the applications of social psychology to contemporary problems." She is also a renowned teacher, who received national recognition as "Professor of the Year" in 1997.

Lawrence R. Murphy, PhD is research psychologist in the Division of Applied Research and Technology, National Institute for Occupational Safety and Health (NIOSH). He received his MA and PhD degrees from DePaul University, Chicago, Illinois, and postdoctoral training at the Institute for Psychosomatic & Psychiatric Research, Michael Reese Medical Center. He has over 25 years experience designing and conducting health and safety research in the areas of job stress, stress management, safety climate, and healthy work organizations. He has published numerous articles in the area of job stress and stress management, and coedited several books, including *Stress Management in Work Settings* (1989), *Stress and Well-Being at Work* (1992), *Organizational Risk Factors for Job Stress* (1995), and *Healthy and Productive Work: An International Perspective* (2000). His current research involves identifying characteristics of healthy and productive work organizations, and assessing the quality of work life using a national sample of U.S. workers.

Debra L. Nelson, PhD, is The CBA associates professor of business administration and professor of management at Oklahoma State University. Dr. Nelson's research has been published in the *Academy of Management Executive, Academy of Management Journal, Academy of Management Review, MIS Quarterly, Journal of Organizational Behavior,* and other journals. Her books include *Stress and Challenge at the Top: The Paradox of the Successful Executive, Organizational Leadership, Preventive Stress Management in Organizations, Gender, Work Stress and Health, Organizational Behavior: Foundations, Realities, and Challenges* and others. Dr. Nelson has received a host of teaching and research awards, including the Regents Distinguished Teaching Award, the Burlington Northern Faculty Achievement Award, and the Greiner Graduate Teaching Award. She has served on the editorial review boards of the *Journal of Occupational Health Psychology, Academy of Management Executive,* and the *Journal of Organizational Behavior.*

Pamela L. Perrewé, PhD, is the distinguished research professor and Jim Moran professor of management in the College of Business at Florida State University. Dr. Perrewé has focused her research interests in the areas of job stress, coping, emotion, and personality. Dr. Perrewé has published in journals such as *Academy of Management Journal, Journal of Management,* and *Journal of Applied Psychology.* She has fellow status with the American Psychological Association, the Society for Industrial and Organizational Psychology, and Southern Management Association. Dr. Perrewé is currently serving on the board of scientific counselors for the National Institute for Occupational Safety and Health. Finally, she is the coeditor of an annual series entitled, *Research in Occupational Stress and Well Being* published by Elsevier Science.

James Campbell Quick is John and Judy Goolsby Distinguished Professor and executive director, Goolsby Leadership Academy, The University of Texas at Arlington. He was an honors graduate, George Cobb fellow, and Harvard Business School Association intern at Colgate University. He earned a PhD from the University of Houston. The American Psychological Foundation honored him with the 2002 Harry and Miriam Levinson Award. He is a fellow of the Society for Industrial and Organizational Psychology, the American Psychological Association (APA), the American Institute of Stress, and was awarded a 2001 APA Presidential Citation. He was APA's stress expert to the National Academy of Sciences for U.S. National Health Objectives 2000. He is listed in *Who's Who in the World* (7th ed.), was awarded *The Maroon Citation* by the Colgate University Alumni Corporation, and *The Legion of Merit* by the U.S. Air Force. He is married to the former Sheri Grimes Schember.

Paul J. Rosch, PhD, is president of The American Institute of Stress, clinical professor of medicine and psychiatry at New York Medical College, honorary vice president of the International Stress Management Association and has served as chair of its U.S. branch. He completed his internship and residency training at Johns Hopkins Hospital, and subsequently at the Walter Reed Army Hospital and Institute of Research, where he was director of the endocrine section in the Department of Metabolism. Dr. Rosch has been involved in stress research for over 50 years. He had a fellowship at the Institute of Experimental Medicine and Surgery at the University of Montreal with Dr. Hans Selye, who originated the term "stress" as it is currently used, and has coauthored works with Dr. Selye as well as Dr. Flanders Dunbar, who introduced "psychosomatic" into American medicine. He has been the recipient of numerous honors and awards in the United States and abroad and is internationally recognized as one of the leading authorities on the effects of stress on human health, productivity, and quality of life. He has contributed numerous articles and book chapters dealing with various aspects of stress, many of which have emphasized that occupational pressures are far and away the leading source of stress for adults in America and other industrialized nations.

Ana Maria Rossi, PhD, president of the International Stress Management Association in Brazil (ISMA-BR). She is the director of the Clínica de Stress and Biofeedback, in Porto Alegre, and is a professor at the MBA Program on Human Resources at the University of São Paulo (USP), in São Paulo. She has written many books and papers published in professional journals and worked in the field of stress management for 30 years. She is the pioneer of self-control and biofeedback techniques in Brazil. Last September she was appointed as a Brazilian representative for the Occupational Health Section of the World Psychiatric Association (WPA). She is a fellow of The American Institute of Stress (AIS).

Steven L. Sauter received his PhD in industrial psychology from the University of Wisconsin-Madison and held an appointment in the University of Wisconsin Department of Preventive Medicine until joining the National Institute for Occupational Safety and Health (NIOSH) in Cincinnati, Ohio in 1985. He currently serves as chief of the Organizational Science and Human Factors Branch at NIOSH, and leads the NIOSH research program on work organization and health. He also holds appointments as adjunct professor of Human Factors Engineering at the University of Cincinnati Department of Industrial Engineering, and adjunct professor of Psychology at the University of Cincinnati. His research interests focus on work organization and occupational stress. He serves on editorial boards of several scholarly journals, including *Work and Stress* and the *Journal of Occupational Health Psychology*, he has prepared several books and articles on psychosocial aspects of occupational health, and he is one of the senior editors of the 4th edition of the International Encyclopedia of Occupational Safety and Health.

Bret L. Simmons, PhD, is an assistant professor of management in the College of Business Administration at North Dakota State University. He teaches classes in organizational behavior, diversity management, and leadership. His research currently focuses on eustress, hope, positive psychology, and worker health.

Jason Stoner is a PhD candidate (ABD) in management at the Florida State University. His research interests are in the areas of occupational stress and identity. He has published his research in *Journal of Leadership and Organizational Studies* and *Journal of Vocational Behavior*. He has also presented his work at Southern Management Association, Society for Industrial and Organizational Psychology, and National Academy of Management. Jason is a member of the Society for Industrial and Organizational Psychology, Southern Management Association, and the Academy of Management.

Mina Westman is a senior lecturer and researcher, at Faculty of Management, Tel Aviv University, Israel (PhD in Organizational Behavior, Tel Aviv University). Her primary research interests include determinants and consequences of job and life stress, negative and positive crossover between partners and team members, work-family interchange, effects of vacation on psychological and behavioral strain and the impact of short business trips on the individual, the family and the organization. She has authored empirical and conceptual articles that have appeared in such journals as the *Journal of Applied Psychology, Human Relations, Journal of Organizational Behavior, Journal of Occupational Health Psychology, Applied Psychology: An International Journal, and Journal of Vocational Psychology.* In addition, she has also contributed to several book chapters and presented numerous scholarly papers at international conferences. She is on the editorial board of *Journal of Organizational Behavior and Applied Psychology: An International Journal*.

Kelly Zellars (PhD Florida State University) is an associate professor of management in the Belk College of Business at the University of North Carolina, Charlotte. She has focused her research on stress, emotion, personality, and organizational justice. Kelly has published articles in *Journal of Applied Psychology, Journal of Organizational Behavior, Academy of Management Journal,* and *Journal of Occupational Health Psychology*. She serves as a reviewer for multiple academic journals and is on the board of the HR division for the Academy of Management.

Printed in the United States
93231LV00003B/282/A

9 781593 114862